MW01702913

7/12/05

Bonnie,

To a fellow Ohioan and Comfort Keeper! Best wishes for much success. Take care of your employees and they'll take care of you!

Sincerely,

[signature]

Zero to $100 Million in Five Years

Zero to $100 Million in Five Years

How I Used 10 Secret Ingredients for Success to Start a Business and Build It into an Empire . . . You Can Too.

Jerry Clum, Jr.

Hudson Books

2005

Published by Hudson Books

Book design by The Floating Gallery
www.thefloatinggallery.com

ISBN 0-9764459-5-6
LCCN 2005920823

PRINTED IN CANADA

Contents

Chapter 5

What Niche Will Make You Rich? · 23

Chapter 6

The Winning Philosophies · 71

Chapter 7

Chapter 8

Chapter 9

Chapter 10

Attitude Determines Altitude · 123

Chapter 11

Market Creation: Getting the Phone to Ring · 133

Chapter 12

Mastering the Art of Selling

PART I: Break A Leg · 179

Chapter 13

Mastering the Art of Selling
PART II: I Object · 191

Chapter 14

Mastering the Art of Selling
PART III: Close It! · 207

Chapter 15

Thinking Outside the Box · 223

Chapter 16

Building Your Team · 237

Chapter 17

Dialing In Your Business · 263

Chapter 18

Business Blackjack · 285

Chapter 19

The Sky Is the Limit · 293

Chapter 20

Chapter 1

It Can Happen to You!

A lot can happen in five years. I sometimes think how different my life would have been had my wife, Kris, and I not taken that giant leap of faith that is at the heart of all new businesses. I had played around with a few ideas in the past — investing a few thousand dollars and then losing interest or the money — sometimes both. So my track record as an entrepreneur was not the best. But this was going to be different. We were fully committed, and nothing was going to stop us. There were many times when we could have given up, many times when critical mistakes could have flattened our house of cards, but we hung in there to beat the odds. And so can you. That's what this book is about.

We started an eldercare business and initially operated it from our home. We would provide caregivers to assist seniors in their activities of daily living. Our services, which were non-medical in nature, would allow seniors to remain in their home, where they wanted to be. I had made good money in the years before and stamped out a decent lifestyle for Kris, our children, Heather and Trey, and myself. But a significant investment was needed to get this business off the ground. By virtually wiping out our life savings — 401k, mutual funds, stocks, and bank accounts — we were able to invest over $70,000 in start-up costs, working capital, and living expenses. It was just enough for us to break even at the end of the first year.

Even though the timing didn't seem quite right, we decided to open a second office in a neighboring city from which we were getting a lot of customer calls. We secured a bank loan of $35,000 on our signature, but with our living expenses still not met, the first office just barely profitable, and our second office just opening, that didn't get us far. And we didn't have the Three Fs — Family, Friends, and/or Fools (i.e., rich family, rich friends, and/or foolish acquaintances with lots of money and nothing to do with it.) For the record, these are the last resort for getting money to finance your new business. What we did have was $40,000 of equity in our home. To get our second office up and running, we borrowed against every drop of it. (Thank goodness for 100 percent loan-to-value equity lines!) We used every penny of the equity line as well.

When we started our business, we thought the concept was unique. It wasn't. Not only were there several other companies in the same business, but also a few had already begun expanding nationally. If we did not follow suit, I felt, we might never get the chance before our competitors cornered the market. Franchising seemed to be the most prudent direction for national expansion. I rewrote our business plan, this time estimating that we would need at least another $250,000 to turn our idea into a franchiseable concept and to keep us afloat until we broke even.

Over the next several weeks we beat on the doors of almost every bank within a 30-mile radius of our office. With all the optimism we could muster, we pleaded with loan officer after loan officer to find it in their hearts (please, no laughter) to loan us the money. But they were less than enthusiastic about loaning money to a couple who:

1. Didn't have a paying job between them
2. Had depleted their savings
3. Had mortgaged their home *beyond* the hilt
4. Had no collateral other than a willingness to work hard
5. Were running a business that was just breaking even, *and*
6. Wanted a quarter of a million dollars to franchise that business in a new industry.

"Banks are more than willing to loan you money as long as you can prove you don't need it. So if you want a friend, get a dog."

HARRY S. TRUMAN

Well, we were in too deep by now. This thing had to work, and we weren't about to let a few obdurate bankers get in the way. We lived, ate, and slept in our new business. I hit the Dog and Pony Show circuit, speaking to venture capitalists and groups of angel investors around the country. But the story was always the same. While they were drawn to our enthusiasm and loved our concept, this was the dot.com age, and all the investment money was flowing in that direction. We had to do something and fast.

Question: Where can you get $250,000 quick with no questions asked?

Answer: Credit cards! Specifically, those two icons of the industry Visa and MasterCard.

All those pre-approved credit card applications we had hoarded over several months paid off (so to speak). We applied for and received 23 credit cards with a combined credit limit of over $256,000, and over the next 12 months, we virtually maxed them out. There was no turning back now — not with an additional $331,000 in debt staring us in the face. Add to that the $70,000 in life savings we had invested up front, and you have the perfect recipe for stress, with a capital "S."

Eighteen months, hundreds of sleepless nights, and countless pounds of antacids later, we had paid off all the credit cards. Two years after that, our company was debt-free, and in three more years we were, personally, debt-free. Looking back, those five years seemed to have passed at the speed of light. We began with an idea and the passion and motivation to turn that idea into a reality. In five years, we turned that idea into an organization with more than 425 offices in 46 states and Canada, and 9,000 employees serving almost 10,000 customers. Annual revenues climbed to more than $100 million dollars a year — small potatoes in the global world business view, but quite an accomplishment for a young couple from the Midwest. I was fortunate enough to be selected as an Ernst & Young Entrepreneur of the Year® 2004 and inducted into the Entrepreneur of the Year Hall of Fame. *Entrepreneur Magazine* selected our company as the number-two top new franchise system in the country, as well as the "Best of the Best" in our industry.

If this sounds as though I am minimizing the difficulty of those five years, nothing could be further from the truth. In fact, they felt more like 20 years. Seventy-hour-plus workweeks began to take their toll. And we missed our kids. Changes had to be made. We sold a majority share of the company, which was valued at eight figures. I stayed on as CEO and Chairman of the Board. Today, we want for nothing and can do just about anything we care to do whenever we want. We have several vested partners to ensure that the company will continue to grow and prosper, and I have turned over the CEO reins to the company's more than capable President so that we could begin enjoying the fruits of our labor.

Is there a direct correlation between risk and reward? You better believe it. The greater the risk, the greater the reward. But it is important to be systematic about it. Risk should always be calculated. For every business success story, there are hundreds of business failures. You have to prepare for success. With motivation, determination, and the right formula for success — *It Can Happen To You!*

> *"If a window of opportunity appears, don't pull down the shade."*
>
> Tom Peters

Chapter 2

Uncovering the Secret Ingredients for Success

To analyze what got me to — and through — the past five incredible years, I had to go back and look at my entire work history. Though I didn't know it at the time, almost every job I'd worked in had provided me with one more ingredient in the formula for success.

I was an average high school student, and after graduation I joined the Air Force. It was an impulse move. Perhaps, like other teens, I was anxious to get away from my hometown and out into the real world. I was trained as a Missile Systems Analyst Specialist to maintain and repair nuclear missiles. (It didn't seem like a big deal at the time, but now I wonder how many teens are out there repairing nuclear missiles. Not a comforting thought.)

Shortly after enlisting, I married Kris, my high school sweetheart, and enrolled in college. My first major was electrical engineering, but it didn't take me long to realize that that was not my forte. I switched to marketing, which felt right, my father having been in sales almost all of his life.

The Air Force moved us six times in four years, and I got to see the world — not the popular vacation spots, but places off the beaten track. That experience taught me something that I believe many Americans don't fully understand — to appreciate everything we have here in this country, especially the abundance of opportunities.

> *"Opportunity passes us by every day. I just learned how to recognize it and do something with it."*
>
> J.P. Morgan

Millions of immigrants came (and still come) to America unable to speak the language and with only a few dollars in their pockets. In a few years, by taking advantage of the opportunities we sometimes take for granted, many have been able to achieve tremendous success.

After I was honorably discharged, we came back home and I took a job as a sales representative and continued working on my education. I worked on straight commission. Translation: No sales? No paycheck. We'd just had our first child, Heather, and there were bills to pay. This is the quintessential definition of motivation. My father took me under his wing and gave me some guidance at first, but I soon left the nest and went out on my own. After the first year, the company felt I had proven myself well enough to give me an office of my own. That was the good news. The bad news was that the office they gave me had been closed down for more than a decade and was in one of the most competitive cities. At its peak this office produced only about 50 percent of the business generated by most of the other 100 or so offices in the company.

Whether by design or out of desperation, I wasn't afraid to try anything and everything to bring in new business. I tweaked and polished my sales presentation, learned and tested new closes and rebuttals, created new advertising methods — and prayed. A lot. In a few years, I was at the top of the sales chart and one of the most valued sales people in the company. To reward the young man in his mid-20s who had turned a defunct office into one of the best in the country, the company offered me a sales management position at divisional headquarters.

Over the next few years, we had our second child, Jerry L. Clum, III (Trey, for short), and I finished college and went on to earn a B.S. in Marketing and an MBA. At work I was spending most of my time helping the other sales offices to duplicate the processes I had implemented in my own office. In only two years we increased the divisional annual sales by more than 40 percent. Financially, I was also doing well. Before accepting the new position, I had negotiated a lucrative compensation package, including a large salary and a bonus package. Also, it was agreed that a certain percentage of any increase in sales revenues would be paid to me as a bonus for my part in achieving that growth. Almost no one expected a 50-year old company, which had had stagnant growth for the previous decade, to grow by over 40 percent in only two years.

In the end, the company president almost seemed angered by the large amount they had agreed to pay me. And, in spite of how well I was doing, I felt empty about the success. The company seemed to focus on the profit margin to the exclusion of concern for employees or customers. In spite of the 40 percent increase in business, there were drastic cuts in employee benefits, and few employees had received a salary increase for several years. I had accepted the new position only with the understanding that once things were turned around, the employees would be rewarded as well. But it began to appear that the company would never be satisfied with their level of profitability, even with the 40 percent increase and after slashing overhead costs to the bone. Soon the differences between my business philosophy and the company's became so wide that I felt I had no choice but to resign. It was a shock to everyone. I was resigning from a position in which I was earning more than I ever had before, or might ever earn again.

(It is interesting to note that this company declared bankruptcy and closed down six years later, after doing more than a half a billion dollars worth of business since its founding. I believe they were blindsided by lust for higher and higher profits and an unwillingness to focus on their employees and customers. Had they addressed these issues, it is likely that the company could have operated successfully for another 50 years.)

So there I was, 29 and unemployed with a wife, two children, and the 4,500-square-foot home of our dreams, which Kris and I had just completed. To say that I felt in over my head is a serious understatement. True, I'd made good money, but we'd spent it as fast as it came in. Bottom line? I needed a new job, and fast. So I went back to sales and working on a straight commission basis. Though I did well, I was still not earning even a quarter of my previous salary. Soon it became obvious that I had two choices: find a new job or sell the house and start over again.

My next job was as a Labor Law Consultant, helping companies to ensure compliance with the Fair Labor Standards Act (FLSA). The number of companies — small, medium, and large — that were not in compliance was astounding. I learned everything I could about labor law, not realizing how crucial that knowledge would be in the future. It was fun, but I still hadn't found my niche.

For years I had been a walking Entrepreneur-Wanna-Be. I tried anything and everything. I bought every stupid get rich quick scheme that came my way — real estate programs, multi-level marketing programs, a publishing company, and a few dozen other bad investments of the kind that dominate late-night television and the pages of the business opportunity rag magazines. As always, I was motivated. I just couldn't seem to find the right vehicle and, more important, the right formula for success. My next job gave me the opportunity to take a different approach and proved to be one of the biggest learning experiences of my life.

I was hired and trained by a company that provided business valuation and advertising services to owners who were considering selling their businesses. My job was to appraise individual businesses and assign a value to them. Along the way, I began studying successful business owners to determine what they had in common. The new job gave me a front-row seat. Like a sponge, I soaked up vast amounts of information. Business owners were more than willing to be candid with me, since the higher value I put on their business the easier it would be for them to sell at a higher price. In short, they shared the secrets of their success. Among the things I learned:

- How businesses create unique selling propositions to outperform and outwit the competition
- The basis for a sound decision making process
- The strongest advertising and marketing techniques
- The long-term value of sparing no expense to find and retain the right employees.

For months I analyzed this information to see how I could use what I learned. Although I had amassed a tremendous amount of experience in sales and marketing, management, the financial aspects of business, operational issues, and labor law, there was one area in which I was not sufficiently knowledgeable: the imperative of recruiting and retaining top employees. To fill this gap in my knowledge base, I accepted a job as a headhunter with one of the top recruiting agencies in the area.

The first time I got a job order I was shocked. An HR Manager with 20-plus years of experience was offering to pay my firm a fee in excess of $20,000 if I, a person with no recruiting experience, could identify a candidate with a specific set of skills. At first I couldn't figure out why, but soon the reason — the true secret to successful recruiting — became crystal clear. I learned that most companies were still using antiquated recruiting processes that no doubt worked back in the day when the motto was "he who has the job holds the gold." The new paradigm can be summed up as "he who is the most marketable candidate calls the shots." Once I understood the process, I was able to fill seven recruitment orders in less than two months, which is not bad for an individual recruiter.

With the employee piece of the puzzle in place, I felt I had uncovered all of the right ingredients to the success formula. I was ready to begin the mixing process.

Life Experience Inventory

What experiences have you had in your life? It's a big question, but if you take time to analyze and answer it you may be surprised at how much you have already learned that is applicable to your success formula. So take a life experience inventory. Write down two or three of the most important lessons you have learned from every job you've had and then apply them to your own formula for success.

> ***"Life is a series of collisions with the future; it is not the sum of what we have been, but what we yearn to be."***
>
> José Ortega y Gasset

Chapter 3

Are You Up To the Challenge?

THE RIDE TO WORK IN THE MORNING HAS BECOME A DAZED ritual. Have you ever pulled into the office parking lot and realized that you don't remember any part of the drive? Or perhaps I should say, "How often?" If the answer is more than you can count, then you may be in the 40-40-40 rut — 40+ hours a week working for someone else, investing 40 years of your life doing it, and, if you're lucky, a gold watch and a pension that equals 40 percent of what you used to earn. For some people, this is a safe and comfortable way of life. For others, it is a recipe for depression.

Success Isn't Easy

"Reality is merely an illusion, albeit a very persistent one."
ALBERT EINSTEIN

Starting a business can be one of the most challenging things you will ever do. Blinded by our desire for the American Dream, we sometimes forget to take off the rose-colored glasses and face reality — warts and all.

Before you consider starting your own business, make sure you recognize the commitment you will be making. You will make many sacrifices before reaping the benefits of owning a successful business. Be brutally honest with yourself. Most of the time, to start your own business, you will have to step outside your comfort zone. Think carefully about whether you are prepared for this. Ask yourself if you are prepared for the inevitable struggles and problems ahead. If you think you are going to start your own business today and by tomorrow be earning six figures annually and spending a lot of free time with your family and playing golf two or three times a week, then step back from the fumes, because that just isn't the way it works!

In the beginning and perhaps for a few years, you are likely to be working 70 to 80 hours a week — or more — for free. A large percentage, if not all, of your savings and more will go into start-up costs and working capital, leaving you further in debt. In addition to the financial costs, be aware of the psychological costs. There will be many times when you will be overworked, fatigued, exhausted, burnt out, in over your head, and depressed. You may forget what your family and friends look like! At least half a dozen times (a day, sometimes), you will say to yourself "I quit!" And here's more encouraging news (NOT!). According to the U.S. Small Business Administration, more than 50 percent of small businesses fail in the first year, and 95 percent fail within the first five years. Before deciding whether you are up to the immense challenge of starting and running your own business, consider that all of these things — and some I haven't thought of — are likely to happen.

The Upside to Business Ownership

Scared? Good! The first thing you need before starting your own business is a taste of reality. The good news is that the light at the end of the tunnel IS NOT, in fact, a speeding train. Go through the mental and physical demands, work through the obstacles, do whatever it takes to be successful, and be patient enough to let it happen, and:

- You'll be your own boss.
- You'll have greater income security.

- You'll be developing *your own* asset(s).
- You may experience a huge adrenaline rush.
- Your income potential is far greater.
- You will have something to pass on to your children.
- You can reach financial independence much faster.
- You can have more flexibility to prioritize your life.

There are ways to reduce the risks and increase your chance of success. So what if 95 percent of businesses fail in the first five years? That doesn't necessarily mean you have only a 5 percent chance of success. There is a reason why 95 percent of businesses fail, and it generally involves something those owners did or didn't do. So:

1. Create your success formula, and
2. Learn from other people's mistakes and successes.

EQA Test

Take a few minutes to complete this simple EQA Test. It will help you determine whether you fit the mold for becoming an entrepreneur. Whereas the IQ test is designed to evaluate your Intelligent Quotient, the EQA Test evaluates your Entrepreneurial Quotient and Aptitude. The results will show whether you possess the specific traits most often found in successful entrepreneurs and at what level. Read the following questions and rate yourself on a scale of 1 to 4 for each. Be brutally honest! No one is looking. You don't have to tell anyone how you scored.

Circle 1 if this rarely describes you.
Circle 2 if this sometimes describes you.
Circle 3 if this almost always describes you.
Circle 4 if this always describes you and it is how most other people would also describe you.

1 2 3 4 Are you a self-starter?

1 2 3 4 Can you handle significant financial risk?

1 2 3 4 Are you a leader?

1 2 3 4 Do you take responsibility?

1 2 3 4 Are you a good problem-solver?

1 2 3 4 Do you possess good organizational ability?

1 2 3 4 Do you have a good tolerance for uncertainty?

1 2 3 4 Do you like a challenge?

1 2 3 4 Are you willing to give the business 60 to 80 hours a week or more of your time?

1 2 3 4 Are you highly motivated?

1 2 3 4 Do you have a burning desire to achieve?

1 2 3 4 Do you exude self-confidence?

1 2 3 4 Are you self-disciplined?

1 2 3 4 Do you like people?

1 2 3 4 Are you a hard worker?

1 2 3 4 Are you trustworthy?

1 2 3 4 Do you have good communication skills?

1 2 3 4 Are you a calculated risk-taker? Would you bet the store on a "Gut Feeling"?

1 2 3 4 Do you have good interpersonal skills and the ability to "read" people?

1 2 3 4 Do you have a positive mental attitude?

1 2 3 4 Are you a good planner?

1 2 3 4 Are you emotionally charged?

1 2 3 4 Are you a control freak?

1 2 3 4 Are you overly energetic?

1 2 3 4 Are you professional?

1 2 3 4 Are you a good manager?

1 2 3 4 Can you market and sell?

1 2 3 4 Do you set and achieve goals?

1 2 3 4 Are you a good decision-maker?

1 2 3 4 Can you handle rejection?

1 2 3 4 Can you handle failure?

1 2 3 4 Do you seek recognition?

1 2 3 4 Are you multi-task oriented?

1 2 3 4 Are you influential and persuasive?

1 2 3 4 Do you have the ability to stick with it and follow through?

1 2 3 4 Are you competitive?

1 2 3 4 Do you tend to believe you are always right?

1 2 3 4 Are you willing to take the initiative?

1 2 3 4 Do you possess a high level of perseverance?

1 2 3 4 Are you a quick learner?

1 2 3 4 Are you visionary, i.e., do you have a clear vision of your future?

1 2 3 4 Do you have a big ego?

1 2 3 4 Are you able to focus on one thing?

1 2 3 4 Do you exude enthusiasm?

1 2 3 4 Are you passionate about the business you are considering?

1 2 3 4 Are you in good mental and physical health?

1 2 3 4 Do you learn from your mistakes?

1 2 3 4 Do you believe you control your own destiny?

1 2 3 4 What level of knowledge do you possess in the area you are considering?

1 2 3 4 Are you willing to make major sacrifices to start your own business?

Now add up all the numbers you circled. Give yourself one point for every number one you circled, two points for every number two you circled, three points for every three, and four points for every four. Compare your total to the Score Evaluation.

Score Evaluation

Total score between 1 and 125

Starting your own business may not be the best vehicle for you. Working for others may provide better opportunities. *Do not think of this as a negative*. It just means your strengths lie elsewhere. Working for others does not preclude you from becoming a multi-millionaire, as any number of people will attest. (*Note:* This test is not The Final Answer. A low score does not mean that you are doomed to failure if you start your own business.) The results are a gauge by which to determine where you stand compared to other entrepreneurs who became successful. The answers to these questions are generalizations, which means they are "generally," but not always, correct. There are exceptions to every rule. A low score may just mean that if you start your own business you *may* have a tougher time than most.

Total score between 126 and 170

You are Entrepreneurial Minded, but should not hesitate to ask for help. Identify and list your strengths and weaknesses. Then find people (e.g., attorneys, accountants, business coaches, marketing consultants, or management consultants) who are strongest in the areas where you are weakest and hire them as employees or advisors.

(*Note:* Do not make a decision about forming a partnership with them at this stage. There is more on partnerships in a later chapter.) A score of 126 to 170 may mean that franchising is a perfect vehicle for you. The franchisor will usually have people to fill certain voids for you and provide the support you need. Thus, if you scored in this range you are likely to be better off starting a business that is part of a successful, tried and true concept vs. starting in a new and unproven arena.

Total score 171 or higher

You seem to have what it takes to be a full-fledged entrepreneur. It would not be surprising that some people find you a bit egotistical and overconfident. You may be so confident that you believe yourself to be infallible. Thus, you judge yourself harshly for even the most minor mistake. Disenchantment with your career is likely to drive you to starting your own business. You are probably a control freak and goal-oriented to a fault. You cannot tolerate mediocrity. Winning is the only acceptable result. In general, you are a "Big Picture" person with little patience for details. Having read this far, you may be wondering if you should be glad to have scored 171 or higher, as the description could be considered less than flattering. This score indicates that you truly are entrepreneurial material because you have a lot in common with many successful entrepreneurs. So don't worry. Be happy!

Is the Feeling Mutual?

Finally, before making the decision to start your own business, consider whether your family is up to the challenge. They live in your world. They will feel the same pleasure and pain you feel even if they are not actively involved in the business. Your better half should be your partner in this new venture. This doesn't mean they must be involved in the day-to-day activities of the business, but you need to be sure that they are fully supportive of the whole idea and are prepared to support you along the way. If your spouse or loved one is against the idea, it may be almost impossible to navigate through all the coming obstacles while keeping a positive attitude. Conversely, this does not mean that he or she must be as entrepreneurial and optimistic as you. In my case, I was the eternal optimist and Kris was the realist. I walked around with my head in the clouds scanning for opportunities. But the air is thin up there, so Kris had to pull me back down for a little oxygenated reality once in a while. We balanced each other well. The support of your family can be one of the most important things you'll need to succeed in your new business venture.

> *"You see, in life, lots of people know what to do, but few people actually do what they know. Knowing is not enough! You must take action."*
>
> Anthony Robbins

Chapter 4

The Recipe for Chocolate

Do you like chocolate? Most people do. There is scientific evidence that suggests we crave chocolate when our magnesium levels are low. This is particularly true for women just prior to their menstruation. Studies have also shown we crave or seek comfort from chocolate when we are emotionally stressed.

The Aztecs discovered cocoa beans in the 15th century and introduced chocolate to Europe. The initial reaction was negative because chocolate was bitter and unappetizing. Hernando Cortes, the leader of the conquering Spaniards, later began mixing other ingredients, including sugar cane, with the cocoa beans. The newly formulated chocolate was an instant success.

Today, chocolate is typically made from things like dried milk, cocoa butter, soy lecithin, pure vanilla extract, and powdered sugar. But have you ever tasted these ingredients individually? Once at a seminar where I was invited to speak I asked a chocolate-loving volunteer from the audience to come up and taste each of these ingredients. Between her facial expressions and the "yuck!" sounds, she made my point. Here was a woman who loved chocolate, but hated the individual ingredients.

Starting and growing a successful business has much in common with the making of chocolate. You can spend a lot of time reading books, listening to tapes, and attending seminars trying to find the key ingredient — the "magic bullet" — that will ensure the success of your business, when the truth is much simpler: There is no one key ingredient to success — no "magic bullet." Like chocolate, a successful business is the right combination of the right proportions of the right ingredients.

Over the years, I have identified the 10 key secret ingredients that have helped me to build a successful business. Each ingredient is as important to the end result as the next. Each process of starting, operating, and taking the business to the next level must include key ingredients or the end result will not be the ultimate success you desire. Think about it. If even one ingredient were left out, would chocolate still taste the same?

TEN SECRET INGREDIENTS FOR SMALL BUSINESS SUCCESS

1. **What Niche Will Make You Rich** — Start by choosing the business that is most likely to succeed for you.
2. **The Winning Philosophy** — Adapt the right philosophies and mission for your particular business and the people in it.
3. **Establishing Goals** — Set goals and create a business plan.
4. **Attitude Determines Altitude** — Have and maintain the right attitude.
5. **Market Creation, Getting The Phone To Ring** — Do the things necessary to create and/or capture a market for your product or service.
6. **Master The Art of Selling** — Develop an effective sales presentation while learning how to deal with objections and close sales.

7. **Think Outside the Box** — Cultivate expert problem-solving skills.

8. **Build Your Team** — Implement the strategies that will allow you to attract the best employees, retain them and properly motivate them.

9. **Dialing In Your Business** — Understand and avoid the operational pitfalls that plague many businesses.

10. **The Sky's The Limit** — Take your business to the next level!

"The most important single ingredient in the formula of success is knowing how to get along with people."

Theodore Roosevelt

Chapter 5

What Niche Will Make You Rich?

"How to succeed: 'Find out where everyone is going, and get there first.' "

Mark Twain

Although picking the right business to start can seem like a colossal challenge, it need not be. With the right formula, you can generally be successful in virtually any business, especially if someone is already doing it successfully now.

You probably already have some idea on what type of businesses may interest you. Before making a final decision, spend a few months investigating the types of businesses you can see yourself in. Begin by listing them. Then go to your local bookstore and pick up every business opportunity magazine or directory available. Here are just a few.

Publications for Researching Business Opportunities

- Black Enterprise Magazine
- Business 2.0

- Business Journal for Entrepreneurs
- Business Opportunities Handbook
- Business Week
- Entrepreneur Magazine
- Family Business
- Fast Company
- Female Entrepreneur
- Forbes
- Fortune
- Franchise and Business Opportunities
- Franchise Annual
- Franchise Canada Magazine
- Franchise International
- Franchise Opportunities Guide
- Franchise Opportunities Handbook
- Franchise Times Magazine
- Home Business Connection Magazine
- Home Business Magazine
- Small Business Opportunities

Use the vast resources of the Internet. Go to any search engine and enter the key words "business opportunities" or "franchises." Try to keep an open mind as you study each industry. Don't spend a great deal of time trying to analyze the pros and cons of each at this stage. This exercise is just to determine your interests, experience, and/or desire to work with a particular concept. Your list should also include any ideas you feel may represent original concepts. Once you have your list of possibilities it is time to begin the weeding process.

15-Item Acid Test for Evaluating Business Concepts

When I was evaluating potential business opportunities I analyzed hundreds of different concepts. Some were new creations I considered inventing. Others were more tried and true ideas on which I felt I could put a different spin. I soon felt as though I was running in circles. There were too many choices, and I couldn't find anything to help me be sure that I made the right one. So I created a method by which I could measure one business idea against another. Using the information I'd collected from the most successful entrepreneurs I'd met, I filtered everything down to 15 items that I felt the ideal business should have to be successful.

15-ITEM ACID TEST FOR EVALUATING BUSINESS CONCEPTS

1. No Collection or Cash Flow Problems
2. Little Competition
3. Residual Income
4. Low Start-up Costs/Access to the Required Capital
5. Duplicability
6. Flexibility
7. Great Market Potential
8. Emerging Trends
9. Low Overhead
10. Volume Intrinsic
11. Something You Would Enjoy and Are Capable of Becoming an Expert In

12. Large Labor Pool or not Labor Intensive
13. Limited Amount of Inventory to Stock
14. Recession Resistant
15. Non-Seasonal

Review and evaluate each of the business ideas on your list against these criteria. (An expanded definition for each of these items is provided later in this chapter.) Be as impartial as possible. Emotional attachment to a particular concept may cause you to squeeze it into a "passing" score. Remember, you don't necessarily have to start the business that scores the best in this evaluation. So be objective and evaluate each business idea honestly.

Scoring Your Potentials

Eight or Fewer Matches — Scrap the concept

A concept that has eight matches or fewer is unlikely to work. That doesn't mean that it isn't valid. It just means that the odds may be stacked against you in terms of reaching the pinnacle of success you desire.

Nine to 11 Matches — Has some potential

A concept with nine to eleven matches has some potential, but if you decide to proceed with it, be prepared for a tough road ahead. Include an additional financial cushion of 35 percent of the total cost for start-up, working capital, and your living expenses. When it comes to business, money can solve a lot of problems.

Twelve to 14 Matches — Deserves much consideration

Concepts that get between 12 and 14 matches deserve the bulk of your consideration because your chances of success are much higher. Not only is it more likely that the business will survive the first five years, but there is also a better chance that the idea will turn into something much bigger than you may have expected.

Fifteen Matches — The Mother lode!

The potential for success with a business concept that matches all 15 items is as great as it's going to get. Out of hundreds of ideas only a handful are likely to match all 15 items.

Now, let's look at each test item and see why it is part of the Acid Test.

No Collection or Cash Flow Problems

"No man's credit is as good as his money."

John Dewey

According to the 2001 report, *National Small Business Poll: The Cash Flow Problem,* almost two-thirds of small businesses experience some cash flow problems, with 19 percent of business owners saying they face "continuing" trouble in this area. For 30 percent of the companies responding, the primary reason for cash flow issues was the difficulty of collecting money owed. Some businesses see their net profit reduced by 50 percent or more due to uncollectibles. So not only can collection and cash flow problems be difficult to overcome, but they can also be devastating to a business. In light of this, the best business to start would be one in which the customers pay for their products or services in advance. This is the Other People's Money (OPM) principle, i.e., using advance payments to cover the majority of overhead. As an individual, your supply of working capital is limited. Under the OPM principle you dramatically expand your capital resource. So why doesn't every business collect in advance of the service performed or product manufactured? A lot depends on what kind of business you're in. Here's a hypothetical example. Suppose you have met with a home improvement salesperson for a project you are considering on your home. He or she gave you a quote for new vinyl siding, windows, and doors. Let's say the total for the job is $25,000 and that you have done your homework to be sure that figure is competitive. What would your reaction be if the salesperson said, "We could get started in three or four weeks. All

I need from you today is your signature on the contract and a check for $25,000." What would you say? You'd set the dogs on them, of course! (If you didn't have dogs, you'd probably get some just for this occasion.) But why wouldn't you pay them up front? In the words of Billy Joel, "It's a matter of trust," you say. But is that really the case? Think about your car insurance, house insurance, life insurance, etc. Periodically you receive an invoice for a payment three, six, or 12 months in advance of any service. Do you call the insurance company and tell them you're not about to pay for a service you have not yet received? No. You put the check in the mail. So the question becomes: Do you really trust insurance companies that much more than contractors? Trust is a factor in this equation, of course. But the more important thing is this: All industries have set standards or generally accepted practices that may have been in place for many years. As long as they don't go too far outside of those standards and practices, then chances are they won't get a lot of pushback from customers.

If you decide to start a business in an industry that is still in its infancy, take advantage of the opportunity to:

1. Set the standards, and
2. Get all or as much of the proceeds as possible in advance.

In the absence of any comparison, customers have no reason not to believe that your way of doing business is the way it's done industry-wide. On the rare occasions when a customer still has concerns about paying in advance, here is a useful response:

> When we started this business we knew there were two ways we could collect for our service. We could collect before the service was performed or we could collect after. We realized if we collected after the service was performed, unfortunately there are some people out there who just don't pay their bills. We would have to factor this into our prices and charge someone like yourself who does pay their bills on time, a higher rate to cover those people who don't. To give everyone the best possible price, we ask everyone to pay in

> advance." *(Of course, if you offer a product rather than a service, you would need to slightly modify this response.)*

In the absence of established industry standards, most people will go along with this. If they still have a problem with it, suggest that you would be willing to change the payment terms *if* they are willing to pay a percentage increase in price to cover potential losses. Given this choice, most people will opt to pay in advance.

Suppose you are going into an industry where standards and practices are in place. Your first step would be to "push the envelope" a bit. Let's go back to our home improvement example, but this time put your self in the place of the contractor. Suppose the industry standard is to ask for a small deposit — perhaps $500 — down, another third after the project is halfway complete, and the balance upon completion. To "push the envelope" you may ask for *a third down*, another third when the project is halfway complete, and the balance upon completion. In the first instance, for a $25,000 project, you would collect $500 down, $8,333 after the project was halfway complete, and the remaining balance, $16,166, upon completion. In the second example, however, you would collect $8,333 down, another $8,333 when the project is halfway complete, and the remaining balance, $8,334, upon completion. That means you would receive approximately $8,000 more up front, which could make a big difference to your cash flow, particularly if you had a dozen or so of these projects under way at the same time.

Here are few additional tips to improve cash flow and reduce collection problems.

- Don't expect your accountant to stay on top of cash flow requirements. You need to be your own bookkeeper. Remember the Five Ps: Proper Preparation Prevents Poor Performance.
- Learn the basics of financial statements, in general, but become an expert on your own.
- When possible, run credit checks on potential customers.

- Stay on top of accounts receivable. Time is of the essence. The quicker you collect, the more you collect. If you allow a customer's payment to be late too long, they may, subconsciously, write it off.
- Establish credit policies and stick to them.
- Allow the use of credit cards whenever possible.

Finally, research the collection history of the industry before you start a business. Determine the prevalence of collection problems and factor this into your decision on whether to start a business in a particular industry. The Internet is an excellent tool for this type of research.

Little Competition

> ***"In business, the competition will bite you if you keep running. If you stand still, they will swallow you."***
>
> Victor Kiam

A highly competitive industry can turn even the most civil person into a barbaric swindler. The last thing you need when trying to build a business with integrity is the constant pressure of cutthroat competitors who will lie, cheat, and steal their way to their next customer. The more competitive an industry gets, the more dirty it seems to be. Although there can be a great deal of opportunity in even the most competitive industries, it is best to avoid them.

That said, however, it is unlikely you will be starting a one-of-a-kind business with no competition. Almost every time someone has told me they have an original idea for a business that has never been done before, we find out that it has. The concept of an original concept may be dead. Still, there is always a way to do something better.

A business with no competitors seems ideal. But even if you do stumble across such an animal, it still may turn out to be the worst business for you. Maybe there's no competition because there's no market for the idea. Even if there is a market, the cost of educating people about the new concept and getting them to accept it could prevent you from realizing a profit for a long time. A perfect of example of this is XM Satellite Radio (or XM Radio), which debuted in 1998. The concept of more than 100 channels (many commercial free) of choice digital programming was, and still is, good. Think about it. You could listen to the same station with crystal clear reception on an auto trip from New York to California, and never have to touch your dial. Of course, this concept would have remained on the drawing board without a great deal of work and capital investment. By the end of 2002, XM Satellite Radio had combined annual net losses exceeding $868,000,000. Although the company will probably increase their subscriber base to recoup the initial investment and begin turning a tidy profit, the amount of the initial investment is far out of range for most of us.

Begin the competitive analysis of your market by checking your list of potential businesses against the local Yellow Pages. How competitive is the market right now? Suppose, for example, that your city has a population of 75,000 and you are considering opening a florist shop. But what if there are already two other florists in town? Where do you draw the line and conclude that the market is close to reaching its saturation point? Conversely, what if there are no competitors? Does that mean your business cannot fail? Like so many other things in life, it's not that simple.

> **Question:** How many snowmobile dealers would you expect to find in Florida?
>
> **Answer:** None, more than likely.

But does that mean there is a market for a snowmobile business in Florida?

To further complicate matters, consider the underserved niche factor. *Harvard Business Review* published a story about a movie theater owner in Europe who set up shop in an area that was saturated with other movie theatres, many of whom were facing financial crisis. But the newcomer put a different spin on things by offering large comfortable seats, convenient valet parking, and other courtesies more often found through concierge services at the finest hotels. The new kid on the block filled his theater night after night.

There is no quick and easy way to determine how competitive a particular market is in a particular area. The process requires an investment of time and money. Start with the local Yellow Pages and make a list of the number of businesses in the line of work you are considering. Determine the population covered by your directory and extrapolate the number of area businesses, like the one you are considering, per thousand people. Then go to the library and repeat the same process using Yellow Pages from other cities. This will give you some indication of what you're up against.

Current business owners themselves are one of the best sources for this type of information. Most entrepreneurs understand what you are going through and will usually be willing to give you some of their time. The key to this information source is tact. A business owner who even suspects that you may be opening up a shop next door is unlikely to be willing to share information about the level of competitiveness in the area. To downplay this factor, try contacting business owners in other cities or states. Posing as a potential customer or employee to gain information about the competition has also been suggested, though you would need to decide how comfortable you would feel using this approach.

Another source is, again, the Internet. Do you sometimes wonder how we ever did research before? I used to spend a great deal of time in the library, but with the Internet you can find vast amounts of information, usually much more than you need, on any subject in a matter of seconds. Here is a list of some of the best web sites for competitive business analysis, demographics, and market research.

- www.claritasmarketing.com
- www.BizStats.com
- www.BizMiner.com
- www.census.gov
- www.hillsearch.org

Although these sites have a wealth of information, in some cases you may be charged a fee to obtain it. For example, www.BizMiner.com offers marketing research profiles for (as of this writing) $99 each. In each profile you can get:

- national and local trends industry-specific to market volume
- start-up activity levels
- high growth rates by sales and employment
- new branch development
- annual sales growth
- staffing levels and growth
- sales per employee
- failure rate
- number of firms in the segment
- growth rate of established firms
- data detail for stable "survivor" firms
- industry sales class breakouts.

With almost a million research reports in their database, your chances of finding what you are looking for are excellent.

A competitive business analysis is time well spent and can save you money — and sometimes heartache — in the long run.

Residual Income

"The reward for work well done is the opportunity to do more."

Jonas Salk

Residual income is earnings you receive for a long period of time even though all of the acquisition costs associated with generating that income have already been recognized.

Most people and businesses earn what is known as linear income. When we do the work, we get paid. When we stop, the income stops. Ask almost any salesperson or business owner what happens at the end of the year. Their answer will usually be, I start all over again. Years ago, as a sales person on straight commission (i.e., I got paid when I sold something), I worked hard to master the art of selling. The one thing I never got used to was the feeling of starting over again and again every year. I would have a good year, perhaps even break a few records along the way, but when January first rolled around I was back at zero. The only way I could get ahead was by working harder.

Earnings from a music CD are a great example of residual income. A song is recorded once, but anytime someone buys the CD or the song is played on the radio, the artist receives a royalty. And this can go on for decades.

Here are a few examples of companies that capitalize on the benefits of residual income:

- Cable TV companies
- Home security companies
- Telephone companies (both local and long distance)
- Internet Service Providers
- Utility companies
- Cellular companies
- Satellite radio

- Satellite TV
- Banks and other lenders
- Credit card companies
- Insurance companies
- Pharmaceutical companies

Do you see a common denominator here? A huge percentage of the *Fortune 500* companies are in residual-based businesses. With residual income, the climb up the ladder is a little different. If you climb a few rungs the first year, at the end of the year you don't have to start at the beginning again. Instead, you start the next year several rungs up the ladder bringing your core base of customers with you into the next calendar year and building progressively on your past efforts. This is working smarter, not harder.

When applying the criteria from the *15-Item Acid Test for Evaluating Business Concepts* to determine which start-up business is best for you, give particular weight to the potential for residual income.

Low Start-up Costs/ Access to the Required Capital

"Capital isn't scarce; vision is."

Sam Walton

WARNING: The next several pages may cause severe drowsiness. Do not operate heavy (or even light) machinery while reading. It is strongly recommended that a large pot of coffee — the kind with caffeine — be kept immediately at hand. Under no circumstances should alcohol be consumed while reading these pages, as this will only exacerbate the side effects.

But seriously, folks . . . I wanted to make this book an enjoyable and entertaining reading experience. I also wanted it to be useful, informative, and practical. The next several pages contain a great deal of financial information that is useful, informative, and practical, and as far from entertaining as you are from Jupiter at this very moment. Mind-numbingly boring though it may be, this information is crucial to starting and growing a new business. You must find a way to comprehensively get through it. Coffee is one way. You could also try having someone stand behind you and beat you over the head with a rubber hammer should you begin to nod off. May The Force Be With You.

The definition of low start-up costs depends on how much you have available to invest and the potential return on investment (ROI). The less you need to invest the better, even if you have substantial financial resources to draw upon. You may be surprised to learn that more than 17 percent of all new businesses are started with less than $5,000. That said, however, remember: the lack of capital is one of the major causes of business failure.

According to Biz$hop, a publishing company in Port Angeles, Washington, the amount of capital used to start companies that are now worth more than a million dollars breaks down as follows:

Less than $5,000	17.5 percent
$5,000–$9,999	14 percent
$10,000–$19,999	15.5 percent
$20,000–$49,999	25 percent
$50,000–$99,999	15 percent
$100,000–$249,999	8 percent
$250,000–$499,999	2 percent
$500,000 and up	1 percent

Before we talk about estimating start-up costs, you need to know that there is a difference between start-up costs and operating costs. Start-up costs are one-time expenses that you shouldn't have to pay again for at least one year — if ever again. Start-up costs include, but are not limited to:

- Your building or office (if you buy)
- Equipment, such as computers, telephones, copier, fax machine, and tools
- Automobiles or trucks
- Any improvements you make in your office
- Signage
- Initial legal costs for setting up your company
- Licensing

Operating costs are expenses that recur on a regular basis. They include:

- Insurance
- Advertising
- Salaries
- Rent
- Telephone bills

To estimate start-up costs, begin with a Pro-Forma and a Break-Even analysis. These calculations are important for many reasons. For now, they will give you an idea of how long it will take for you to begin turning a profit. This, in turn, will allow you to estimate how many months of working capital and living expenses should be included in your initial start-up costs.

The person who invents a crystal ball that can accurately tell you whether your new business idea will be profitable will make a fortune all their own. In the absence of any means to see into the future, however, there is no way to determine the outcome, of a certainty. You can, however, use the information you collect researching the industry to make an educated guess.

Pro-Forma Analysis

A Pro-Forma Analysis is a projection of sales over a period of time. For the first three years of your business, it is best to do this analysis monthly. You will need to estimate, based on your research, what you expect your average percentage of monthly growth will be over the first full year, then the second and third years. Because you are starting at zero, your first year growth is usually much larger than later years. You may see a monthly increase of 20 to 30 percent or more in the first year, but over time the monthly growth rate will level off. By year three, your monthly growth rate may drop to between two and 10 percent or lower.

Break-Even Analysis

A Break-Even Analysis will show how much revenue you'll need to bring in each month to cover expenses. The money that you earn *after expenses* is profit. Most successful entrepreneurs use a Break-Even Analysis to screen new business ideas. For now, you can use it to estimate expenses and revenues based on the industry research you did earlier. On the Internet, you can also go to www.BizStats.com, select their "Benchmark Your Business in Five Seconds" option, click on a particular industry, and enter an estimated annual sales figure to find the average profitability and expense percentages for that industry.

For the Break-Even Analysis, you will need to make the following estimates:

Sales Revenue

This is your projected monthly sales — what you expect, *not* what you hope to do. Be careful not to overestimate this number.

Fixed Costs/Overhead

Fixed costs are exactly that, i.e., they don't change much from month to month. Fixed costs include:

- Rent
- Utilities

- Administrative staff salaries w/burden
- Insurance
- Advertising (budgeted)
- Telephone (budgeted)
- Office Supplies (budgeted)
- Printing (budgeted)
- Any other fixed costs

Costs of Goods Sold (COGS)

This is what you pay for the product or service you sell. For example, if you started a retail computer shop and you were able to buy computers wholesale for $500. That $500 would represent your COGS.

Average Gross Profit for Each Sale

This is what you would have left after paying direct sales costs. For example, if the retail price of that computer you sold was $800, you would have $300 left after COGS was deducted. That $300 would be your gross profit for the sale.

Average Gross Profit Percentage

This denotes how much of each dollar of the sales revenue is gross profit. Divide your average gross profit figure by the average selling price. In our computer example, $300 divided by $800 would equal .375 or 37.5 percent.

After you have determined all these figures, you are ready to calculate your break-even point. Divide your estimated monthly fixed costs by your gross profit percentage to determine the amount of sales revenue you'll need to break even. For example, if your computer business has fixed costs of $20,000 per month and your projected profit margin is 37.5 percent, your break-even point would be $53,333 in monthly sales revenue, i.e., $20,000 divided by .375. In short, you would need to do $53,333 in sales each month to cover your expenses. (*Remember:* This does *not* include profit or your salary.)

Next, using your research information on the industry, determine how probable it is that you can reach this point in revenues and how long it will take to get there. Will it happen in six months or three years? The faster you get to break even the better. Then you can stop borrowing from your own pocket (a.k.a. "Hip National Bank").

Estimating Required Working Capital

Now that you know your break-even point and you have estimated how many months it will take you to get there and become profitable, you can begin estimating start-up costs. This list must be specific and comprehensive. The sample list provided here is fairly common for many businesses; however, some items may not be applicable. In those places, enter zero. You may also have additional costs that are not listed here. Enter those costs under "Other."

Now enter your estimated cost(s) for each item. The total of these numbers is your estimated start-up cost.

CHECKLIST FOR ESTIMATED START-UP COSTS

Furniture, Fixtures & Equipment	Amount
Answering machine	
Cash registers	
Coffee maker	
Computers	
Copier	
Desks, chairs, tables, décor, window treatment, etc.	
Fax	
File cabinets	
Microwave	

Furniture, Fixtures & Equipment	**Amount**
Printers	
Refrigerator	
Safe	
Shelving	
Signage	
Telephone system	
Time clock	
Vacuum, mops, buckets	
Legal	
Accountant fees for initial set-up	
Attorney fees or retainers for initial set-up	
Board of Health license	
Business, vendor's, and other licenses	
Copyrights	
Fictitious name or doing business as (DBA) application fee	
Incorporation / LLC fees	
Liquor license	
Seller's permit	
Trademarks	
Land & Building	
Building and Zoning Permits	
Building plans	
Deposit on lease	
Deposits for utilities	
Down payments on mortgage, closing costs, and other fees	
Property taxes	

Remodeling & Improvements	Amount
Alarm system	
DSL and/or Internet installation fees	
Electrical	
Fire sprinkler system	
Installation of new heating and/or A/C system	
Landscaping	
Making needed items handicapped-accessible	
Plumbing	
Repaving or repair of parking lots	
Restrooms	
Telephone installation fees	
Research & Development	
Initial test marketing	
Patents	
Product testing	
Prototyping	
Inventory	
Initial inventory	
Storage	
Office supplies	
Personnel	
Deposit for worker's compensation	
On-the-job training	
Orientation	
Recruitment costs	
Up-front worker's compensation insurance payment	

Cash	Amount
Initial cash for cash register drawers	
Opening minimum balance in checking	
Petty cash fund	
Reserve for cash flow (i.e., two to three months of operating expenses)	
Six to 18 months of working capital	
Other	
Bonding	
Design of logos, business cards, initial advertising, etc.	
General liability insurance	
Grand opening advertising	
Initial inventory of office supplies	
Security personnel	
Living Expenses:	
Six to18 months of minimum monthly living expenses	
Total Start-up Costs	

Now compare the total start-up costs to the capital you have available to invest or that you can get your hands on (legally!) to determine whether it is feasible for you to pursue this particular business idea.

If you have the financial wherewithal to pull it off, next decide if the return on investment (ROI) makes sense. For example, a $500,000 investment in a venture that is likely to return no more than $10,000 per year in net profit over the next five years is not very appealing, as that return is less than a two percent annual ROI. Conversely, a $75,000 investment that returns an average of $50,000 per year in net profit over the first five years would equate to a 66 percent annual ROI. This would be much more attractive especially if, after the first two years or so, you can begin to minimize your own personal involvement. (*Note:* There aren't too many investments with an ROI that good.)

As you can see, this section was devoted to number-crunching. Start-up costs, Pro-formas, and Break-Even analyses will be part of your Business Plan, which is covered in greater detail in Chapter 8.

Duplicability — Run Your Business like a Franchise

"Discover what works best and do it again, but do it better."

Jerry L. Clum, Jr.

Webster defines "duplicate" as "to do or perform again." Find a business that is duplicable. The success or failure of the business should not continually depend on your involvement with the primary activities of the business. People often start businesses only to find themselves in a situation that is the opposite of what they intended. Maybe they've been working several years in a particular industry and they are good at what they do. One morning they wake up and say to themselves, "I'm tired of putting in 40 to 50 hours a week for that company and only being paid a fraction of what the company is earning from my work. I'm good at what I do. I'll start my own business — earn three times as much, work half as many hours, and make my own decisions." So they quit the job, start their own business and, three years later, find themselves working 60 to 80 hours a week with net earnings a little more than minimum wage. What went wrong?

As the owner, "they" were the business. If they took a day off, the business took the day off. If they were burned out, the business suffered. They lost focus and commitment, and the business failed. So, with savings likely depleted and now carrying even more debt, they find themselves looking for a new job.

"*Go to work* on *your business, rather than* in *your business.*"

Michael Gerber

Many small business owners work "in" their business. In addition to the day-to-day activities, the owner is also the HR Department, the Sales and Marketing Department, Accounts Payable, Accounts Receivable, Finance, and Customer Service. To avoid this trap:

- Hire the right people.
- Don't be afraid to delegate.
- Get out of their way.

Kris and I take at least 10 trips every year secure in the knowledge that our businesses will run smoothly without us. We don't have to worry about what will happen to the business should one of us become ill or have to leave on short notice for some reason. These are things that can cause major problems in businesses that rely too heavily on the owner. So, design duplicable processes, procedures, and systems.

You can order a hamburger from a McDonalds in Chicago and it looks, smells, and tastes the same as one ordered in Beijing, China. McDonalds has mastered the art of process. Every activity is broken down into steps that have proven to be the most efficient and effective way of performing that activity. These steps were then assembled into an Operations and/or Policies and Procedures Manual. It may take a great deal of time to pull together an Operations Manual for your business, and it is likely that you will never stop modifying it. But it is imperative for the success of your business.

One of the reasons I chose franchising as the vehicle to expand my own business was its duplicability. Setting up processes and systems allows you to reach your goals more consistently and efficiently. In the beginning, most business owners must do the majority of the work themselves. This is called "sweat equity," and it's inevitable unless you have a great deal of start-up capital on hand. But as soon as possible start bringing in the right people to take over different functions of the business. Also, be careful when deciding which work you will do and which you will delegate. If your goal is to earn at least a six-figure income, then don't do the $6 per hour work! Instead, you should be doing the $50-plus per hour work. Delegate less critical activities of your business. And don't make the mistake of waiting until the time is right, i.e., until you are making a little more money or until you get that one big deal you've been counting on. It is unlikely that the time will ever feel "right." Sometimes you will have to take two steps forward and three steps back to make progress. You may have to hire someone who is out of your price range and before you feel you can afford him or her. But hiring a less experienced person just because he or she is willing to work for half as much is not a good idea. One of my franchisees said, "I feel like I'm the conductor of an orchestra." That is the way to approach building a business. Find and hire the best "musicians" money can buy. Then learn to be the best possible conductor. If you try to "play all the instruments" yourself, the result will not be music to anybody's ears.

> ***"I'd rather have one percent of the efforts of 100 men than 100 percent of my own efforts."***
>
> J. Paul Getty

This approach, i.e., leading vs. being in the middle of the day-to-day firefights, will allow you to see the overall picture with near-perfect clarity. From that vantage point you can more easily identify problems and find creative ways to solve them.

Almost as soon as my company became profitable, and even before I was paying myself very much, I hired a President/COO and a Vice President of Operations/CFO. These are things you need to do before you get too comfortable performing those functions yourself and spending excess cash flow on other things. Invest the profits wisely, rather than spending them foolishly.

Franchises are the epiphany of duplicability, and a quality franchise is a proven system. By investing in one, you are starting well ahead of where you would be on your own. Franchising has made a name for itself. Although less than five percent of all businesses in the United States are franchised, 41 cents of every retail dollar is spent on products and services offered by franchises.

To decide whether you should consider investing in a franchise vs. starting your own independent business, you need to weigh the pros and cons.

PROS AND CONS OF FRANCHISING

Pros

1. You have a road map to follow. The processes have already been developed.
2. Other people are there to support you. You are in business for yourself, but not by yourself.
3. The franchisor will provide your initial training.
4. Less experimentation is required.
5. Ramp-up time is much quicker.
6. Franchises are usually much less expensive to start.
7. Lower overhead due to volume buying by the franchisor.
8. Other franchisees can provide support, provide motivation and share ideas.
9. The brand name is usually more easily recognized.
10. You feel like part of a team and, thus, less alone than when starting an independent business.
11. There are many things the franchisor may do for you that you could never afford to do on your own. These include national public relations, customized software, national strategic alliances with other companies, and even national advertising, if the franchise system has an advertising fund.

Cons

1. You will (usually) have to pay a royalty (typically three to eight percent or more of your gross revenues) to the franchisor. It is important to weigh the amount of support they provide and other benefits against the royalty you pay. In many cases, it can be well worth the investment.

2. You will be committed by a written contract to follow the franchisor's system.

3. You will (usually) be limited in the size of territory you can cover.

4. If the franchisor has a national advertising fund, you will have to pay additional fees (typically two to five percent of gross revenues) that the franchisor will spend on national advertising.

5. Even franchises can fail, though not as often as independent businesses. Just remember, there is still no guarantee of success.

If the business you are considering has been franchised, it is prudent to investigate the opportunities that may already exist with franchisors in that industry. You may decide that it makes more sense to invest in a franchise than to start your own independent business.

Flexibility

> *"Without work, all life goes rotten, but when work is soulless, life stifles and dies."*
>
> Albert Camus

Burnout is rarely mentioned as one of the top reasons for business failure. On the surface, this seems illogical. Why would a person who has created a successful, profitable business close down? Well, the truth is, it happens all the time. A business failure may be blamed on lack of sales, poor profit performance, or lack of additional capital, but burnout was probably the catalyst. The owner may simply have lost the focus, interest, and determination to persevere.

To reduce the chance of burnout, look for a business that will not require your undivided attention every minute of every day of every week. You must be able to take a break once in a while. Retail businesses or restaurants can require a great deal of your time depending on how long you are expected to be open for business each day and how many days of the week. For example, in a restaurant that serves breakfast, lunch, and dinner you may have to open as early as 6:00 a.m. and stay open as late as 11:00 p.m. Factor in an extra hour or more preparing to open and another hour or more to close, and that could mean having customers and/or employees in your establishment 19 hours of every day. And if your restaurant is open seven days a week, that would mean a staff requirement of 133 hours per week. With the right employees you may not need to be there every minute, but to some extent you will be "on call" anytime there are customers or employees in your restaurant, at least until you have recruited an outstanding General Manager.

Realize that no matter what business you decide to open, you will be burning the early morning, midday, and midnight oil for at least the first 18 to 24 months. It is important to factor this into your decision making process. At what point will there be some light at the end of the tunnel so that you will not have to spend the rest of your life working 70 to 80 hours a week? This is a crucial question because the likelihood of burnout goes up in direct proportion to the number of hours per week you will need to put in.

Great Market Potential

> ***"A market is never saturated with a good product, but it is quickly saturated with a bad one."***
>
> Henry Ford

How big can your company get? Many factors will determine what level of success you can achieve. Among the most important are the market and the need and/or desire for your product or service. Suppose, for example, you went into the typewriter business. The consensus would be that you are unlikely to find a market large enough to take your business to the level of success you may desire. But mere size of the market is not the only factor in play. The market for typewriters may have plunged, but $140 million worth of new typewriters and word processors are still being produced and sold. This is not meant to suggest that the typewriter business is viable. Rather, it illustrates the point that, with limited competition, even the most unlikely of industries can still hold some opportunity. Still, as a general rule, the better opportunities are to be found in industries with the larger potential market.

If the business you are starting has any potential for becoming the next "big thing," then you should be thinking in terms of a global market. We are fast becoming a global economy; thus, the businesses with the greatest chance for tremendous success will be those that provide products and services that can be marketed not only in the United States, but also in Hong Kong, Singapore, South Korea, China, Chile, India, Mexico, Thailand, Malaysia, Philippines, South Africa, Indonesia and Venezuela — i.e., countries with huge potential for economic growth.

But let's not put the cart before the horse. Before you can determine market potential, you must decide how big you want your business to become. If you would be happy with an upside potential of less than $10 million, then it may be feasible to confine yourself to doing business in your own city. If, however, you envision growing your revenues into the billions, then you must expand your research accordingly.

The Trade Area Analysis is a common and fairly simple formula for estimating the potential market for a product or service.

$$\text{MSP} = \text{POP} \times \text{PCE} \times (\text{TPI}/\text{MPI})$$

MSP = Market Sales Potential

POP = Area Population

PCE = State Per Capita Expenditure for
Type of Store or Product or Service

TPI = County Per Capita Income

MPI = State Per Capita Income

Relax. It looks more complicated than it is. Before you tackle this, however, you need to do a little more investigative work to:

1. Identify the population of the area you wish to serve
2. Determine the per capita expenditure for the type of store, product, or service you will provide
3. Determine the per capita income of your area relative to the state average, and
4. Estimate the market share you expect to capture.

Sources for this information include the Small Business Administration, Small Business Development Center, SCORE offices, local Chamber of Commerce, local, state and federal agencies, libraries, the Internet, and universities.

Suppose, for example, you want to open a large grocery store in Anywhere, USA. Your research shows that the population is 30,000 (POP) and that there are three other grocery stores in the area. The average per capita expenditure for grocery store products in your state is $1,200 (PCE); the per capita income in your county is $20,000 (TPI); and the per capita income in your state is $22,500 (MPI). For your Trade Area Analysis, plug these figures into that forbidding formula.

$$\text{MSP} = 30{,}000 \times \$1{,}200 \times (20{,}000/22{,}500 = .89)$$

$$\text{Thus, MSP} = \$32{,}040{,}000$$

Since you are about to open the fourth grocery store in an area that has three other established grocers, let's assume that you will initially be able to take over an equal share (in this case 25 percent) of the market. So —

$$.25 \times \$32{,}040{,}00 = \$8{,}010{,}000.$$

Next you need to determine the average percentage of net profit for this type of business. In this case, we have learned that larger grocery stores realize an average 1.4 percent net income as a percentage of sales.

Question: What would you end up putting in your pocket each year if you could maintain the average percentage of profit?

Answer: $112,140 (i.e., $8,010,000 × 1.4 percent)

Now decide whether the reward is big enough to justify the risk of your initial investment in time and money. If so, then the market potential exists for that particular business concept. If not, run the same formula on your next idea. *Note:* It is not easy to apply this formula to new businesses ideas. You can, however, compare figures on other similar existing business concepts to get a fair estimate.

Emerging Trends

"Advertising generally works to reinforce consumer trends rather than to initiate them."

Michael Schudson

While identifying the next "big thing" would be great, finding it (without the aid of that crystal ball) is difficult. However, you can draw some reasonable conclusions about the future, i.e., emerging trends, by looking at the past and following demographic population shifts. For example, if you trace the Baby Boomer generation (those born between 1946 and 1964) through the decades, it is easy to see the tremendous impact they have had on different industries.

One of the best-selling products in the world — the Hula Hoop — was produced in the late 1950s. In 1957, the proverbial light bulb came on over the heads of Richard Knerr and Arthur "Spud" Melin, founders of the Wham-O Company, after a conversation with an Australian who was visiting California. He told them that in his home country, children twirled bamboo hoops around their waists in gym class. Knerr and Melin had a winner. The following year, the Hula Hoop (named after the Hawaiian dance its use more or less resembles) was rolled out internationally. In this country alone, the company sold 25 million in two months. Approximately 100 million orders came in from other countries. By the end of 1958, the Hula Hoop fad was beginning to fizzle. But by then Knerr and Melin had rung up over $45 million in profits. And, just in case you think lightning never strikes twice in the same place, Knerr had also just come up with another winning idea — the Frisbee. Have you ever asked yourself why such a simple product was so successful? The answer is timing — the right idea at the right time.

As the Boomers grew up, they began to spend their money a little differently. There were more than 5,000 drive-in movie theatres during the 1960s, compared to less than 500 today. Why? The Baby Boomers were dating in the '60's. And, because they needed some place to sit at the drive-in, they were also buying cars — Firebird, Chevelle, Camaro, Road Runner, Corvette, Corvair, Malibu, Nova, Impala, El Camino, Charger, Hemi, Mustang, Thunderbird, 442, Cutlass, Hurst, and the GTO — to name a few. Industry giants in the Motor City (a.k.a. Detroit) designed "muscle" cars for the 18-to-34 year-old segment of the market. How many cars can you name today that are designed to appeal to that same market segment?

The 1970s ushered in one of the largest real estate booms in our history. The Boomers were growing up and starting families. Their need for housing ignited a buying frenzy.

In 1985, just minutes away from bankruptcy, CEO Richard Teerlink convinced lenders to accept a restructuring plan. Using management principles adopted from the Japanese, along with new marketing strategies and manufacturing techniques, Harley Davidson Motorcycles began its journey to regain market share. By the 1990s, demand was so high that there were two-year waiting lists for some models. And they were able to sell most of their bikes for twice as much as their Japanese competitors. What role did the Boomer generation play in this industry? They had reached a collective mid-life crisis, and the big boys needed new toys.

Historically, it has always been easy to assign blame or take credit for economic conditions. Thus, politicians occasionally wanted to take credit for the economic boom in the 1990s. But sometimes politics has nothing to do with it. The booming economy of the 1990s was largely due to basic market conditions. When there are more people buying than selling, the market goes up. Those were peak earning years for many of the Boomers. They were putting more into the equities market than ever before, and the market responded by growing. They were also buying luxury cars. Sales at Chrysler, Ford, and GM declined 9, 10 and 13 percent, respectively, while BMW, Mercedes, Lexus, and Audi were enjoying record sales — up 16, 19, 10 and 2.5 percent, also respectively. Finally, the 1990s were also "Boom" years for the diet, exercise, vitamin, and herbal products industries, as a generation began to see and feel the signs of age.

Hindsight is always 20/20. Indeed, it doesn't take a rocket scientist to recognize mistakes 10, 20, or 30 years after they're made. But is it really surprising to see how much the Baby Boomers have affected specific industries during specific time periods?

Few, if any, businesses are taking advantage of the indicators of market potential to determine what products or services they should be bringing to future markets. What will the Boomers be spending their money on in the future? Answer that question, and you may be on the right track to predicting an emerging trend and to identifying the kind of business you want to start.

Of course, the Baby Boomers are not the only barometers of demographic shift in America today. What about the Echo Boomers (a.k.a. the Millennial Generation, Millennials, or Generation Y)? Born between 1977 and 1994, these are the children and (sometimes) the grandchildren of the Baby Boomers. Weaned on video games and computers, this generation is more in touch with cutting-edge technology than any generation before. Having been slammed with advertising messages since birth, they are also more brand-conscious, although not as loyal to one product or service as their parents and grandparents may have been. There are abundant opportunities in this demographic as well.

LOW OVERHEAD

> *"Beware of little expenses. A small leak will sink a great ship."*
>
> BENJAMIN FRANKLIN

Question: What is overhead?

Answer: The costs of doing business that cannot be directly attributed to the product or service you provide, but are still necessary for the business to function.

Suppose, for example, that you start a business manufacturing computers. Your overhead costs would include rent, insurance, advertising, equipment maintenance, administrative salaries, etc. Direct labor costs would include manufacturing the computers themselves and the materials used in that those computers. Rather than overhead, these fall under COGS (see section on *Low Start-up Costs/Access to Required Capital*) or Cost of Sales (COS), and they are calculated on a different line on financial statements.

Although there are profitable businesses that have enormous overhead costs, typically the percentage of overhead is in direct proportion to the percentage of net income — the lower the overhead, the higher the profit.

According to BizStats.com, the average management consulting firm (proprietorship) has a net income of 62.8 percent, while gasoline stations (proprietorships) have an average of 3.3 percent net income. Which do you think has a larger overhead? The answer, of course, is gas stations because of the substantial costs including (typically) expensive real estate, pumps, storage tanks, building, and signage. Management consulting, which is really just the sale of information, has a much lower overhead.

VOLUME-INTRINSIC

As sales go up, so do expenses. But in businesses that are volume-intrinsic, the growth in expenses is not necessarily in direct proportion to the growth in sales. This means that as your sales volume goes up, the percentage going to expenses is reduced, which gives you a higher net profit percentage. The most profitable businesses are those that are most volume-intrinsic.

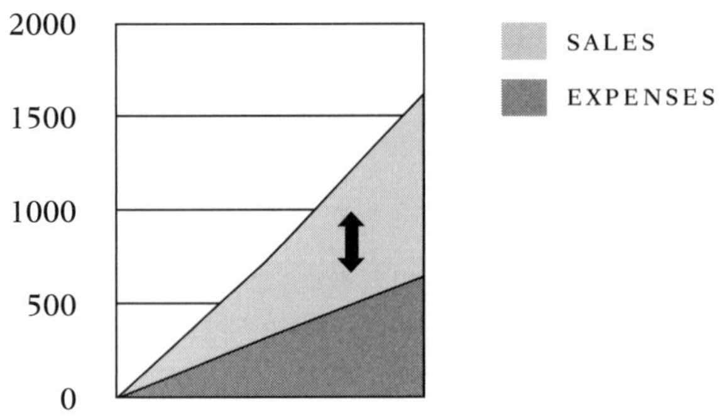

To determine how volume-intrinsic your business idea may be you need to perform a Cost, Volume, and Profitability Analysis (CVP). This is a tool for examining the relationship between *fixed and variable costs,* volume, and profits. Fixed costs (e.g., rent, insurance, salary of administrative personnel) generally do not change regardless of the level of sales. Variable costs (e.g., materials, direct labor, commissions), on the other hand, generally increase in direct proportion to sales. Using your research and/or estimates for a particular business idea, you can determine whether each estimated expense is variable or fixed. Total each category to obtain the Contribution Margin, i.e., the percentage of each sales dollar that remains after the *variable costs* are deducted. In short, subtract your estimated annual variable expenses from estimated annual revenues. The remainder is the Contribution Margin. Divide that by annual revenues to get the *percentage* of Contribution Margin. By way of example, here is an analysis of a fictitious computer manufacturing company called ABC Computers.

ABC COMPUTER COMPANY
CONTRIBUTION FORMAT INCOME STATEMENT
FOR YEAR ENDED DECEMBER 31, 20XX

Sales	$1,894,865	
Variable Costs:		
Cost of Goods Sold	970,675	
Commissions	189,420	
Total Variable Costs	$1,160,095	
Contribution Margin	$734,770	39 percent
Fixed Costs:		
Rent	84,000	
Depreciation	68,843	
Insurance	12,370	
Payroll and Burden	207,430	
Advertising	45,000	
Total Fixed Costs	$417,643	
Net Operating Income	$317,127	17 percent

In general, the higher the percentage of Contribution Margin the better, because as business volume increases the business will be more profitable. Here, I have increased the sales of the ABC Computer Company by 100 percent. Note that this changes the dollar amount of the variable costs, but *not* the dollar amount of the fixed costs.

ABC COMPUTER COMPANY
CONTRIBUTION FORMAT INCOME STATEMENT
FOR YEAR ENDED DECEMBER 31, 20XX

Sales	$3,789,730	
Variable Costs:		
Cost of Goods Sold	1,941,350	
Commissions	378,840	
Total Variable Costs	$2,320,190	
Contribution Margin	$1,469,540	39 percent
Fixed Costs:		
Rent	84,000	
Depreciation	68,843	
Insurance	12,370	
Payroll and Burden	207,430	
Advertising	45,000	
Total Fixed Costs	$417,643	
Net Operating Income	$1,051,897	28 percent

As you can see, when the sales doubled, so did variable costs. However, Net Operating Income (in dollars) more than tripled, from $317,127 in the first example to over $1 million in the second example. This is the advantage of businesses that are more volume-intrinsic. So be sure to perform a CVP analysis before deciding what business to start.

Something You Would Enjoy and Are Capable of Becoming an Expert In

> *"Chose a job you love, and you will never have to work a day in your life."*
>
> Confucius

The few people who have or have had the opportunity to do what they love for a living can attest to the fact that it is much easier to roll out of bed in the morning. So choose a business that fits your personality and philosophies. That said, however, it is important to remember these two axioms:

1. You won't be successful just because the business is something you love to do or are good at. (*This is only one piece of the puzzle.*)
2. It is almost impossible to be successful if the business is something you hate and aren't good at. (*But, it's a very important piece of the puzzle.*)

Now *that's* inscrutable! You can see why I chose to begin this section with a quote from Confucius. Just bear with me here.

If you go back and look at the *15-Item Acid Test for Evaluating Business Concepts* you will see that there are two parts — two pieces — to this puzzle. The first, "something you would enjoy," is straightforward and self-explanatory. The second, "and are capable of becoming an expert in," is somewhat more complicated. While advanced knowledge of the industry you're considering is helpful, you need not already be an expert in it *provided you feel you can become one*. No doubt there are certain industries for which you know you are better suited. Pick your business from among those industries. Then be prepared to become a walking sponge — soaking up as much knowledge and information as is humanly possible. Do extensive research, learn all you can about your competitors, and know your product (or service) inside and out, forward and backward.

Finally, it is not uncommon for people to overestimate what it takes to become an expert. If you know just a fraction more than most of the other people in your competitive area, you're an expert!

> ***"You don't have to be faster than the bear, you just have to be faster than the slowest guy running from the bear."***
>
> GROUCHO MARX

Large Labor Pool or not Labor-Intensive

I've often heard business owners lament the necessity for — and expense of — employees. While having no employees would make many things less complicated, it is doubtful you would be able to start a business, at least not a big business, without them. Moreover, the right employees, properly trained and motivated, can help exponentially in the growth of your business.

Because industries vary so much, it is difficult to set acceptable limits on what would be defined as labor-intensive. Begin by determining the percentage of labor costs vs. total revenues for each business you are considering. This will help you to gauge which are more labor-intensive. A business with 40 full and part-time employees, a total payroll expense of $750,000, and sales of $1 million would certainly be considered labor-intensive. On the other hand, a business with 40 full-time employees doing all the work needed in a business grossing $100 million in revenues — now that's a horse of another (and much more pleasant) color.

Here are some examples of industries that are considered labor-intensive.

- Most manufacturing
- Some agricultural, where automated equipment cannot be used
- Heavy construction
- Transportation industry (air, bus, taxis, and rail)
- Most service oriented businesses

- Hotel industry
- Education and training
- Restaurants
- Wholesale trade
- Housekeeping and cleaning services
- Child care facilities
- Food processing
- Hospitals and health care
- Many retail stores, especially the larger discount stores

If your business concept falls within these categories, that doesn't necessarily mean you should not move forward. It does mean that you need to do some more homework. Specifically, you need to evaluate how difficult it will be to recruit the type of employees who have the skill levels your business requires. Here again, you will need to do extensive research on your market area and its current employment conditions. Excellent resources include your state office of employment, the Chamber of Commerce, libraries, and local colleges or universities. Often you will find that comprehensive studies have already been done on labor conditions in your state and/or county. Check with your state employment bureau to see if a study has been completed. (*Note:* Employment bureaus are known by different names in different states. These can include Department of Human Resources, Department of Job and Family Services, Workforce Commission, Job Services, Department of Employment, Unemployment Office, Bureau of State Employment, Employment Security Department, Career and Employment Center, Department of Labor, or Department of Career Development.)

With information from these studies, you can determine the number of potential employees that will be available to you at different pay thresholds. For example, if your business plan projects that you will need to hire 20 sales clerks over the next two years, and you have estimated your average starting wage at $8 to $10 per hour, the study may show you there are 2,500 people in the available workforce who may meet the skill level you require. On the other hand, at $8 per hour there may only be 500 available workers, whereas at $15 per hour that number may jump to 10,000. The available workforce consists of people who are actively seeking employment or those who would be willing to shift to a higher-paying job if the circumstances were right. So, not only will this research shed some light on the availability of potential employees in your area, it may also give you an estimate of what you will need to pay to attract the best and brightest.

Limited Amount of Inventory to Stock

"The inventory goes down the elevator every night."

Fairfax Cone

Starting a business in which you must keep a significant amount of inventory will add a great deal of aggravation to an effort that is already pregnant with the stuff! It will usually mean a substantial increase in overhead costs as well. Of course, the products and materials of which inventory is actually composed make up a large portion of the overhead costs. There are, however, many other costs — Inventory Carrying Costs — which you would have to factor in. These include:

- Depreciation
- Cost of insuring inventory
- Warehouse costs (rent, utilities, etc.)
- Cost of theft
- Cost of damage
- Cost of inventory that becomes obsolete
- Financing costs
- Opportunity costs (what you might have earned if the funds tied up in inventory were instead invested)
- Other types of shrinkage
- Taxes on inventory
- Material handling costs

Because of the many complex problems that come with a business in which a substantial amount of inventory is required, it is best to avoid that type of business, if possible. If a substantial inventory is a requirement of the business you have selected, then you will need to include a considerable "cushion" in your start-up costs, as well as an additional 30 percent in carrying costs above and beyond the cost of the inventory. For example, if you must maintain $150,000 worth of inventory, factor in an additional $45,000 annually to cover carrying costs.

RECESSION-RESISTANT

"It's a recession when your neighbor loses his job; it's a depression when you lose yours."

HARRY S. TRUMAN

When I was conducting business valuations, inevitably the owner would show me a line chart indicating business growth, and there was always a logical explanation for every year the sales went up or down. Sometimes sales went down because of a problem in the sales department. Sometimes sales went up because the company had hired a new VP of Sales. Whatever the direction of the sales, the owner always had a good reason for it.

Later on, back at my hotel, I used my laptop to compare the owner's chart to general economic conditions in the same time periods. Often the owners chart would mimic the economic chart almost exactly, which meant that the owner thought he or she was controlling the business when in fact the economy was a major controlling factor.

You could probably count on one hand the number of businesses that are 100 percent recession-proof. If it were true that death and taxes are the only two certainties in life, then funeral directors who specialize in selling their services to the surviving spouses of IRS agents would be in a recession-proof line of work. The rest of us have to settle for making our businesses recession-resistant.

Some types of businesses are less affected by economic events than others. Here is a partial list of businesses that are generally considered to be recession resistant.

- Upscale products (catering to clients who have a surplus of disposable income)
- Upscale services (catering to clients who have a surplus of disposable income)
- Automotive oil change
- Automotive tune-up centers
- Automotive transmission centers
- Health care-related companies
- Vending businesses
- Home repair services
- Businesses catering to the vices (alcohol, tobacco, gambling, adult entertainment, etc.)
- Security system services
- Business brokering
- Bookkeeping services
- Computer consulting
- Computer repair
- Medical claims assistance
- Medical transcriptionist
- Résumé writer
- Secretarial and office support services
- Tax preparation
- Hair care services
- Food related companies
- Retailing to the teen market
- Self-storage facilities
- Hearing aid centers
- Carpet cleaning services
- Recruiting services in specialized niches

- Gasoline stations (limited resistance to recessionary times)
- Commercial cleaning
- Debit and ATM card processing
- Used car sales
- Pharmacies
- Law firms
- Dental care
- Defense contractors
- Services catering to the senior population
- Retail sleep specialty market (bedding, mattresses, etc.)
- Gold and precious metal mining
- Dry cleaning
- Bars and taverns
- Supermarkets
- Some restaurants
- Educational services

See any common characteristics? In general, the businesses that do well, regardless of economic conditions, are those that provide products or services that are wanted and/or needed regardless of economic conditions. Come recession or high water, people still have to eat, drink, take care of their health, and repair and maintain their cars and houses.

Businesses whose customers come from higher income brackets are, in general, recession-resistant. The wealthy and the uppermost middle class almost always keep a surplus of cash in reserve. During tough economic times they may have to cut back a little, but rarely will they have to tighten their belts to the same degree as their less fortunate brethren.

Businesses that cater primarily to a teenage market can also, in general, weather tough economic times. Most teenagers live and eat at home, have few household expenses, and often have jobs with restaurants and retailers. In short, they are up to their designer jeans — and beyond — in disposable income. A *Harris Interactive* study showed that 75 percent of bulk earnings for girls and 52 percent of bulk earnings for boys is spent on clothing. According to Larry Leeds, an investment manager at Buckingham Capital Management, Inc., "teentailers" are the most recession-resistant market for American retailing.

Use these common characteristics and the exceptions to your advantage when deciding on the type of business you want to start. Research your concept, and lean toward those businesses that are less economy-driven and more market-driven. This will not only better your chances of success, but it will also increase the odds of continued growth for many years to come.

Non-Seasonal

Would you be comfortable in a business in which 50 percent of annual sales had to be earned in one month? That is the case for many retailers. According to the Retail Council of New York, merchants rely on the 30-day period between Thanksgiving and Christmas for up to half of their total annual revenues. Think about it. One really bad month could cut your revenues almost in half for the entire year!

In general, a business is considered to be seasonal if it must make more than 75 percent of its sales for the year in a time period equal to or less than six months. Unlike non-seasonal businesses, seasonal businesses must always have a cash reserve available to get through the off-season. Sales may slow to a trickle during the off-season, but many of the monthly expenses still remain. It doesn't take a Harvard MBA to figure out that when you have expenses, yet no income, you can have problems.

Ski resorts, snow removal businesses, and snowmobile sales are not real moneymakers in many parts of the country in August, nor are swimming pool sales, water skiing, and boat sales in January in other parts of the country. In short, avoid cyclical businesses if at all possible. If you do decide to enter a seasonal industry, your business plan must include a means by which you can diversify your business into multiple income streams, which you can leverage during the slow months. For a seasonal business, this is critical.

Now that we have fully expanded the items within our *15-Item Acid Test For Evaluating Business Concepts*, it should make it easier for you to evaluate your selected business ideas to determine which ones have the best possible chance of succeeding.

Learn from the Masters

> *"The secret of business is to know something that nobody else knows."*
>
> Aristotle Onassis

In this chapter, you have learned various ways to evaluate different businesses before choosing one to open on your own. Here are five additional points to consider. If they're good enough for — James Pierpont Morgan, Ray Kroc, Donald Trump, Bill Gates, John D. Rockefeller, Robert Morris, Walt Disney, Mary Kay Ash, Henry Ford, David Sarnoff, Sam Walton, David Ogilvy, Cyrus McCormick, Stephen Girard, Cornelia Vanderbilt, Mark Cuban, Frederick Weyerhaeuser, and John Jacob Astor — then they're good enough for us.

1. Learn from the masters. Every major business success has at least one thing in common: supply and demand. The founder saw a major opportunity when they uncovered or created a demand for a particular product or service where the supply was not being met. They found ways to meet that demand and became rich in doing so.
2. Learn from the masters. Timing is everything. It is easy to be too early or too late getting into the marketplace. If Alexander Graham Bell had invented the telephone 200 years earlier, he might have been burned at the stake for practicing witchcraft.
3. Learn from the masters. Find a niche and fill it. You don't need a completely new idea to come up with the next "big thing." You can be just as successful, perhaps even more

so, if you find a specific and narrow market, and penetrate it deeply rather than trying to be a jack-of-all-trades with a broad group of products and services.

4. Learn from the masters. Passion. They all had passion for what they were doing.

5. Learn from the masters. They all found something they were good at and then capitalized on that strength.

What if Bill Gates had not become a Harvard pre-law dropout in the mid-70s and, thus, had never started Microsoft? How much different would his life be today? How much different would your life be? For that matter, how much different would the world be? Like the other masters, Bill Gates recognized his strengths and made them work for him. You may have that elusive pot of gold right now in the palm of your hand. Learn to capitalize on your strengths and you may never again have to search for greener pastures.

Your Acres of Diamonds

In the late 19th century lived a man by the name of Russell Conwell. He began his professional career as a lawyer, but later decided to become a Baptist minister. His life's goal was to build a university for students who might not otherwise have been able to afford a college education. He achieved this goal by delivering a speech called "Acres of Diamonds" more than 6,000 times. Many consider it to be the best motivational speech ever written. Dr. Conwell made a great deal of money from this speech over the years — enough to provide most of the funds for the founding of Temple University in Philadelphia in 1884. Temple is now the 36th-largest university in the United States.

The story that Dr. Conwell told was about a farmer named Al Hafed who lived in Africa. It is a true story.

Hafed was a wealthy and content farmer, but after a conversation with an old priest who had visited him, he began to think that perhaps he wasn't as wealthy as he could be. The priest told him all about diamonds — how they were formed and how valuable they really were. Hafed, no longer content with his wealth from farming, decided to begin searching for diamonds and become wealthy beyond his widest dreams. At the time, diamonds were being discovered in abundance on the African continent. Hafed got so excited about the idea of finding diamonds that could potentially be worth millions of dollars that he immediately sold his farm and began his search for those valuable gems. He spent many years roaming the African continent spending every waking hour searching for his new wealth. He never found his diamonds and finally spent the last of his money he had received from selling his farm. He was thought to have committed suicide by casting himself into a tidal wave and drowning. As all of this was happening, the old priest happened to visit the new owner of Hafed's farm. During his visit, the old priest caught a flash of light coming from an unusual-looking rock on the new owner's mantel. The old priest rushed over to the rock and told the new owner he was certain that it was a diamond. In his excitement, he asked the new owner if Hafed had returned. The new owner told the priest that he had not and that the rock was nothing but a stone that he found right out in his garden on the farm. The priest told the new owner that he knew a diamond when he saw one, and this was definitely a diamond. The new owner of the farm told the priest that the entire farm was covered with them — and wouldn't you know it, it really was. That farm is known today as the Golconda Diamond Mines, and it turned out to be one of the richest diamond mines in the world. The great Kohinoor diamond in England's crown jewels and the largest crown diamond in the world, which is in Russia's crown jewels, came from that mine. Unfortunately, Hafed was literally standing on "Acres of Diamonds" until he sold his farm. All of us may well be standing right in the middle of our own "Acre of Diamonds" — we just need to recognize it and do something with it before we begin our search for greener pastures. What are you really good at? Can you turn it into a successful business?

> *"It is easy to have passion for something you are truly passionate about."*
>
> Jerry L. Clum, Jr.

Chapter 6

The Winning Philosophies

"If winning isn't everything, why do they keep score?"

Vince Lombardi

What does it mean to win? According to Webster's, it is to finish first in a race, a contest, or the like. But if you have to lie, cheat, steal, or push someone down to win, is it still winning? Now, more than ever in our history, we need to revisit the true definition of winning.

I believe winning is the act of progressing towards your goals and doing the best you can while not sacrificing your character or integrity. The Enron scandal — and WorldCom and Global Crossing and Tyco — might have been avoided had winning been redefined in time. Corruption, greed, and the desire to win by fair means or foul have become a sign of our times.

I believe the root for much of this turmoil can be traced to the compensation received by key officers in big corporations. When 80 to 90 percent of the total value of a CEO's salary is composed of stock option plans and the like, bad decision-making is almost a sure thing. Think about it. How many presidents of big companies make critical decisions every day based on the effect of immediate profitability, which usually translates into short-term stock prices? It is the quintessential definition of not seeing the forest for the trees.

Perhaps we should take a lesson from Japanese management philosophy and focus on the big picture. The Japanese seem less concerned about short-term profitability if they can see higher long-term profitability in the future. This may be one of the reasons they have successfully taken over market share in so many of the product areas where we were once the dominating force. While we seem to worry about the next quarterly returns, they focus on the next quarter century. They believe in investing in the future.

> ***"Someone's sitting in the shade today because someone planted a tree a long time ago."***
>
> Les Brown

I don't believe this is an original concept. Even a brief look at American business history shows that many of our biggest success stories are based on the concept of long-term thinking and investing in the future. Visionary founders established these philosophies very early in their start-ups.

Fast-forward to the present, and we sometimes discover that many of these early start-ups have become enormous public companies where the founder's original vision may have become a little fuzzy. In many cases, this is due to the need for instant financial gratification. But I believe that the most successful businesses of the future will be those that adopt the early philosophies that are part of our rich corporate legacy. As the song says, "Everything old is new again." So in addition to hanging on to those old bell bottoms for round three, I am predicting that the old business philosophy of long-term thinking and investing in the future will come back into style, at least among those business owners who want to be around in another 50 years.

In the next few pages, I will discuss Winning Philosophies that are crucial to any successful business.

People-First Philosophy

"If you treat people right, they will treat you right... ninety percent of the time."

Franklin D. Roosevelt

During the years I spent evaluating businesses, I was privileged to meet some of the most respected small businesspeople in the world. Of the many things I learned, by far the most important is the People-First Philosophy. The business owners for whom this was a core principle were personally happier and earned greater financial rewards, as well.

Today when a CEO or other corporate executive of a large public company has a major decision to make, they may evaluate the ramifications based on how that decision will affect:

1. Profitability
2. Customers
3. Employees

And they normally prioritize their evaluation in that order.

Thus, if one decision will have a more favorable affect on profitability, that decision becomes the flavor of the week, many times even if the effect on customers and/or employees will be negative. For example, when a company lays off 10,000 employees, the executives will usually cite profitability as the key reason for the decision. Will customers benefit from 10,000 fewer employees? Unlikely. And we know that this certainly is not beneficial to the employees! Sometimes a certain decision may be positive in terms of profitability and the customers, but less so for employees. For instance, a company decides to automate a manufacturing process with the use of robotics and thus is "forced" to terminate all of the employees who had performed that function. The results are in and profitability is the bigger winner — hands down.

Not that profitability is a bad thing. No, sir! It is one of the more important reasons to be in business. But it should not be the *only* reason.

Read most company Mission Statements and you may come away believing that profitability is not a major player on the corporate stage after all.

"We're going to produce high-quality goods or services and satisfy our customers, and we consider our employees as our greatest asset."

See? The word profitability isn't even used. Yet a huge contradiction exists, as it remains the primary consideration in almost every corporate decision.

This is where the People-First Philosophy differs. If you want to establish a business that will grow and prosper, while at the same time, nurturing loyalty and pride of workmanship in your employees, you need to invert the former equation and instead evaluate the ramifications of decisions based on how they will affect:

1. Employees
2. Customers
3. Profitability

Is it important to take profitability into account when making a decision? Absolutely. But the first consideration should be how the decision will affect your employees and your customers. Thus, if the decision will have a major negative effect to the employees it generally would not be implemented even if it would have a positive effect on the customers and/or profitability. It has been my experience that when you put your employees and customers above your profit concerns, the profit is still there, and (typically) there is more of it.

The idea of placing consideration of employees ahead of customers contradicts an older school of thought in which the customer was the most important piece of the puzzle. After all, the customer pays everyone's salary. Although this is true, I have found that if you put the well- being of your employees first, they in turn will provide what all customers are looking for — the highest level of service, artificially making the customer the most important element of the three.

If I have made the People-First Philosophy sound like a walk in the park, nothing could be further from the truth.

There may come a time when you have to "fire" a profitable customer because they are being too hard on some of your employees. The urge to tell your employees to suck it up and deal with it will be powerful. But for the sake of the employees, your business, and yourself, you must have the courage to do what is right. There will also be times when you'll have to pony up the cash and dip into your profits to do the right thing for your employees or your customers. This is where the philosophical rubber meets the road. This is when you find out if your commitment to the People-First Philosophy is more than skin-deep.

The first Christmas after Kris and I started our business, we wanted to do something for our 18 employees. We had been open a little more than nine months, and the business was not yet realizing a profit. But I had worked for other companies — some quite large — where employees did not so much as receive a Christmas card, let alone any tangible token of appreciation. I knew we needed to do something. In the end, we gave each employee a bonus of $150 to $200. That may not seem like a lot, but with nearly $70,000 of our life savings in a business that had yet to turn a profit, handing out $3,200 in cash to relatively new employees who were earning between $6.50 to $7.00 an hour was a true test of our faith in the People-First Philosophy, particularly if you consider the fact that we used a cash advance from one of our not-yet-maxed-out credit cards to do it! In addition, we weren't certain how much we were going to be able to do for own family that year. So the People-First Philosophy isn't always easy. But if it was, it probably wouldn't be that special.

We have always made it a point to celebrate birthdays, holidays, and employment anniversary dates with our employees. For birthdays, we try to be sure the gift has some thought behind it. If you get to know your employees well, this isn't so difficult. One of our employees is a NASCAR fan who idolizes Jeff Gordon. For her birthday one year we got her tickets to the Brickyard 400 and an autographed picture of Gordon, and presented it to her at a staff meeting. She had tears in her eyes for the rest of the meeting. I also remember the first-year anniversary party we had with our first four employees. We told them we were taking them out to dinner and that we would pick them up at home. What we didn't tell them is that we would be arriving in an elegant white stretch limousine, with a dozen roses for each of them. (Not to mention several bottles of champagne!) The same thing happened at each house. We rolled up in the limo and jumped out of the car carrying champagne and roses, and scores of neighbors would peek through doors and windows to see what was going on — probably expecting to see Ed McMahon from the Publisher's Clearinghouse. When our employee came out and the driver opened the door, a family member would usually run out and ask us to wait so they could take a picture. Four employees, four homes, 120 miles round trip and a meal at one of the best restaurants in the state, for a grand total of about $1,000. And worth every penny for an evening we will never forget. Remember. These were $6.50 an hour employees, not six-figure salaried executives. A couple of them had never even been in a limousine before, yet they were experiencing this grand evening because of their employer. To really get a full appreciation of this you have to ask yourself a question. Have you ever worked for a company where you never received so much as a thanks or a "job well done" or a congratulations on your one-year anniversary — let alone been given the royal treatment? As an employer, you will be remembered for the things that you do, not necessarily the things you say.

Once in a while an employee would call to tell me their car had broken down and they couldn't get to work that day. In my mind, I could hear the voices of some of my old managers. "Hey, that's not my problem. That's your problem. You better find a way to get to work or you're not going to have a job to come to." It doesn't take a rocket scientist to know that a dictatorial approach — ruling with an iron fist — is not a way to retain employees. If you hire the best and the brightest, and you want to keep them, then learn to think outside that outdated management box. Get creative. I once rented a car for an employee who was having car trouble!

If I sound like a cross between Pollyanna and Donald Trump, you're missing the point. I believe in the People-First Philosophy because it works. It's good for the employees and it's good for business. Will you get stabbed in the back once in a while? Yes. But this philosophical carrot still works better than any managerial stick. You just have to apply it, live by it, and not lose faith in it.

Employees will work their fingers to the bone for an employer who cares about them and shows it. Any fool can "demand" respect. But the smart — and most successful — business owners know that the only way to get it is to *earn it*.

> *"A good manager is a man who isn't worried about his own career, but rather the careers of those who work for him. My advice: Don't worry about yourself. Take care of those who work for you and you'll float to greatness on their achievements."*
>
> H.S.M. Burns

One of the most often-touted personal financial strategies is: Pay yourself first. While this may be effective in terms of giving yourself more control of your income, paying down debt, and building up savings, alas, it does not fit well with our People-First Philosophy.

When you are operating with a limited amount of cash flow, you need to invest that cash in the areas of your business where the investment will provide the biggest return, i.e., sales and marketing, your suppliers, and — surprise — your employees. This may mean having to tighten your personal belt a little further to get through hard times.

Some new business owners mistakenly pull out every dime they can to live a lifestyle that does not reflect the true picture of the company. This is often a guaranteed formula for failure. I have seen business owners take money from the business to pay a personal expense and not have enough left to meet their payroll!

AFNC

Then there is the All Flash, but No Cash (AFNC) syndrome. (In Texas, this is referred to All Hat, but No Cattle (AHNC).) Business owners set up lavish offices with all the bells and whistles and pronounce to the world they have started their own successful business. Six months later they are selling everything off for pennies on the dollar and closing their doors. Fortunately, this is one of the easiest business traps to avoid. *Invest only in items that are absolutely necessary*. Hold the flash until you really have the cash.

Do not confuse this with the necessity of maintaining the professional image as required in your industry. In the beginning, our business was home-based. Clients never had a need to visit my office. Even so, my literature, business cards, letterhead, and brochures were all top-of-the-line, full-color professional pieces. This was not overkill. Rather it was a necessary expenditure to meet expectations in my industry.

Dress for Success

No doubt you've heard the expression "dress for success." Well, it's corny, but it's true. If you want to be successful, you need to look successful. You don't need $1,000 suits, but you do need to keep your shirts ironed, pants pressed, and shoes shined.

I have a pet peeve about my shoes, and I (conveniently) blame this on my grandmother. She lived through the Depression and, like most people, she didn't have much, but she took care of what she had. One day she caught sight of my shoes and was not a happy camper. First, she lectured me about the importance of keeping them polished. Then, before I left, she made me polish them until I could see my face in them. Years later, in the Air Force, shoe shining was again reinforced. To this day, even when there isn't a melody in my heart, there's a shine on my shoes!

It sounds like a small thing, I'm sure, but people notice small things, and you can tell a lot about a person from the way their shoes look. In general, I dress one notch up from what is expected for any function I am attending. Better to be a little overdressed than a little underdressed. Of course, at some point, this all becomes a matter of sartorial taste. For example, I have a thing for expensive rings and watches. Now many of the dress for success books advise against wearing expensive jewelry for business occasions. They believe such trinkets make you look a bit flashy. While I am sure there is some truth in this, and I definitely draw the line at nose rings and any other pierced body parts that are readily observable, I can't see where wearing a nice watch or a ring has ever done me any harm.

Is it fair for people to judge others and treat them differently based on first impressions? No. But if you're waiting for the world to be fair, don't hold your breath.

Exit Strategy

"Every exit is an entry somewhere else."

Tom Stoppard

Another Winning Philosophy is the Exit Strategy. It may seem premature to talk about how you will leave your business before you even get started. Nevertheless, an Exit Strategy is mandatory, and you should work it out well ahead of the time when you'll need it. Many of the decisions you will make along the way can, and should, be influenced by the initial Exit Strategy. Some of the more common exit strategies are:

1. Selling 100 percent of your ownership interests and leaving the business completely.
2. Selling all or part of your business and remaining as an employee or consultant.
3. Recruiting key officers, managers, or partners to take over day-to-day responsibilities, while you act as an advisor and pursue other business interests or retire.
4. Taking your business public.
5. Merging your business with another business.
6. Acquiring other businesses under your existing business.
7. Building your business and turning it over to your children or other family members.
8. Closing your doors and selling off its assets.

Your business plan, which we will talk about in a later chapter, should include your proposed exit strategy, and now is a good time to start thinking about it. It's like planning a vacation. You don't usually say, "I think I'll go on vacation today," then jump into your car and head to the nearest airport. Instead, you plan where you are going, buy the tickets ahead of time, reserve your room, and maybe even check out the activities that will be available when you get there. Put another way, you don't start the journey until you have decided on the destination.

A Quest for Knowledge

The final Winning Philosophy is to never stop learning or growing. Knowledge (and the quest for knowledge) is the fuel that sparks imagination. Knowledge and imagination combined are the fuel that sparks success.

Read at least 15 new books each year. Pick topics that interest you and seem to stimulate your thinking. The average book contains 70,000 words. The average reader can read 250 to 300 words per minute. This means the average book should take about 4½ hours to read. So you should be able to read 15 new books per year with a time investment of about 68 hours, or 11 minutes per day, or by giving up one 30-minute television show three days a week. (If you're a television junky and that seems to be too much of a sacrifice, then read during the commercials of one 30-minute television show each day, and you will still get in 15 books by the end of the year. Hopefully, the story lines won't start running together.)

Another great learning opportunity is the time you spend driving. The average American now spends 443 hours per year behind the wheel of a car. Most of the time is spent listening to music or talk shows (or perhaps yelling at other drivers.) There are better ways to invest that time.

For more than half my life I have listened to personal development audio cassette tapes and CDs covering topics such as selling and marketing, advertising, leadership, management, motivation, psychology, goal-setting, wealth-building, time management, learning techniques, and spiritual growth. My library includes more than 400 programs with nearly 2,300 tapes and CDs, totaling an investment of more than

$27,000. I have listened to most of the programs at least five times and some more than 20. If this sounds a little compulsive, so be it. But I can assure you that what I have gained from these programs has proven more valuable over the years than what I learned obtaining my MBA.

> *"Turn your car into a University on wheels!"*
>
> Brian Tracy

> *"I wouldn't take $100,000 for my cassette recorder if I were not allowed to replace it."*
>
> Zig Ziglar

> *"Work harder on yourself than you do on your job. If you work hard on your job you'll make a living; if you work hard on yourself you'll make a fortune!"*
>
> Jim Rohn

A UCLA study concluded that you could gain the equivalent of one year of college by listening to educational tapes in your car over the course of a year.

Tracy, Ziglar, and Rohn are three of the best selling authors and motivational speakers in their field. If they are still finding new things to learn, why should you and I be any different?

"Birds of a feather flock together" is an adage with a good deal of truth behind it. If you want to be successful, choose your friends well and surround yourself with successful people. Since most of us will never have the opportunity to surround ourselves with famous and successful authors, speakers, and businesspeople, reading and listening to their ideas will have to do. Here is a list of my favorite authors and speakers. I have listened to their material more times than I can begin to count. My advice? Buy their books, tapes, CDs, and/or videotapes. Attend a seminar if there is one in or near your hometown. It's an investment in your business and yourself.

Jay Abraham	www.abraham.com
Les Brown	www.lesbrown.com
Dale Carnegie	www.dalecarnegie.com
Stephen Covey	www.stevencovey.com
Michael Gerber	www.e-myth.com
Napoleon Hill	www.naphill.org
Tom Hopkins	www.tomhopkins.com
Harvey Mackay	www.mackay.com
Earl Nightingale	www.nightingaleconant.com
Tom Peters	www.tompeters.com
Anthony Robbins	www.anthonyrobbins.com
Jim Rohn	www.jimrohn.com
Brian Tracy	www.briantracy.com
Donald Trump	www.trumponline.com
Denis Waitley	www.waitley.com
Zig Ziglar	www.ziglartraining.com

"Time invested in yourself is an investment well worth your time."

Jerry L. Clum, Jr.

Chapter 7

Establishing Goals

"Setting goals is the first step in turning the invisible into the visible."

Anthony Robbins

Goal-setting works. Goal-setting programs your brain for success. Set goals and you will, almost subconsciously, move toward achieving them. Goal-setting helps you focus your thoughts and organize your efforts for maximum results. Many people — myself included — have turned their dreams into reality using proper goal-setting techniques.

One day, about four years ago, when Kris and I were doing some spring cleaning in our attic, I noticed a large box under the Christmas decorations. After removing several years of dust, I discovered it was our memorabilia box — old pictures, letters, scrapbooks, my old football jersey, etc. For the next few minutes, we had some fun reliving the past. As I thumbed through the pages of my high school yearbook, a piece of paper slipped out. It was a list of ten goals I had set for myself 20 years ago. I instantly remembered the exact day I'd created the list. It was the day before I graduated from high school. As I read down the list, I grew more dumbfounded with each word. To my great surprise, I had fulfilled eight of the ten goals I'd listed, and all well within the time frame I'd projected. It was eerie, as though I had psychically predicted my own future.

There were two goals left to be met. Number 9 was, "I will own a new BMW 7 series." Well, you can guess what happened. The next day I bought a brand new 740il. I didn't even bother to test-drive it. The tenth and final goal was monetary in nature, and 15 months later I had achieved it — two years earlier than I had projected.

Goal-setting can be an amazing thing. Looking back on the 10 goals I set for myself, I realize that my success story was somewhat atypical in that I had not continued to evaluate the list over the years. Of course, it's hard to evaluate a list when it's in the attic in a box under some Christmas decorations and an entire generation of dust bunnies. When you make your list (you knew that was coming, didn't you?), keep it handy, and refer to and revise it often. I now have a new list —"100 Things To Do Before I Die." It is broken down into seven categories: Material, Spiritual, Travel, Adventure, Skill, Health, and Physical. Given how well it worked the first time, I can't wait to get started. Actually, writing this book accomplishes one of those 100 goals.

In the face of overwhelming evidence, I have to wonder why there are still so many people who do not take goal-setting seriously. Yet the results of a Harvard Business School study showed that:

- 83 percent of the population have *no* clearly defined goals
- 14 percent have goals, but have not written them down, and
- only *three percent* have clearly defined, *written* goals.

The study also concluded that the three percent of the population with clearly defined, written goals were earning, on average, almost ten times more than the 83 percent of the population who have no goals. If that's not enough to send you scurrying for a pad and pencil, then heed this: studies have also shown that those with written goals tend to be in better health and have happier relationships than those who have no goals. Sounds like a wake-up call to me. Got your pencil?

An initial goal-setting session should not take more than 30 minutes to an hour. By investing this first hour in yourself and your goals, you will be surprised how much more you can and will accomplish. Success becomes virtually inevitable.

A comprehensive guide to goal-setting would be a book in itself, so I will just cover the basics for now. Let's start with my 10-step process of goal-setting.

10-Step Process of Goal-Setting

1. Make sure you understand what actually constitutes a goal. Goals must be:

   - **Specific**: Describe what you want to accomplish in as much detail as possible. Details make it easier to visualize your goals, and exponentially increase the likelihood of achievement.

   - **Measurable**: You must be able to measure your progress. So describe your goals in measurable terms. Thus, it's not just "I want to lose weight." It's "I want to lose __ pounds by ___."

   - **Realistic**: "I want to lose 100 pounds by the end of the week." Not going to happen! Translation: Be sure your goal is something you are capable of achieving.

   - **Challenging**: If it is too easy, it probably isn't worth doing. A goal is something you must push yourself to achieve.

2. Decide on the specific goals you want to set and that you have a major desire to fulfill. Achieving these goals will require focus, intensity, and passion. Think about the things you always "talk" about, but somehow never manage to do. Remember: Goals begin as desires and desires start in your mind. Sure, "It would be nice to be financially independent." But that is not a goal. There is a Grand Canyon of difference between something "that would be nice to have" and something you "have passion

to achieve." That difference *will be the difference* between success and failure. Of course, it's not always easy to distinguish between what you merely want and what you'd crawl over hot coals to have. So get a piece of paper and start writing down anything and everything that comes to mind in terms of what you feel you'd like to accomplish professionally and personally. Don't think too much. Just let the words flow from your mind to the paper. This is just an internal brainstorming session where any idea is an idea worth writing down. Try to come up with at least 50 things, but not more than 100.

3. Now read each item on your list. Spend a little more time thinking about each one and how badly you really want it. How far would you drive yourself to achieve that goal? Rate each item on a scale of one to five, with five being the highest. A goal that rates a "five" is something you always seem to be thinking about and you feel you're ready to begin achieving.

4. Next, delete all the items you rated as one or two. What's left are the things that are most important to you right now, and therefore will require all your concentration and energy. This doesn't mean that you are discarding forever the goals that rated one or two. Those things may become more important to you in the future, particularly once you begin to achieve the goals that rated three, four, and five. For now, you need to prioritize.

5. With the remaining goals, the threes, fours and fives, look at each one to see if it meets the criteria discussed early. Is it specific, measurable, realistic, and challenging? Do the words on the paper accurately express your true feelings? Could you modify or better describe any of these goals to make them more precise? Turn your intangible thoughts into something that is tangible which you can now see rather than just think about.

6. Write down the obstacles you will need to overcome to achieve each goal. This will allow you to begin building a strategy or strategies for success.

7. Set projected target dates for completion. Some goals may take only a few days or a week. Others may take 10 years. So it is important to be realistic in setting these dates. Depending on the goal, you may need to break down the timelines into manageable segments. A goal that will take five years could be broken down into several smaller goals to be completed within the five-year time-frame. These smaller goals then become checkpoints to keep you on track along the road to achievement.

8. Now it is time to build a Strategy Flow Chart. Use one piece of paper for each of your goals and create a flow chart that shows where you are when you start, the obstacles you may encounter, how you will overcome those obstacles, and the management timelines you have created to complete different steps or portions of the goal. Then add the projected target date you have set for completion. This chart will be your road map along the way.

9. Now you must program your mind toward achieving each goal. No doubt you've heard the saying, "a picture is worth a thousand words." Well there is, in fact, a great deal of truth in that. Begin this step by going through magazines, photos, newspapers, and any other materials to find pictures that best represents each of your goals. It is easier to find pictures that represent tangible goals, e.g., a car or the type of house you would like to own. To find pictures that represent intangible goals, you will need to be more creative. But with a little extra thinking and work, you will find an image that will create the mental picture you need. These images are important because you will attach them to the individual Strategy Flow Charts. *You must see yourself owning and living that*

goal. Remember: Anything the mind can believe, it can achieve.

10. Be passionate. You must be persistent and committed. Nothing must stand in your way. Problems become opportunities that inspire creative thinking to develop effective solutions. Keep these goals in mind every day. Refer to your Strategy Flow Charts often and modify them as necessary. On any trip, there may be unexpected detours. Recalculate your route and keep going until you reach the destination.

You now have your list of goals. Your mission, should you decide to accept it, is to fulfill your dreams and live your life to its fullest!

Chapter 8

Writing a Business Plan

"A good plan is like a road map: it shows the final destination and usually the best way to get there."

H. Stanley Judd

A business plan is a well thought-out and comprehensively documented goal. It is vital to create a business plan early in the start-up phase of your business. Make it one of the first steps you take. New entrepreneurs often either hire someone to write their business plan for them or, worse yet, gloss over or skip this step completely. The best person to write your business plan is the one you see in the mirror every morning. This plan will be the foundation for your entire business. No one can visualize that better than you. By writing the business plan, you set the foundation in place and you know how strong it is.

Your business plan should encompass your goals and strategies for growing the business and the specific steps you need to take along the way. These steps should include marketing strategies and demographics, a competitive analysis, staffing requirements, financial requirements, and backup plans. After you have the basis of your plan, and if you think you need to, only then should you hire others to start building on top of that foundation by writing the final business plan. According to the Small Business Administration and the American's Women Economic

Development Corporation, to develop an effective business plan, you must:

- Use a typewritten 8½" × 11" format and a loose-leaf binder to package the plan and facilitate any revisions.
- Begin with a cover sheet that includes the name, location, and telephone number of the business, and the name of the person who wrote the business plan.
- Keep it short and crisp without compromising the description of the venture.
- Keep it simple.
- Organize it appropriately, with a table of contents, logically arranged sections, and appendices.
- Identify a target market and demonstrate evidence of marketability.
- Demonstrate the benefits of your product or service to the user or customer.
- **Orient the plan toward the future.** Develop forecasts of developing trends and use these forecasts to help you describe what you intend to do — not only what has been done — over the next three to five years.
- **Do not be too optimistic in estimating sales potential.** Develop best-case, worst-case, and most-likely case scenarios. Base sales estimates on market analysis, not on production facilities. Develop production needs based on that information rather than vice versa.
- **Highlight current and potential problems and demonstrate how they will be overcome.** By identifying problems ahead of time, you enhance your credibility with investors and lenders.
- **Demonstrate that you have an effective management team.** Your team must not only have the necessary busi-

ness skills to manage the venture, but they must also work effectively as a team.

(American Woman's Economic Development Corporation, Stamford, CT, 6/97)

You don't have to write your business plan from scratch. Many software programs can give you a good head start. Two of my favorites are Business Plan Pro from Palo Alto Software, Inc., which can be found at www.bplans.com, and BizPlanBuilder from JIAN, which can be found at www.jian.com. These programs cost about $100 each, but will save you countless hours and provide an outline for a proper business plan. Either one is a wise investment.

CHAPTER 9

Start-Up

"A journey of a thousand miles begins with a single step."
CONFUCIUS

STARTING A BUSINESS CAN BE AN EXCITING VENTURE THAT OFFERS many rewards. Or it can be a stressful, expensive, and time-consuming process. The key to making it the former, rather than the latter, is planning. Armed with your business plan, you should have a good road map to follow. In this chapter, we will cover a few areas that may not always be addressed in your business plan, but which are important to the success of your business. This list is not all-inclusive. Depending on the industry you are entering and the strategy you have identified in your business plan, you may need to add some items.

Always use a Start-up Checklist to outline the actions required to complete your start-up. Include the projected date for completion of each step and the actual date of completion. This will be a tool with which you can measure where you are compared to where you want to be.

START-UP CHECKLIST FOR NEW BUSINESS

Checklist Items	Completion Date	
	PROJECTED	ACTUAL
Required Capital Secured		
Name Creation		
Logo Creation		
Attorneys, Accountants, and Other Advisors		
Trademark Protection, Patents, and Copyrights		
Legal Form of Business		
Federal Employer Identification Number		
Secure Your Location		
Vanity Phone Numbers and Domain Names		
Utilities and Internet Access		
Business Accounts		
Licensing, Business Codes, Registering, and Zoning		
Insurance		
Payroll Services		
Business Records and Accounting		
Create Your 30-Second Elevator Speech		
Brochures, Business Cards and Sales Literature		
Supplies, Furniture and Equipment		
Set up Required Suppliers and Vendors		
Professional Organizations, Memberships, and Affiliations		

Required Capital Secured

"Money is better than poverty, if only for financial reasons."
Woody Allen

One of the most challenging steps in starting a business is getting the money to start it. The rule seems to be that no one wants to loan you the money until your business is already successful and you don't really need it (refer to Truman quotation, Chapter 1).

Complete your Business and Marketing Plan *before* you start looking for capital. That way you will know exactly how much you need. Below are some of the most common resources for capital to start small to medium-sized businesses.

Personal Savings

While this may contradict the OPM principle (see Chapters 5 and 17), when possible, it is always better to use your own money to start a business. Since there are no required payback terms, you can wait until the business comes out of the most vulnerable phase before you pay yourself back. Also, by using your own capital you do not have to give up any ownership in your business. One hundred percent of your success — or failure — is yours alone.

Personal savings include bank accounts, bonds, CDs, stocks, 401 (k)'s, retirement accounts, loans against life insurance policies, collectibles, or anything else that holds a great value that can be liquidated into cash. If you can't bring yourself to tap into your own savings to capitalize your business, you may not be ready to start a business.

Banks

Going into debt for any reason can be depressing. But it is a lot more palatable if it is for something that has an upside potential for making money.

There are two basic forms of loans: unsecured and secured. Unless you have a great deal of business experience and have started successful businesses in the past, chances are your loan will be based more on your personal ability to pay than on the potential success of your business. Even if they call it a "business loan," it will be approved or disapproved based on your personal financial history.

In the absence of collateral, you will need to apply for an unsecured or signature loan. This is a loan that is given to you on your signature alone and based on your past credit history. Banks and other lending institutions will rarely lend more than $50,000 on a signature loan ($10,000 to $15,000 is more common.) If you have collateral, e.g., real estate, you may qualify for a secured loan, which may take the form of an equity line or second mortgage.

Next to your own savings, I believe an equity line of credit is the best way to finance a business start-up, assuming you have adequate equity in your home. Some of the advantages are that you do not have to give up any ownership interest in your business, an equity loan can be tax deductible, and you do not have to borrow it all as one lump sum. Instead, you have a credit line with a maximum amount established, you borrow what you need when you need it, and you only have to make payments on the *portion* you borrow. Conversely, with a conventional loan you are borrowing the full amount, and regardless of whether you end up having to use it all, you are still making payments on the full amount.

Venture Capitalists & Angel Investors

Most VC firms and angel investors prefer to get involved after a business has made it past the start-up phase. But if you find the right firm or investor and you have the right idea or concept, there is a chance (albeit a small one) that you will be able to secure funds. *But* be prepared to give up a large percentage, in most cases a majority share, of your business ownership. On the Internet, go to www.vccontacts.com for one of the most comprehensive lists of Venture Capitalists and angel investors and their contact information.

Credit Cards

While I cannot condone using credit cards to finance a business start-up, my own business history would make me hypocritical if I did not mention them.

Many new business owners use credit cards as a business start-up tool. Some use credit cards to make some of their initial purchases to save cash. Others use the cash advance option to supplement working capital. If you decide to take this option, remember: Not all credit cards are alike. For instance, if you have a $10,000 credit limit on one of your cards, you may only have a $5,000 cash advance limit. So if you are planning to use cash advances, you will need to obtain the cards that have the highest cash advance limits. Needless to say, it is also wise to use the cards that have the lowest interest rates. Many credit cards carry promotional rates as low as one to two percent for the first six months to a year. Depending on your business plan, this may be enough time to pay them off before the rate kicks up an additional seven to 15 percent to the normal usurious levels.

Also, keep in mind that every time you apply for a credit card, an inquiry goes on your credit report. Too many inquiries may reduce your likelihood for credit approval in the future.

Advertise for It

Some new business owners have successfully secured start-up funds by advertising. A number of national publications feature ads from owners looking for start-up funds. If you go this route, remember to state the type of business you are entering and the amount of funding you need, which should be overstated to give yourself negotiating room. Again, be prepared to give up some ownership interest.

Small Business Investment Companies (SBIC)

These are firms that exist for the sole purpose of lending money to businesses they feel have a good upside potential. SBICs are private investment companies licensed by the Small Business Administration. The funds are generated through private investors. Companies in which the SBICs invest must meet stringent guidelines. Thus, it may be more difficult to secure start-up funds. Once again, be prepared to give up some percentage of ownership in your company.

Small Business Development Commissions

Many states and local municipalities have programs available to help new businesses get started. These programs may include tax breaks, financial assistance, and consulting services. Consider visiting the nearest center before jumping into some other form of financing.

Money Broker

Money brokers are middlemen who assist you in packaging your loan to give it a better chance of approval. Also, they will usually know which lenders are best suited to your needs. Money brokers often require an up-front fee and, in general, offer no guarantees that they will be successful in finding you the required capital. Still, as the next-to-the-last resort, this may be worth a try.

Family and Friends

This is the absolute dead-last resort. Borrowing money from the Three FFFs (see Chapter 1) is a serrated double-edged sword. If things go bad, you will not only have a debt to repay, but in many cases a serious dent in your relationship to repair. Even if your business is a huge success and you do repay the loan, the relationship may still suffer. While you are enjoying the fruits of your labor, the person who loaned you the money may become envious, feeling that, without their help, you would not have been successful. Of course, your situation could be quite different, and everything could turn out for the best, but unless it is your absolute last resort, why take the risk?

> ***"O, beware, my lord of jealousy; It is the green-ey'd monster which doth mock the meat it feeds on."***
>
> William Shakespeare

For many new business owners, securing start-up capital is the first step outside their comfort zone. If you are not comfortable with going further in debt or tapping into your life savings, starting a business may not be the best thing for you.

> *"I started my first several companies with no money at all. It's a misconception that you have to go out and raise money to start a company. Sweat Equity is the best capital for a company. When you have an idea, or a dream for a company, the first thing to do is not go out and raise money, it's to find customers. If you have a customer, then you have someone willing to pay for your product or service, and that makes it easy to start."*
>
> MARK CUBAN

NAME CREATION

> *"The difference between the old ballplayer and the new ballplayer is the jersey. The old ballplayer cared about the name on the front. The new ballplayer cares about the name on the back."*
>
> STEVE GARVEY

How important is it to have the right name for your business? Extremely. It can be the difference between success and failure. Large companies, which may be opening another division or preparing a new product for market, often spend millions looking for just the right name, which should give you a pretty good idea of how important the right name can be. Your name will become one of your biggest assets. (*Note*: Even after Pan-Am went out of business, they were still able to sell their name for more than $1.3 million.)

An effective business name:

- Creates a positive outlook for your customers
- Is easy to remember, spell, and pronounce. (Simpler is better).
- Is rational for the business you are in and reflects your products or services

- Builds value for your business
- Is distinctive
- Matches your image
- Is meaningful
- Reaches your potential customers on an emotional level
- Excels visually as well as verbally
- Is not something you may quickly outgrow
- Is available to be trademarked and is not confusingly similar to anything else

There are two other things to remember about choosing a name for your business. Be sure the .com domain name, or a slight derivative thereof, is still available. Also, keeping the first letter of your business name early in the alphabet can be beneficial. Many times, your business may be found on an alphabetized list with other companies, and it never hurts to be toward the top of the list

The first step is to create a long list of names. Then put it aside until the next morning and see how many of those names you can throw out once you are fresh and awake. Next, check your list against the United States Patent and Trademark Office (USPTO) database at www.uspto.gov. More than likely several of the names you listed are already in use or come too close to yours for comfort. Narrow your list down to about 10, then start getting input from anyone you can. Explain what your business is about and ask them which of the 10 is their favorite. After you have received at least 50 opinions, take the top three and begin tinkering with potential logos that may work with each one.

Depending on how tight you are on start-up capital, you may want to consider hiring a professional to assist you in the process of choosing a name for your business. Even if you are particularly creative, you may find professional assistance helpful. Many companies can provide this service. To find them, go to any Internet search engine and put in "creating business names." Fees for these services vary from as low as a few thousand dollars to as much as $50,000 or more. A few final tips for using this type of service:

- Review the company terms closely.
- Ensure that any fee advanced will be refunded should they not come up with a name that you find satisfactory.
- Make sure you get all rights to the name.

Logo Creation

"A logo should look just as good in 15-foot letters on top of company headquarters as it does one sixteenth of an inch tall on company stationery."

Steven Gilliatt

Creating your logo is as important as choosing a name. A good logo can almost tell your story without words. It is the image or drawing that represents your company and establishes your customers' first impression. Often, your business name is an integral part of the logo. Most of the tips for creating your business name are applicable to creating your logo as well, but here are a few more.

- Use easy-to-reproduce colors. *Always use* Pantone colors, also known as PMS colors. They have a numerical code for each color.
- If possible, limit your logo to two colors. A lot of colors may look great, but the cost of putting them on everything (stationery, business cards, buildings, the broad side of the QE2 . . .) can be high.
- Keep the logo simple and clean. If it is too complicated, the name of the company may be lost.

- Look at your competitors' logos to determine how you want to differentiate yours.
- Illustrate your company's key benefit with your logo.
- Never use clip art to build your logo. It is too common and not at all professional.

For creating a logo, professional help is almost mandatory. Costs vary, but $1,000 to $3,500 should get you professional help that is more than satisfactory. Again, do an Internet search to find firms that provide this service.

Trademark Protection, Patents, and Copyrights

Let's say you have checked your new business name against the U.S. Patent and Trademark database. You may think the name you have chosen is unique, but the USPTO may not agree. So before you get too involved in the final name and logo decisions, you need to start the application process. Retain a trademark attorney for this. However capable you may be, it is not a good idea to do this yourself. The process is not difficult, but using a trademark attorney will give you more credibility should you later run into problems with other companies, including those that may feel your name and logo are confusingly similar to theirs. Make sure that your trademark attorney performs trademark searches on state and federal levels. Once the attorney has concluded that in his or her opinion your name is safe to trademark, he or she will complete the required forms and submit them to the USPTO for approval. The approval process can take over a year before registration is complete, but in the interim you can use the TM or SM symbol to signify that your registration is pending. (TM stands for Trademark, which comprises products and services. SM stands for Service Mark and is used by companies offering only services defined by the USPTO.) After your registration is official, use the ® symbol. It is a good idea to submit at least two applications: a Word Mark, for your business name, and a Design Mark, for the logo you created.

If your business concept revolves around an original product, service, device, process, or composition of matter created by a human, have it patented. A patent is a right given by the U.S. government to stop others from making, selling, using, or importing something on which you are the Patent Holder. The patent process is somewhat more complicated and a lot more expensive than the Trademark process. A full utility patent can cost between $15,000 and $20,000 or more. To temporarily reduce the initial cost, apply for a provisional patent (PPT), which gives you a Patent Pending number and protects your invention for one year. This may be enough time for you to determine whether it is prudent to get the full utility patent. Also, PPT filing and attorney fees are more affordable, usually under $2,500.

Copyrights are much easier to obtain than Trademarks and Patents. A copyright is protection provided by the U.S. government that gives exclusive rights to the author. For something to be copyrightable, it must be defined as an original work of authorship. Just about anything that can be put to paper can be copyrighted, including literary works, musical works, dramatic works, movies and audiovisual works, pantomimes, choreographic works, pictorial works, graphic works, sculptural works, sound recordings, and architectural works. You do not have to register a work for it to be considered copyrighted. Although, according to the Copyright Act, just the condition of creating the work creates the copyright, it is still prudent to register your work with the U.S. Copyright Office at www.copyright.gov.

Attorneys, Accountants, and Other Advisors

"He who can take advice is sometimes superior to him who can give it."

Erica Jong

Selecting trusted advisors to assist you in starting and growing your business is vital. Find professionals who have some experience in your particular industry. Ideally, choose a larger law firm with partners in various specialties of the law. That way you won't have to go outside your firm every time a new legal question comes up in a different area of the law.

As in a number of other arenas, cheaper isn't always better when it comes to hiring professionals. One attorney's hourly rate may be much higher than another's, but you may end up spending less in the long run. You are paying a higher rate because of their experience and knowledge, and because of that experience and knowledge they may not need as much time to research the problem on which you need help. Most important, make sure you are comfortable with the advisors you retain.

When it comes to hiring accountants, let your fingers do the walking. Get out the Yellow Pages and start calling accountants. Ask one question: "What is two plus two?" When you get to the accountant who answers: "What do you want it to be?" hire him (or her).

O.K. So I'm trying to be funny. But there is more than a whole grain of truth here, too. You need an accountant who knows every available (legal) tax advantage and, most important, knows how you can use them to benefit your business. Two plus two is four everywhere except at the IRS, where the answer depends on what they allow.

In addition to attorneys and accountants, find a good mentor or advisor, preferably someone who has owned and grown a successful business or two (or seven). This is a person who will listen to your ideas — someone who likes you well enough to give you good advice, but not so much that they will steer you in the wrong direction to avoid telling you that your latest idea has more holes in it than a pound of Swiss cheese.

Legal Forms Of Business

What follows is a list of the various types of legal businesses along with a definition and a brief discussion of each one. Your attorney, accountant, advisor — or all three — can give you the best advice on choosing the type of business under which to organize your company.

Sole Proprietorships

Although this is the cheapest and easiest type of business to open, there are significant disadvantages. These include tax consequences and the fact that your personal assets may be attached should you become involved in litigation or collection for bills your business may not be able to pay.

General Partnership

General Partnerships are like sole proprietorships. The only difference is that the business has two or more people who bear personal responsibility for the liabilities of the business.

Limited Partnerships

In this type of business, one or more "General" partners run the company while "Limited" partners invest capital and share in the profits. Limited partners have no responsibilities in operating the business. General partners are still personally liable for the debts of the business. Limited partners incur no liability beyond their capital investments. This form of business is designed to encourage investors to invest without risking anything beyond their capital investment.

Limited Liability Partnerships (LLPs)

LLPs are similar to limited partnerships, except that under an LLP all owners have some protection against business liabilities. LLPs allow the owner to operate somewhat more informally than is required in a corporation. Many attorneys and accountants operate their businesses under LLPs.

Limited Liability Companies (LLCs)

An amalgam of corporations and limited partnerships, LLCs are one of the newest legal forms of business. The tax consequences are similar to those for Sole Proprietorships and General Partnerships. Although LLCs are somewhat more complicated than other forms of business, they do have the advantage of personal liability protection for the owners. LLCs must be privately held companies and are considered separate "entities" from their members. To a certain degree, the business has taken on a "life" of its own. Professionals most often use this form of business. Usually, you will be required to file annual reports with your Secretary of State. You must keep minutes of your meetings and produce periodic financial statements.

C-Corporation

C-Corporations are organized with ownership of stock that is usually assignable and transferable. The "C" indicates a standard, for-profit, state formed corporation. A corporation pays taxes at its own corporate rate. To incorporate, you must file articles of incorporation with your Secretary of State, elect board members, have regular board meetings, and elect corporate officers, usually including a president, vice president, secretary, and treasurer. You will be required to periodically file reports with your Secretary of State.

There are many tax advantages to operating a business as a corporation. Also, a corporation provides the owners with the maximum protection against personal liability. The down side of incorporation (for a small business) is that you will be required to operate with the same complicated formalities as a Fortune 500 company.

S-Corporation

An S-corporation starts its life as a C-corporation. The owners then elect to request S-corporation status by filing a Form 2553 with the IRS.

The primary difference between an S-corporation and a C-corporation lies in the way each is taxed. The net income for a C-corporation is taxed at its own corporate rate. Any net profit that remains after taxes are paid could be given to the shareholders as a dividend, which would then be taxed again as part of the shareholder's personal income. In an S-corporation, net income is passed through directly to the shareholders, and taxed only once at the shareholder's rate. This option could be highly advantageous if your company is closely held with very few owners.

Under no circumstances should you select the legal form under which your company will be organized without first consulting your attorney, your accountant, and/or your business advisor.

Federal Employer Identification Number

Every organization that has a bank account must have a Federal Employer Identification Number (FEIN), also known as a Federal Tax ID number. To get one, obtain a Form SS-4 from your accountant or from the IRS website. You can complete the form and send it to the IRS, or, if you are in a hurry, call the IRS, ask for a FEIN number, and give them the Form SS-4 information. Then write the FEIN number in the correct space on the form, mark it "by phone," and mail the completed form to the IRS. Phone numbers may be different from state to state. You can also apply online at

www.irs.gov/businesses/index.html

Click on "Employer ID Numbers" and download the SS-4 form and/or get the correct phone number for your state.

Secure Your Location

The type of business you are starting will be the single most important factor in determining an appropriate location. For most small businesses, locations are divided into four general categories.

1. Home-based
2. Office-based

3. Retail-based
4. Manufacturing- or industrial-based

Home-Based Businesses

Home-based businesses are booming. I started my business from home and, in time, turned it into a $100 million dollar a year operation. So working from home is possible for the right business. Of course, any type of retail business that depends on customer traffic would not fare well in a home-based business, nor would any business requiring a great deal of manufacturing. Businesses where the actual work is performed at the customer's site and which, as a result, do not generate much customer traffic, are the most applicable type of business to operate from your home.

The advantages of a home-based business are obvious, but there are some disadvantages.

1. If you are a workaholic, working from home can be likened to an alcoholic owning a bar. Burnout can occur quickly in a home-based business. Kris and I found we were working as many as 18 hours a day. But if you work in an office at another location, your home can still be the sanctuary from which to retrieve your sanity.
2. There can be many distractions in working from home, especially if you have children.
3. Working at home may not provide the professional appearance that is likely to attract customers and the right employees. Home-based businesses are often thought of as small-time or, worse, "fly-by-night."
4. There is likely to be very little drive-by exposure, since you won't have a sign out front.
5. Working from home can have a negative psychological effect on you and the growth of your business. Subconsciously, you may begin to view your business as more of

a hobby than your livelihood. Thus, you may tend not to take the business seriously.

6. In general, it is not professional to have the employees of your business working at home with you. Thus, you may be unable to hire staff as quickly.
7. Let's face it. You may not want just anyone coming into your home.
8. Zoning issues and/or difficult neighbors could present problems.
9. In general, home-based businesses do not grow as fast.

When capital permits, it is advisable to start your business out of an office rather than from home. If you do decide to start your business at home, however, take precautions to avoid or at least minimize the disadvantages.

Office-Based Businesses

If customers or potential customers need to visit your office, then it must reflect a professional image. In short, keep it clean and organized. Remember: A professional image does not require tens of thousands of dollars worth of furniture and lavish décor (see Chapter 6, the *AFNC* Syndrome).

The first step in locating office space is: know exactly what you need. On a piece of paper, lay out your ideal office space, including the number of separate offices you feel you need, reception area, storage areas, and break room. Then try to locate office space that comes as close as possible to matching your layout. (*Note:* Put yourself in your customers' shoes. Look at the space through their eyes.) Don't sign a lease for the first place you see. Finding the ideal space will take time, so don't get in a hurry and settle for something that may not work. When you do find the right place, visit it several times before making the final commitment. You may see things you didn't see before.

Office space is generally rented at a price per square foot on an annual rate. If you find space for $15 per square foot and the office is 2,000 square feet, then your total annual lease will be $30,000, or $2,500 per month. Remember also that the first lease a landlord presents to you is usually just a starting point. Never sign that first lease without trying to negotiate a better deal. If you don't hear the word "No" on your first offer, you made the wrong first offer. You may be able to reduce your price per square foot by entering into a longer-term lease.

If you are not strapped for cash, offer to pay a certain number of months' rent in advance. I once reduced my annual lease amount by over 35 percent by writing the landlord a check for a year's rent up front. Cash is king!

Negotiating is a critical tool. You will be amazed at how many things may be negotiable, including the lease rate, office improvements (e.g., initial painting and carpet cleaning or replacement), tenant allowances (i.e., things you do yourself for which the landlord may reimburse you), free rental periods, the deposit, maintenance fees, and rent reductions.

Before signing, go over the lease agreement with the proverbial fine-toothed comb. Have your attorney do so as well. Negotiate as much flexibility as possible. Make sure you understand *all* of the costs involved. There are usually other costs you need to consider in addition to the lease payment. For example, are there common areas that are being included in your rent? Always measure the space yourself.

If you have limited experience in leasing office space, consider engaging a real estate professional to assist you. The cost may be worth the long-term savings in time and potential aggravation.

Retail-Based Businesses

"Location, location, location" is another adage with more truth than fiction. Good businesses have failed in bad locations. Poor businesses have succeeded in good locations.

Location is the single most important factor for success in a retail business. Although most of the negotiating tips for leasing regular office space apply to leasing retail space as well, there are some additional factors to consider.

One of the most important considerations for determining the best space for starting a retail business is "retail compatibility." Start your business next to another business that will generate targeted traffic similar to your business. If you will be selling items such as clothing, jewelry, shoes, or housewares, start your business next door to other businesses that sell these types of goods. If you're going to sell convenience goods such as groceries, baked goods, hardware, or pharmaceuticals, open your doors next to other like businesses.

Since location is so important to the success of a retail business, here is one more tip. Hire a consulting firm that specializes in site selection. If you are planning to open a retail business, this will be one of the best investments you can make.

Manufacturing or Industrial Based

Leasing industrial or manufacturing space is more complicated than leasing office or retail space. That's the bad news. The good news is that there is usually more industrial and manufacturing space around in many parts of the country.

Manufacturing, as an industry, has been through some tough economic times in the past few years. Many manufacturers, some of which have been around for 100 years or more, have closed their doors. This has left many facilities available for sale or lease.

If you are considering opening a business in the manufacturing or industrial sector, it is likely that you have had previous experience in this industry. So you may not need advice about leasing space.

If, on the other hand, this is your first experience starting a business in this industry, then I strongly recommend that you hire a consulting firm that specializes in site selection.

Vanity Phone Numbers and Domain Names

Vanity numbers are phone numbers that translate into messages. As a consumer, I know that many people dislike having to dial vanity numbers. But as an experienced business owner, I also know that there can be benefits to having them.

In 1987, 1-800 Flowers was launched. The company now brings in over $200,000,000 in annual sales, most of which goes through that number. The simple fact is that words are easier to remember than numbers for most of us. Use that to your advantage, and you are likely to see a significant impact on the growth of your business.

If you are going to use a vanity number and/or Internet site, look into obtaining them NOW in the conception stage of your business start-up. Don't wait until you are ready to roll out the red carpet. The cyber woods are full of vanity number speculators and domain squatters who pay close attention to the business world so that they can quickly buy anything they feel they can later resell for a tidy profit.

Depending on the type of business you are starting, you may have different needs for vanity numbers and domain names. If, initially, your business will be a local one, then you may decide not to obtain a toll-free number. But suppose that in five years you decide to go national and the number you want is no longer available. For the modest monthly investment it takes to own a toll-free number, it probably makes more sense to get it now.

There are instances when a new business owner may not need a vanity number. For example, if you will be providing a product or service primarily to the elderly, a vanity number may be more of a disadvantage than an advantage. Many senior citizens already find it difficult to read the numbers on the keys, let alone the (much smaller) letters. Thus, for a business marketing to the elderly, repetitive, ascending, or descending numbers may be more appropriate. For example, the first three digits after the area code is called the local exchange. The number of local exchanges that will exist in your area code depends on the size of the market. Let's say that one of your local exchanges is 555. Then good repetitive ascending or descending numbers might include: 555-1234, 555-4321, 555-1010, 555-5555, or 555-4444.

Depending on your business, you may be able to take this concept one step further. Suppose, for example, you are opening an optical shop. A good number could be 555-2020. One advantage of using local exchanges is that you feel more like a neighbor to your customer base. Most people are familiar with the different three-digit exchanges in their area.

For local business, it is not absolutely necessary that the entire number spell something out to accommodate partial vanity numbers. In a partial vanity number you would use the first three digits of the local exchange and then create a word or message after that. For example, in a health-related business you might choose a number like 555-CARE or 555-HEALTH. If you can make it work out within your local exchange, 554-HEALTH would be even better because it sounds like call 55 *For* Health. Avoid complete vanity numbers such as FOR-HEALTH where all seven digits are represented by a letter versus a number or potential customers may not recognize it as a phone number.

Remember too that even though there are only four more digits after the local exchange, you do not necessarily have to limit yourself to only four-letter words. The seven-digit phone number is not as much of a constraint as you might think. A customer can dial eight, nine, or even 10 numbers and the telephone will only recognize the first seven and ignore the rest. Still, it's best not to get too carried away. More than nine numbers total will just confuse (and possibly annoy) your customers because many may not realize that they only have to punch in the first seven digits.

The same general guidelines apply for toll-free numbers, which have been around for more than 30 years. The first toll-free numbers were 1-800 numbers. About 25 years later 1-888 was created, then 1-877, 1-866, and 1-855.

For your business, it is a good idea to go after a 1-800 number, or a 1-800 vanity number, first. Getting one, especially the latter, will be difficult, but in terms of attracting customers it's worth a try. After 30 years of dialing 800 numbers, it has become a subconscious habit for consumers. Potential customers may dial 1-800 when they meant to dial your advertised 1-888 number.

Here is the most successful method I have found for obtaining the best local phone numbers.

1. Compile an exhaustive list of every possible variation of numbers and words you can think of that provide a meaningful word or message for your business. Don't be concerned about availability at this point. Locate all

three-digit exchanges that may be available for the address of your business. Then, create meaningful words or messages using four, five or six letter words that would follow those first three digits of your local exchange. Again, you can use more than four digits or characters, if necessary, for the last four numbers. But try to keep it to no more than six.

2. Call all of the numbers you have created. If you get *anything other than* a recording stating that it is a non-working number, cross it off your list.

3. Having narrowed down the list, call your local phone company to select your number. Go through the list to see if any of the numbers you have created are available. This process takes time. If the phone company representative who is assisting is impatient, politely tell him or her that you will need to call back. Then do it, and hope you get a kinder, gentler representative the next time.

4. If you have identified a non-working number and you are told it is not available, politely ask why. In many cases, the phone company may not allow you to use it because it was recently disconnected. This is usually a phone company policy that prevents new customers from getting a slew of annoying phone calls from people attempting to reach the previous owner of the number. You can try to negotiate a deal whereby you sign a release agreeing not to hold the phone company liable for nuisance calls. This rarely works, but you never know.

5. If, after going through your list, you still haven't found an available number, ask the representative if the phone company has a way to find out whether any of the numbers you have mentioned are owned by a reseller, i.e., a company that buys vanity numbers for the purpose of reselling them.

6. Still no luck? Find out if there are other local phone service providers. They may have been issued blocks of numbers to assign to their customers that the first local phone company you contacted would not be able to assign.

7. If you've still had no success, go back to step one and try again, or you may decide to settle for a repetitive, ascending, or descending numerical phone number instead.

The process for getting a toll-free number is similar to the local number process except that you can go directly to the AT&T Toll-Free Database to search for available numbers. This database can be found on the web: www.att.com and click on Small to Medium Businesses.

If you wish to use it, there is one more possibility. There are companies that do nothing but help business owners get toll-free vanity numbers. Prices vary, but some of them have good records of success. To locate many of these companies, go to any Internet search engine and type the words "toll-free vanity numbers."

With the advent of the Internet, domain names have become gold to many companies. Regardless of the size of your company, you should have an Internet presence. The dot.com domain names are usually the best, which is why they are the hardest to find. I would rather have a poor dot.com address than a great dot.net, dot.org, dot.cc, dot.us, dot.tv, dot.ws, dot.info or dot.biz address, for the same reason I would choose a 1-800 number over a 1-888 number: Consumer habit.

Various companies can be found on the Internet to register domain names, and searching the database for availability is a fairly simple process. One of the larger and more successful companies is www.register.com. As with the toll-free number resellers, there are hundreds, if not thousands, of companies that register domain names for the sole purpose of reselling them. I don't condone this activity, but you may find yourself having to pay their ransom or not get the domain name you want. Even so, don't be afraid to negotiate. There are an abundance of .com domain names available for resale, in fact, there are more domain names available for resale than there are domains registered to companies that are actually using them.

Utilities and Internet Access

Get your utilities set up — water, sewage, electric, gas, telephone, etc. High-speed Internet access is best for business. Every extra minute costs you money, so the faster information can be retrieved, the more money you are saving.

Bankers and Business Accounts

Establish a working relationship with a local bank as soon as possible. This involves more than just opening an account. Make an appointment with a representative in their small business or corporate department. Give them a copy of your business plan and explain your strategy. Even if you do not need additional capital at this time, consider setting up a line of credit for your business. Thus, if (when!) you run into unexpected obstacles, you may be in a better financial position to deal with them.

Keep your business finances (including the business checking account) entirely separate from your personal finances. This is particularly important for corporations and LLCs. Banks usually require a corporate resolution to open a checking account in your business name. If you are a corporation, your Board of Directors will authorize this resolution. If you are an LLC, the authorization will come from the members or managers.

Licensing, Business Codes, Registering, and Zoning

Your attorney and/or accountant can help you to navigate these waters. Depending on the type of business you are starting and its location, the process may or may not be complicated. In many states, you can request a business start-up package, which will include many of the forms you need to file, along with contact information for all of the agencies with which you will be involved. Generally, you can request this start-up package from your Secretary of State or a state or local Business or Economic Development Center.

Insurance

> *"I don't want to tell you how much insurance I carry with the Prudential, but all I can say is: when I go, they go, too."*
>
> Jack Benny

The type of business you are starting will dictate the types and amounts of insurance you should carry. Many states will also have minimum requirements. Regardless of state law, it is prudent to at least carry a minimum of $1 million of comprehensive general liability insurance. If you have employees, you will also need to secure workers' compensation and unemployment insurance. In many industries, you may also need professional liability insurance, which may also be called errors and omissions insurance. In some instances, you may even want to have some or all of your employees bonded. Finally, don't forget about property insurance to cover your building, equipment, and furnishings. This is just a partial list of the types of coverage you may need. *It is imperative that you discuss insurance needs with your attorney, accountant, and insurance specialist.*

Payroll Services

> *"I don't mind having a big payroll. A bigger payroll usually nets a bigger payoff."*
>
> Jerry L. Clum, Jr.

Depending on the number of employees you will have and the type of business you have selected, payroll can be simple or complex. In most cases, I recommend using a payroll service provider such as ADP or

Paychex. They are comparatively inexpensive, and the number of hours you will save per month can be enormous.

Using a payroll service provider drastically reduces your payroll responsibilities. For the most part, your job will be keeping track of the hours worked, reporting those hours, reviewing their reports, and passing out the paychecks. In a small- to medium-sized business, if you handled it all yourself, payroll management could take almost 40 hours a month.

Payroll is a good example of the philosophy discussed in Chapter 5. If you want to earn a six-figure income, then you need to do the $50 plus per hour work yourself and hire staff or outsource the lower rate activities of your business. You may be able hire a payroll service provider for as little as $250 to $300 per month, which translates into less than $6 to $7.50 per hour. Those extra 40 hours you would have spent doing the payroll can be put to better and more cost-effective use in growing your business.

Business Records and Accounting

Many small business owners never realize the importance of keeping good, organized business records until it's too late. You are required by law to keep payroll records, tax information, and contracts for a specified period of time. Consult your accountant right from the beginning of your business and set up a proper record-keeping system. Find out what needs to be kept, for how long, and the best way to keep it.

Create Your 30-Second Elevator Speech

Not that you will be conducting a great deal of your meetings in elevators, but you never know. A 30-second elevator speech is your story — condensed for telling in the shortest amount of time possible. Because of your business, you will be meeting many new people, e.g., employees, vendors, potential customers, and business professionals. Learn to tell your story completely and *with enthusiasm* in less than one minute.

What goes into this 30-second monologue? Your name and the name of your company, what you do, why you do it the way you do, and how you are different from your competitors. There is an adage: you have only one chance to make a great first impression. Create the best possible 30-second commercial for your business. Then rehearse it relentlessly — until you reach a point where you could tell it perfectly if you were awakened from a sound sleep at 3 a.m. It should be automatic, but it should not sound automatic. It should be brief and to the point, but engaging. And, as they say in show business, leave 'em wantin' [to hear] more!

BROCHURES, BUSINESS CARDS, AND SALES LITERATURE

"If it doesn't sell, it isn't creative."

DAVID OGILVY

Brochures and sales literature can be another double-edged sword.

On the one hand, you must assemble the highest quality materials money can buy. Cut corners to save money somewhere else in the business — not here. My preference is top of the line, full-color, glossy brochures with lots of exclusive photos (as opposed to pictures someone is licensing to you and 200 other businesses.) Have this material — sales literature, brochures, agreements, and business cards — printed by a professional. Regardless of how good you are with publishing programs, it's just not good enough. Anyone with a halfway-practiced eye will recognize an amateur job, even a better than average amateur job, when they see it.

It's a pet peeve of mine, but business materials generated on somebody's home computer make my teeth itch. The company behind the materials may well be top-drawer, but I'll probably never know because I have already formed a negative impression.

If you are starting your business out of your home, it is even more important that your sales literature look first-class.

All of that said, however, (here comes the other edge of that sword), it is unwise to put too much faith in brochures and sales literature — even first-class, professionally-done brochures and sales literature.

Brochures will not sell anything. Period. Paragraph. They can generate and influence interest, but they will not close the deal. This is a common misunderstanding among new business owners and sales people. Too many believe their literature will make the sale for them. Here is a hard fact: ninety percent of the time when someone asks for literature it is nothing more than a stall to put off making the final buying decision. The other 10 percent of the time, it is their way of politely disappearing without buying anything at all.

Sales literature is a great tool, but it must be used in combination with a great sales presentation, proper rebuttals, and closing techniques, as well as good follow-up, including keeping your promises.

Many years ago I was in the home improvement business. In checking sales figures of our sales force, my boss discovered that only one out of every eight inquiry calls resulted in an appointment. He was, to say the least, not happy, so he began listening to the calls that were coming in. In most instances the salesperson never asked to set up an appointment. Even when they did, the prospective customer put them off by asking for a brochure, which the salesperson would dutifully send out believing that they were on the brink of some real business. In most cases, we never heard from the prospect again. To solve this problem, my boss made a unique decision. He took every piece of literature we had and locked it away in the supply room. From then on when a prospect asked for a brochure, the salesperson would reply, "We really don't have anything I can send to you, but I would be happy to come out and show you some actual pictures and explain everything in person." The number of appointments immediately doubled. My boss had recognized what the salespeople had yet to learn: Nothing [in that industry] is sold unless you have a chance to meet with the customer face to face.

By no means am I suggesting that you lock up your sales literature. Just don't be too eager to send it out. Go for the appointment several times in different ways. Don't be pushy. Be persistent and give logical reasons as to why you should meet the prospective customer personally. And make the visit sound as noncommittal and low-key as possible.

Rarely, if ever, will a customer decide they can't live without your product or service based solely on looking at your brochure. Sales literature doesn't close deals. People do.

Supplies, Furniture, and Equipment

Get only what you need and use what you take. In general, you will not need a year's worth of supplies just to get started. Get enough to last through the first two or three months, when things will be too hectic for quick trips to the office supply store.

Just as with grocery shopping, before you go out to buy office supplies, make a list of what you need. Then stick to it. If you don't, you are likely to end up spending twice as much as you budgeted.

Good quality furniture and equipment does not have to be expensive. Try warehouse retailers such as Sam's Club or Costco for good quality merchandise at affordable prices.

Set up Required Suppliers and Vendors

Depending on the type of business you are starting, this can be a short step or a long one. At a minimum you will probably need to set up advertising accounts with the local newspaper and television and radio stations. Also, getting a business credit card from your local office supply store is a good way to begin establishing a credit history for your business.

Professional Organizations, Memberships, and Affiliations

As an adamant supporter of the Chamber of Commerce, I recommend that all new business owners join their local Chamber. Not only can the contacts you make help your business grow, but most local Chambers also have discount programs on a variety of products and services you are likely to need. Finally, the Chamber will help you spread the word that you are open for business.

Although it may be more necessary for some businesses than others, I believe it is prudent for the majority of new businesses to join the Better Business Bureau.

I also recommend that you join a business referral group such as Business Network International (BNI). These groups meet periodically to exchange ideas and potential leads. In essence, a membership gives you dozens of extra "salespeople" who are predisposed to think of your business should they run into someone who expresses a need for the service or product you provide.

Based on the industry you are getting into, there may be other professional organizations you should consider joining. Do some research to find them.

Chapter 10

Attitude Determines Altitude

"Attitude is a little thing that makes a big difference."

WINSTON CHURCHILL

WINNING THE LOTTERY IS A MATTER OF LUCK. BEYOND THAT, I don't believe luck is a factor in most success stories, though it is easier to attribute our failures to bad luck and our successes to good luck. In either case, if you analyze the facts objectively, you will probably find that hard work and persistence — or the absence of one or both — were the pivotal factors.

"Genius is one percent inspiration and 99 percent perspiration."

THOMAS EDISON

Was Thomas Edison just lucky when he invented the first working light bulb in 1879? (*Note:* Joseph Swan, a British inventor, actually obtained the first patent for the light bulb in Britain one year prior to Edison's patent date. Edison's true claim to fame was improving the design and then building an entire power company around the idea.)

If the device had worked the first time Edison plugged it in, then the invention may have been considered just a matter of luck. But it didn't. In fact, Edison failed more than 6,000 times in two years before he finally got it right.

> *"I am not judged by the number of times I fail, but by the number of times I succeed; and the number of times I succeed is in direct proportion to the number of times I can fail and keep trying."*
>
> **Tom Hopkins**

The Harder I Work, The Luckier I Get

To a large degree, we make our own luck in life. It is our perseverance, goals, attitudes, philosophies, how we think and behave, and our willingness to turn potential failure into success that has a much larger impact on how we fare in life. You must go into any situation with the mindset that you will absolutely prevail.

> *"Try not. There is only do or do not. There is no try."*
>
> **Yoda, the Jedi Master from**
> ***Star Wars: The Empire Strikes Back***

Okay. So Yoda is a fiction of George Lucas's brilliant imagination. But that doesn't depreciate the truth in what Yoda said. In any endeavor — business or personal — you either will or you won't. Never say you're going to "try." That just leaves the door open for failure. You must go into any situation with the mindset that you will absolutely prevail.

Now let's talk about worry. Worry is unhealthy. It is also something new business owners have a tendency to do more often than necessary. Worry is counterproductive, as it induces a mindset that blocks clear, creative thinking.

Think back to the times in your life when you were worried about something, perhaps to the point of panic. You were Chicken Little and the sky was crashing directly toward your head. And there was no hope of recovery. But you're still here. So you must have found a way to recover — to pull those chestnuts out of the fire. And now you look back on those times with a different feeling and much-needed perspective. Of course, truly terrible events are supposed to feel terrible. But how many times have you let your mind take you to a point of absolute panic only to realize later on that you had overreacted and that, in fact, there was very little to worry about at all?

Your mind is a program, and you are the programmer. Learn how to program your mind to expect good fortune, rather than lingering over potential negative outcomes. Does that mean you will always succeed? Of course not, but you will dramatically increase your chances of success.

Sound farfetched? Well, you're not the only one who thinks so, although there is no scientific evidence to categorically prove or refute the idea. For all the advances that have been made, science is still awed by how the human mind works. The power of our conscious and subconscious mind has yet to be fully explored, let alone explained. One school of thought says the average human being uses only five to 12 percent of their mental capacity. Scientists have come to some conclusions on the functions of different parts of the brain, even though vast areas, such as the pituitary gland, the pineal gland, and parts of the midbrain limbic system, remain a mystery.

My point is this: until there is more definitive evidence to the contrary, I operate under the assumption that there is still some upside potential between our ears. Hundreds, if not thousands, of books have been written on the power of positive thinking. More importantly, almost everyone who has excelled in their particular field — entrepreneurs, senior corporate executives, generals, politicians, and athletes — cite a positive mental attitude as a crucial part of their success.

Even professional gamblers give credit to a positive mental outlook, which may surprise you, given the varying degrees of skill required in different venues. Of course, this is one area where luck is still a major factor, but it is interesting to note that a select few players always seem to come out well ahead.

Texas Hold 'Em Poker tournaments have gained a great deal of popularity over the last few years. Tournaments are now being regularly televised. The best players will tell you that, in spite of the skill required to calculate the odds, strategize your next move, and read the other players, they still hope "luck will be a lady." But consider this. Some of those tournaments start with more than 500 participants, yet when they get down to the final table of eight or nine players, you almost always see some of the same faces. Simply put, in spite of luck, the winners always seem to figure out a way to win. More important, they *expect* to win. Losing is possible, but for winners it's not considered an option.

It comes down to this: attitude is the key factor that separates winners from losers. We all have choices in life. Attitude is one of them. You can get out of bed in the morning and say to yourself "This is going to be a great day!" or you can say, "This is going to be one of those days when I should have stayed in bed." Either way, you'll be right because you have already programmed your mind. If you believe you're going to have a bad day, anything and everything that happens all day that may be even remotely negative reinforces your "prediction." You were looking for bad things to happen, you expected them, so you're not at all surprised when they do. Conversely, if you are looking for good things to happen, if you expect them, everything seems to click.

> *"Optimists are right. So are pessimists. It's up to you to choose which you will be."*
>
> Harvey Mackay

Good things and bad things happen to each of us and every day. But if you dwell on the negative, you will subconsciously gravitate toward it, whereas if you dwell on the positive you will almost automatically move in that direction. Those people who tend to dwell on the negative seem to gravitate towards it, versus those people who focus on the positive.

> *"Reality is not so much what happens to us; rather, it is how we think about those events that create the reality we experience. In a real sense, this means that we each create the reality in which we live."*
>
> Albert Ellis

Positive thinking is not easy. In fact, it can be a tremendous challenge. We all wonder why bad things happen to good people or vice versa. But a positive attitude will make it much easier to get through even the worst of times.

> *"Positive thinking won't let you do* anything, *but it will help you do* everything *better than negative thinking will."*
>
> Zig Ziglar

So how can you improve your attitude? Here are my top 15 suggestions.

Improving Your Attitude

1. Surround yourself with positive people. Constantly talk to them and motivate each other. You will rub off on each other.

2. Conversely, stay away from negative people. You don't want what they are selling. They can take any minor problem and in a matter of minutes have you feel as though it is time to call a suicide hotline. Also, stay away from those people who feel they have your best intentions in mind when they try and talk you out of starting your own business. If you are committed and this is what you want to do, don't let anyone talk you out of it, even if it may be a loved one.

> *"Keep away from those who try to belittle your ambitions. Small people always do that, but the really great make you believe that you too can become great."*
>
> Mark Twain

3. Program your mind with the right information. Read motivational books and listen to tapes or CDs. Even a small

investment of your time each day can have phenomenal results. You should become a regular customer of companies such as Nightingale Conant that sell affordable motivational and self-help audiotape and CD programs from hundreds of authors and speakers. You can contact Nightingale Conant through their website at www.nightingaleconant.com.

4. Live optimistically and shape your perspective. The glass really is half full or half empty. You get to decide. Focus on the positives and stop dwelling on the negatives. When you have setbacks, don't search for excuses; instead move on. Remember, those who want to be successful will find a way; those that do not will find an excuse.

"Losers live in the past. Winners learn from the past and enjoy working in the present toward the future."

Denis Waitley

5. Practice Self-Talk. You know, that subconscious voice that chatters away all day long. Turn it into your own best friend. Motivate yourself every step of the way. Identify when you are truly encouraging yourself and those times when you are pushing yourself towards self-destruction. Learn to manipulate your own subconscious mind to think the way you want it to.

6. Expect positive results. You must know deep down that you are going to win. If you can convince yourself of this, you can convince others, and eventually it will happen.

7. Reduce or eliminate those things in your life that seem to bring you down. Obviously, this can be quite different for each of us, but you must identify those things in your life that seem to bring you the most doom and gloom and reduce or eliminate them. It could be something as simple as not reading the newspaper anymore because

the way the negative stories influence you, or it could be as complex as a bad marriage. Whatever these things might be, until you resolve them you may find yourself in a vicious circle of stress and negativity you can never break free from.

8. Build your self-esteem and confidence. Low self-esteem and a lack of self-confidence can be a major source of negativity in our lives. Quite often it is the most common cause of poor attitudes. We must first start believing in ourselves if we are ever going to get others to believe in us. This may explain why so many people who have huge egos end up being so successful. Having a big ego may not be something you want to include on your resumé. It is, however, something that a great number of winners and successful people have in common. A large percentage of wealthy and successful entrepreneurs may seem to be a little egotistical. Was it the success, fame, and money that changed them? More often than not, these same people had big egos even before their success. Their ego reflects the confidence in themselves. They have total confidence in their abilities and don't mind telling everyone about it, but they usually win.

9. Start each morning with your own self-mantra. Tell yourself over and over again it is going to be a great day. Perform mental exercises in which you see yourself accomplishing specific tasks you have set out for yourself for that day. This may seem a little odd, but don't worry, you don't have to tell anyone you're doing it if you don't want to. It is yet another method of programming your mind for success, and many successful people will eventually admit they have been doing it for years. I even made up a picture and had it framed and hung in my bathroom that said, "Attitude Determines Altitude". Every morning it was the first message I saw. This served as a constant reminder to me.

10. Get in touch with your spiritual side. No matter what your religious beliefs may be or your level of spirituality, we all need to concentrate that energy and draw on it to continue to grow, help eliminate our fears, and accomplish the things in life we set out to accomplish.

11. Fake it until you make it. Act successful and ultimately you will be successful. This starts with your attitude. If you find yourself in a bad mood, act as though you are in a good mood. No one has to know you are in a bad mood. Sometimes, you may even fake yourself out and you'll end up in a good mood.

12. The grass isn't always greener. When the chips are down and we are having trouble in our business, we may start thinking about other opportunities that may seem a little easier. The truth is that all businesses have good parts and bad parts to them. There are things you will love to do and things you hate. When you are doing the bad parts your attitude might make a 180-degree change for the worse. Just get through it and move on to the parts you like. Don't let this bring you down.

13. Take better care of yourself. Eating right, getting some exercise, and getting the right amount of sleep each night will do wonders for your attitude.

14. Keep a good sense of humor. Having fun is great for your attitude. Make sure you make time to have fun every day. Life is too short not to.

15. Take a time out. When things looked as though they were becoming a little too stressful in the office, I would do something crazy. One afternoon I shut the entire office down, brought everyone into the conference room, and we ordered pizzas and watched a DVD on our multi-media system. Another time I sent different staff members at different times to go get a relaxation massage — anything to break down the stress and get everyone focused again.

In this mixed-up, crazy world we live in, maintaining a positive mental attitude is a tremendous challenge. Make it your mission to do it anyway!

> ***"Perpetual optimism is a force multiplier. [In the military, one always looks for ways to increase or multiply your forces.]"***
>
> **Colin Powell**

The Victor

by C. W. Longenecker

If you think you are beaten, you are.
If you think you dare not, you don't.
If you like to win, but think you can't,
It's almost a cinch you won't.

If you think you'll lose, you're lost.
For out in the world we find
success begins with a fellow's will.
It's all in the state of mind.

If you think you're outclassed, you are.
You've got to think high to rise.
You've got to be sure of yourself before
you ever can win the prize.

Life's battles don't always go
to the stronger or faster man.
But sooner or later, the man who wins
is the man who thinks he can!

Chapter 11

Market Creation: Getting the Phone to Ring

"The aim of marketing is to know and understand the customer so well that the product or service fits him and sells itself."

Peter F. Drucker

No matter what type of business you may decide to start, if you can't find enough customers you will fail. Many a great idea has never turned a profit.

No amount of market research can, with 100 percent certainty, predict the viability of a specific product or service, no matter how great it may be. On the other hand, some really crummy products and services have produced tremendous sales success simply because of a fantastic marketing campaign. The infomercial is one of the finest examples of this principle at work.

Tell the truth. How often have you ordered some new gadget you saw on a late night infomercial that seemed to offer the perfect solution to a particular problem, only to end up with an item marginally less useful than an extra cup of sand in the Sahara? For better or for worse, some of the best, most talented, savvy salespeople are making a mint the size of Fort Knox by selling junk.

Obviously, I'm not suggesting you become a junk huckster, too. The point is, in the absence of a well thought-out professional marketing campaign, even the best products or services can fail, while the duplicitous purveyors of the Easy Burn Bun, Thigh, and Hedge Trimmer are raking in the dough.

Thousands of books have been written about marketing, and there are tens of thousands of theories about the best way to get your message across to your target audience. But I sometimes think we have gotten so lost in the "tree" market of catchy phrases, funny advertisements, and appearances that we have lost sight of the basic "forest." Ask 100 business owners, whatever the business, what they would want most if they could wave a magic wand and get it, 95 out of 100 will say higher sales and profits. In short, we want more customers!

One of the exercises I use when I speak at meetings and seminars is about effective marketing campaigns. I begin by asking the participants about some of the television commercials we've all seen hundreds of times. For example, if I ask them to name the first battery company that comes to mind when I say, "pink bunny." On average 30 percent of the participants will say Eveready, 35 percent will say Duracell, 30 percent will say Energizer and the final 5 percent will name a lesser known brand or have no answer. So, based on these figures, approximately 70 percent of the participants did not know it was the Energizer Bunny! Since Eveready actually owns the Energizer brand, perhaps it doesn't matter. But the Energizer Bunny was introduced back in 1989 and, after 115 different commercial spots that have aired thousands of times, I am still amazed that everyone on the planet would not recognize one of the top five advertising icons of the 20th and 21st centuries.

The Eveready/Energizer Company invested countless millions of dollars in developing and marketing the bunny. Corporate America can afford such an investment. As a small business owner, you cannot. You must focus on the basics, i.e., getting more customers by ensuring that your message comes across loud and clear and that you get the biggest bang for your advertising buck. Start by identifying:

1. What your customers want
2. Where they are
3. The most effective and attractive ways of telling them you have what they want, *and*
4. The most effective and attractive ways of persuading them to buy it from you instead of someone else.

Emotion vs. Logic

No one buys a car just to have a two-ton hunk of metal sitting in the driveway. They buy a car because it can take them where they want to go more comfortably and efficiently than walking. Put another way, people do not buy products or services. They buy the benefits of owning and/or using those products or services. They buy the "sizzle," not the steak.

People also do not buy for logical reasons. Instead, they buy for emotional reasons and justify their purchase with logic. So if you want to sell something, appeal to the customer on an emotional level, then give them logical reasons to back it up.

Years ago I leased a Lincoln Navigator. I was never emotionally connected to it, but my kids loved the third row of seats and all the cup holders. I worked out an agreement under which I paid for the 24-month lease in advance, which left me with no future payments for the term of the lease. One day, about a year after I'd leased the Navigator, I was driving by a Cadillac dealer when I glimpsed a beautiful STS. I immediately saw myself in that car, so I decided to drop by and have a quick look. With nearly a year remaining on the Navigator lease, I knew there was no way I would buy the STS, because the Lincoln dealer was certainly not going to give me back a year's worth of my advance payments — approximately, $8,500.

As I walked around the Cadillac, the dealer finally convinced me (as if he had to twist my arm!) to take it out for a spin. When I told him I didn't really have the time, he suggested that I take it overnight and bring it back in the morning. I grabbed the keys and hit the road. In sales circles, this is called the "Puppy Dog Close." Pet storeowners would encourage would-be customers to take a puppy home overnight just to see if the puppy would mesh well with the family. Of course, by the next morning the puppy had a name and the kids had fallen in love with it.

Well, I was not about to get caught in that trap. Given all the money I had prepaid on the Navigator lease, buying the STS was illogical and out of the question. Period.

Then I began to notice how comfortable it was, the way you could barely feel the road, the effortless drive and, of course, the way it looked. Or rather, the way I looked in it. Cool personified, at least in one man's opinion.

The next morning on the way back to the dealer to drop off the car I yanked out my calculator and started running some figures. I had already put more miles on the Navigator than I had expected, which meant I was likely to double the miles stated in the lease agreement. And I would certainly have to pay for those extra miles. Then I looked at the gas gauge on the STS and noted how little it had moved since the previous afternoon. Using the on-board computer, I found that the STS was delivering almost twice the gas mileage as the Navigator. With my trusty calculator, I quickly calculated the annual gas savings. The rest, as they say, is history. By the time I got back to the Cadillac dealer my mathematical calculations had convinced me I could *save* money by buying the STS. I probably don't have to tell you what I ended up driving home.

This is a classic example of how people allow emotions to influence their purchases. The Cadillac was an emotional desire, which I allowed myself to justify logically based on projected gasoline and mileage savings. The logic may have still been there even without the emotion, but logic alone would never have convinced me to make the purchase.

So, find out who your customers are, what makes them tick, and how to satisfy their emotional needs. Then back it all up with logic. Wham! They'll be hooked like so many starving catfish.

"The Devil made me do it."

Flip Wilson

AIDA Format For Advertising

The Attention, Interest, Desire, and Action (AIDA) format is one of the most tried and true methods of advertising. St. Elmo Lewis first proposed the AIDA model in 1898. By 1925 an estimated 90 percent of businesses were using AIDA, which had become the most prominent form of advertising.

I first heard of AIDA from my father. He had attended a Dale Carnegie training class about 40 years ago where they discussed it. AIDA encompasses the four *critical* elements of effective advertising.

Attention

Find out what the reader wants most, then create a headline that includes it. In seconds, the reader will decide whether the rest of your advertisement is worth reading. What is a good headline? Here are 101 of the best of all time. Many are somewhat dated for this day and age, but you will get the idea. *Note:* Some of these headlines ran continuously for more than 35 *years* and sold millions of dollars worth of products and services.

> ***"On the average, five times as many people read the headline as read the body copy. When you have written your headline, you have spent eighty cents out of your dollar."***
>
> David Ogilvy

101 Best-Written Headlines of All Time
(as selected by Jerry L. Clum, Jr.)

161 New Ways to a Man's Heart — In This Fascinating Book

Seven Ways To Collect Your Unpaid Bills

A $10,000 Mistake!

A Little Mistake That Cost a Farmer $3,000 a Year

A Startling Fact about Money

A WARNING to Men Who Want to Be Independent in the Next Five Years

A Wonderful Two-Year Trip at Full Pay — but Only Men With Imagination Can Take It

Advice to Wives Whose Husbands Don't Save Money

Are You Ever Tongue-tied at a Party?

As Seen on TV

At 60 Miles an Hour the Loudest Noise in This New Rolls-Royce Comes from the Electric Clock

Break Out of Jail!

Car Owners . . . Save One Gallon of Gas for Every Ten

Check the Kind of Body You Want

Dare To Be Rich!

Dear American Tourister: You Saved My Life

Do You Do Any of These Embarrassing Things?

Do You Make This Mistakes in English? *[Purposely contained incorrect grammar]*

Do Your Employees Work as Slowly as They Read?

Does Your Child Ever Embarrass You?

Don't Even Think about Buying a New Home without Reading This Report!

For People Who Don't Have Time for Unimportant Books

For the Woman Who Looks Younger than She Is

Free to Brides — $2 to Others

Get Rid of Money Worries for Good

Girls! Want Quick Curls?

Great New Discovery Kills Kitchen Odors Quick!

Greatest Bible News in 341 Years

Have You Ever Seen a Grown Man Cry?

Here Is a Quick Way to Break up a Cold

How a New Discovery Made a Plain Girl Beautiful

How I Improved My Memory in One Evening

How I Made a Fortune with a Fool Idea

How Much Is Your Working "Tension" Costing Your Company?

How the Experts Buy and Sell Gold and Silver

How the Next 90 Days Can Change Your Life

How to Avoid Mental Hazards

How to Beat Tension Without Pills

How to Burn Off Body Fat, Hour-by-Hour

How to Discover What You Are Really Good At

How to Form Your Corporation Without a Lawyer for Under $50

How to Get More Energy From the Food You Eat

How to Get Rich Reading Classified Ads

How to Give Your Children Extra Iron — 3 Delicious Ways

How to Rob Banks Legally

How to Start from Scratch and Become a P.O. Box Millionaire

How to Swim with the Sharks without Being Eaten Alive

How to Win Friends and Influence People

How to Write a Business Letter.

How to Write a Good Advertisement

How to Write a Hit Song and Sell It

How You can Get a Quick Loan of $1,000

I Gambled with 3 Cents and Won $35,850 In Two Years

I Liked This Product So Much — That I Bought The Company!

I Lost My Bulges — And Saved Money Too!

Imagine Harry and Me Advertising our Pears in *Fortune*!

Imagine Me . . . Holding an Audience Spellbound for 30 Minutes

Is the Life of a Child Worth $1 to You?

It Seems Impossible That You Can Offer These Signed Original Etchings for Only $5 Each

Keep Your Dog Safe This Summer!

Little Leaks That Keep Men Poor

Men Who "Know It All" Are Not Invited To Read This Page

My Sears Kenmore Sewing Machine has 9 Different Stitches — Imagine!

Need More Money?

New Shampoo Leaves Your Hair Smoother — Easier to Manage

Often a Bridesmaid — Never a Bride!

Pierced by 301 Nails and It Still Retains Full Air Pressure

Play Guitar in 7 Days or Money Back

Quick Relief for Tired Eyes

Seven Steps to Financial Freedom

Six Types of Investors — Which Group Are You In?

Suppose This Happened On Your Wedding Day!

Take This One-Minute Test!

The Child Who Won the Hearts of All

The Crimes We Commit Against Our Stomachs

The Greatest Reason in the World

The Instrument of the Immortals

The Last Two Hours are the Longest — and Those are the Two Hours You Save

The Lazy Man's Way To Riches — Most people are too busy earning a living to make any money

The Man in the Hathaway Shirt

The Most Expensive Mistake of Your Life

The Secret of Having Good Luck

The Secret to Being Wealthy

The Secrets of Making People Like You

The Truth About Getting Rich

They Grinned When the Waiter Spoke to Me in French

They Laughed When I Sat Down at the Piano — But When I Started to Play!

Thousands Have This Priceless Gift — but Never Discover It!

To a Mother Whose Child Is Three Years Old

To Men Who Want to Quit Working Some Day

To People Who Want To Write — But Can't Get Started

Want to Be a Legal Investigator?

What Makes a Woman Lovable?

What Your Lawyer Doesn't Want You to Know

When Doctors "Feel Rotten" This Is What They Do

Who Is Making a Bundle and How

Why Some Foods "Explode" in Your Stomach

Why *Wall Street Journal* Readers Live Better

Will You Help Me Free Gina?

You Can Laugh at Money Worries — If You Follow This Simple Plan

You Can Make Big Money Easily

Notice any common denominators? All of these headlines describe benefits to the reader and usually on an emotional as opposed to a logical level. For example, the headline "Pierced by 301 Nails and it Still Retains Full Air Pressure" was used to sell a particular brand of tires. As you can see, they weren't attempting to sell the tire in the headline, but rather one of the primary *benefits* of the tire. That headline grabbed customer attention and was intriguing enough to draw them further into the advertisement.

While you should never copy any headlines verbatim, you may modify them to fit your particular product or service. Regardless, it is good to review existing headlines to get a general idea of what you want in the headline you create.

In 1979, the psychology department at Yale University revealed that the 12 most influential words in advertising are:

- Guarantee
- New
- Save
- Health
- Discovery
- Love
- Results
- Easy

- Proven
- You
- Money
- Safety

Here are 30 additional highly effective words.

- Advice
- Alternative
- Announcing
- Benefits
- Comfort
- Dependable
- Easy
- Effective
- Fast
- Free
- Fun
- Gain
- Happy
- How To
- Introducing
- Most
- Now
- People
- Proud
- Right
- Sale
- Secret
- Security
- Strategy
- Success
- Trustworthy
- Value
- Wanted
- Why
- Win

Although you may find these words useful in your headline or in the content of your advertisement, don't try to shove in as many as you can just for the sake of having them there.

Interest

Because people, by nature, have a short attention span, you cannot bask in the success of your headline for long. You have to draw them in further.

To create interesting content that explains why your particular product or service fits your customers' needs, you must first fully know and understand your customers.

One effective way to create interest and to get the reader to read further is by using questions in your advertisement. A question implies that an answer will be forthcoming later in the text. That may not always be true, but, depending on the question, the reader may want to find out if his or her answer is the same one you provided.

Another rule of thumb is not to be overly concerned with the length of your copy. There is an old advertising myth that suggests that the best advertisement is the one with the fewest number of words. That is not necessarily true. Use as many words as necessary to build interest and value for your product or service.

This is also a good time to begin exploring your Unique Selling Proposition (USP). A more detailed discussion of the USP is provided later in this section. For now, here are two examples of statements that will cause a reader to read further: "Want To Win A Free Gift?" or "Having Trouble With…?". These are almost guaranteed attention-getters.

Desire

This is the clutch shot. Now that you have the reader's interest, it's time to create a desire for your product or service. Your best efforts to this point will have been wasted if you are unable to create or build on the customer's emotional need and influence them to contact you. You must convince the reader of the benefits they can obtain from your product or service. Be as bold as you can, but be honest. The worst mistake you can make is to over-promise and then under-deliver.

Testimonials are an excellent vehicle for letting potential customers know what to expect from you. A testimonial is a written affirmation from someone who has successfully used your product or service. Hearing others sing the praises of your product or talk about how your service changed their lives is both credible and believable to potential customers. It is also much more powerful than anything you can say on your own behalf.

Action

If you scored on the previous steps, this one should not be too difficult. It is now time to ask for the sale or get the customer to take the next step, which is contacting you. Something as simple as "Call Today, Don't Delay," followed by your phone number or "Visit Us on the Web," followed by your web address may be all you need. Statements such as "Call Toll-Free," "Out of Town Call Collect," "Call 24 Hours a Day, Operators Standing By," "For a Free Color Brochure," "For Free Information," "For A Free Consultation," or "For a Free Quote" will remove obstacles and make it even easier for people to call you.

Unique Selling Propositions (USPs)

What separates Federal Express from other package delivery companies, or Avis from other car rental companies, or Wal-Mart from other retailers, or Domino's from other pizza chains? USPs.

Almost every major company in America has used a well thought-out and well-devised USP to achieve domination in their industry. USPs turn small companies into industry leaders.

When Domino's was founded, the pizza market was already saturated and highly competitive. To grow and prosper, they had to find a way to differentiate themselves from their competitors. A comprehensive study of their target audience showed that the strongest and most frequent purchasers of their product line were busy moms. With the increase in dual-income families, millions of moms were coming home from work exhausted and facing hungry families who demanded to know "what's for dinner?" The answer? A hot meal delivered to the family doorstep in a lot less time than it would take Mom to prepare one. Enter Domino's with the soon-to-be-famous USP "Fresh Pizza Delivered to Your Door in 30 Minutes or Less." Mom could pick up the phone, punch in seven numbers, and have a quick shower before dinner was delivered. No muss. No fuss.

Here is another now familiar success story. In the early 70s, there was an enormous opportunity in the package delivery industry in the form of a service gap that the post office and independent delivery companies had been unable to fill. The founders of Federal Express (or FedEx, as they are now called) based their entire business concept on that opportunity. Their USP, "When It Absolutely, Positively Has to be There Overnight," not only changed the entire postal delivery industry, but also the world as we know it.

The founders of Avis Car Rental knew that Hertz was the number one car rental company in the world. They also knew that Hertz was far too big for them to successfully compete with head-on. So they instead positioned themselves as the number two car rental company, the "underdog" that would work harder to keep your business. Their USP, "We're Number Two. We Try Harder," is one of the most brilliant ever devised. They made being second best almost sound better than being the number one company, and over time it enabled them to do what had not been possible in the beginning: compete head-to-head with Hertz.

No other industry in the world has had such a massive face-lift as retailing. The lead plastic surgeon? Wal-Mart. The typical American Main Street of small shops as far as the eye could see has all but disappeared because industry giants such as Wal-Mart established one of the most efficient and cost-effective distribution systems ever devised. This system allowed them to offer many of the same or similar products as other retailers but at a drastically reduced and hence more affordable price. Their USP, "Always Low Prices," has allowed them to dominate the retailing industry with sales of approximately one-quarter-of-a-trillion dollars annually!

Does this mean that your business has to be the biggest and best in your chosen industry? Not necessarily. To dominate the industry, make your business unique, find an underserved niche in the marketplace, and develop the strongest USP.

If that sounds like a tall order, you're right. But the reward is well worth the effort.

WHY IS YOUR USP SO IMPORTANT?

- It will differentiate you from the competition.
- It will distinguish your company.
- It will give you an advantage.
- It will make your company unique.
- It will help increase your brand awareness.
- It will help you fill a void in the marketplace.
- It will give you vision to drive your company to greater success.

To create your USP, begin with a little brainstorming about the industry you have chosen. If you are already in business, find out why your customers use your service or bought your product in the past. If you can find a common denominator, you may be able to polish it and come up with a solid USP. If you are just starting a business, find out why customers would want to use your service or buy your product rather than going to one of your competitors. Think about it long enough and you may find the real gem: a void in the market that you can fill.

Whether you are already in business or just starting out, your USP must be:

- Specific
- Measurable
- Unique
- Based on industry performance gaps or voids
- Bold, yet realistic.
- Crystal Clear

"Fresh Pizza Delivered to Your Door in 30 Minutes or Less." That's specific, measurable, and unique. No other company was making the same promise, so this USP was about filling a gap or void in the industry. And you have to admit it was bold. Can you imagine the tens of thousands of customers who called in for a pizza and then sat around watching the clock only to be amazed when the driver pulled up in less than 30 minutes? (To say nothing of the drivers who pulled over when they saw the pizza car coming!)

Take as much time as you need to decide on a USP. It is too critical for a rush to judgment. Your USP may not change for decades, and you will be spending thousands of dollars, if not more, in advertising and promotion.

Although changing a USP is not impossible, it can be extremely difficult and expensive. Still, if a business is barely making a profit, it may be because they have no USP or because the one they have is composed of old worn-out phrases. How many times have you heard or seen these phrases in advertisements?

- The Best Selection in Town
- Our Prices Can't Be Beat
- We'll Match Our Competitors
- Come See Our Friendly Staff of Professionals
- We Won't Be Undersold
- Best Service in Town
- Serving You Since 1990 *[or even before then]*
- Service Second to None
- Don't Miss This Once-in-a-Lifetime Opportunity
- Hurry In Today
- But Hurry…With Prices Like These, Selections Won't Last Long
- Prices Have Never Been Lower
- Five Locations to Serve You

- Our Loss Is Your Gain
- You've Got to See It to Believe It
- But Wait, There's More
- Absolutely Everything Must Be Sold
- Everything Drastically Reduced. It's Our Biggest Sales Event of the Year
- You'll Save Like Never Before
- Everything Must Go
- We're Declaring War on High Prices
- This Is One Sale You Don't Want to Miss

Each of these USPs was unique when it was introduced. Now they have become so common they're almost clichés, and customers are likely to ignore them.

Again, take your time creating a USP. Make sure that it identifies your business as unique in the industry. Then integrate it into all of your advertising and promotional materials.

Last, but you better believe not least: *Make sure you can deliver what you say*. You want this USP to become synonymous with your company name. A company that fails to deliver what its USP promises is probably not long for the business world.

NEWSPAPER ADVERTISING

For many industries, newspaper advertising can be effective — provided it is done correctly.

I love to critique advertisements. Fortunately, for me, there are a host of bad ones out there. Looking at most advertisements, it is reasonable to conclude that a majority of small business owners, and not a few advertising agencies, have forgotten the basic purpose of an advertisement: getting potential customers to call!

Too much cuteness and too much cleverness can sometimes lead to terrible results in advertising. The same is true of ads that seem to be ego-driven, leaving the customer to wonder if the business is trying to sell a product or the owner. In many advertisements, the AIDA format (discussed earlier) has been entirely ignored, assuming the perpetrators of the ad were even aware of AIDA.

When it comes to newspaper advertising, start by considering your audience. Who are you trying to target? Whose eye do you want to catch? This brings us back to the importance of knowing your customer base. If you don't, successful newspaper advertising is almost impossible.

Most newspapers in America are divided into sections: Main News, Local News, Health, Community, Real Estate, Sports, Entertainment, and Classifieds. Some people read the newspaper, front to back, and never miss a page. Others read the Main News and then skip to whatever other section interests them most. So, if your product is sports-related, you run your advertisement in the Sports Section.

But suppose your product or service is designed for the masses, so you want as many people as possible to read your advertisement. I have found that, regardless of particular interests, most people read the front-page news. Of course the likelihood of getting a newspaper to run your ad on its front page is too small to be calculated. But remember: most front-page stories are continued on pages deeper into the first section of the newspaper. You may be able to get your ad on one of those pages. Now, your advertising representative will probably tell you that, while they can guarantee that your ad will appear in a particular section, they cannot guarantee page placement. Well, maybe and maybe not. The trick here is to find a good, aggressive ad rep and then develop a good relationship with him or her. Sometimes they can create miracles for you when it comes to ad placement.

In the marketing training seminars I used to conduct, I often used the following exercise. I would pick a paper, hand it to one of the participants, and ask them to open it to any page at random. Seconds later, I would grab the paper back and then ask them what they remembered seeing. With only a quick glance, obviously their memory was not always perfect. But whatever they remembered, it was invariably something they'd glimpsed in the upper right hand corner of the right hand page. Since the majority of people initially focus on that area, requesting and getting your ad in that area can increase its effectiveness.

So remember that the placement of an ad can have a significant effect on the results, i.e., the business, you are likely to get as a result.

Finally, focus your ad on the *benefits* of your product or service rather than the product or service itself. Remember: "sell the sizzle, not the steak." Always include your USP, follow the rules of the AIDA format, and don't try too hard to entertain the customer. Laughs they can get on the comic page.

Direct Mail

Over four million tons (or eight *billion* pounds) of junk mail is sent each year and most people hate it. Which raises the question: why do businesses send the stuff?

Well, if it weren't working somewhere on some level, they wouldn't. I would never advise a business owner to send junk mail. But there is a big difference between sending junk mail and initiating an effective direct mail program. Here are a few suggestions that will help to increase your success rate if you decide to set up such a program.

1. Never send items at the bulk rates. Use first-class postage. Yes, it's more expensive. But more people are likely to open it, rather than pitching it, unopened, into the nearest "round file."

2. Don't use address labels. Print or write the names and addresses on the letters. Is this time-consuming? Yes. But it can be quite effective. You could even hire a few high school students with good penmanship to do this for you. Also, consider using red ink. It has a slight psychological effect in that it will usually get your letter opened more quickly than others.

3. Avoid having a great deal of printing on the outside of the envelope. If it looks like junk mail, the person is more likely to treat it as such.

4. Use envelopes instead of folding and stapling your offer.

5. Include a cover letter with your mailings — even if you are including a brochure. Address the cover letter and the envelope to the person's name. Most word-processing programs have a mail-merge option that makes it easy to do this. Never address your mail to Occupant, Resident, etc. The person sees those right away, and they think "junk mail."

6. Make sure your message follows the AIDA format. Especially the Attention step, which would be your headline, and the Action step, which gets the prospect to move to the next step of the sales process. Remember your USP and sell the sizzle.

7. Use a P.S. on every letter. This alone can increase your results by 20% or more.

8. Whenever possible, make your offer tie in with current events. This will make it seem timely.

9. If you are using an alphabetized mailing list, start with the "Z's" and work backwards. I know that sounds odd, but bear with me. Almost every company that uses direct mail and mailing lists starts with the names beginning with "A" and then works alphabetically. Many times they never end up getting to the end of their list before they have given up on the project. I honestly believe that the "A," "B," and "C" people get more direct mail and telemarketing calls than the "X," "Y," and "Z" people.

10. Test market first with smaller mailings before spending the time and money rolling out large ones.

11. Give your prospects several ways to pay for your product or service.

12. Use a good mailing list. Make sure the list is fresh and targeted to your qualified potential customers. If you are

going to purchase a mailing list, make sure they have a guaranteed deliverable policy that, at a minimum, replaces undelivered pieces at the rate of five new names for every undelivered piece.

13. Whenever possible, provide money-back guarantees.

14. Always use photos of your products or services. A picture really is worth a thousand words. Try to use photos that depict how someone is benefiting from your product or service.

15. To eliminate as many concerns as possible, cover the most popular objections in the letter.

Four-Step Direct Mail Marketing Program

This is one of the best ways to increase the effectiveness of your direct mail program. Traditional programs have a response rate of one-half percent to three percent for cold mailings — and the three percent is rare. With this program, you could increase your response rate to 10 percent or more.

Step One

Separate the cold prospects from the warm prospects. Create what is called a "Soft Offer" via direct mail, postcards, Internet advertising, or classified ads in publications your target prospects are likely to read. Rather than creating a direct mail piece that solicits your specific product or service, instead offer something that is less ominous, but still of interest to the customer you are attempting to target. Suppose, for example, you sell financial planning services. Your "Soft Offer" might be to send them a free report on how to save up to $10,000 on their taxes this year. A free report sounds less threatening to a prospective customer, and is likely to generate a much larger number of warm prospects. And make sure you give them an easy way to contact you, e.g., a toll-free number, website, email, fax, or a form they can fill out and return. Better yet, all of the above!

Step Two

Using those warm prospects that responded in Step One, send out the first of three direct mail pieces. Use the AIDA format, include your USP, and send any brochures that are applicable to your offer. Then follow up, by phone or in person, to market your product or service to those who respond.

Step Three

After one to two weeks, send another piece to those who *did not* respond to the piece you mailed in Step Two. Put "Second Notice" or "Second Chance" somewhere on the letter and the envelope. You may change the offer a little, but be sure it builds on the first offer, and that your central message remains the same. Again, follow up, by phone or in person, to market your product or service.

Step Four

After another one to two weeks, send one last piece to those who *did not* respond to the material you sent in Step Three. Put "Final Notice" or "Last Chance" somewhere on the letter and the envelope. Then follow up with those who respond as you did in Step Two and Three.

This four-step program can be extremely effective. One of the reasons traditional direct mail programs have such a limited response rate is that they do not take into account those people who may have an interest in the product or service, but who decided not to take immediate action. Marketing is about timing. Multiple mailings increase the yield exponentially.

Chased vs. Chasing Principle

"If my choices are to be chased or to be the one doing the chasing . . . tag, you're it."

Jerry L. Clum, Jr.

What usually happens when you are chasing someone? They run away. But if you can get someone to chase you and then tactfully allow them to catch you, you're in business. (Historically, women used this tactic for years, as many a husband may or may not willingly attest.)

I call this the Chased vs. Chasing Principle. Put simply, make the potential customer want your service or product so strongly that he or she will go to great lengths to get it.

As a consumer, how often have you felt that a company has gone beyond selling to pushing their product or service down your throat? Your defenses go up and they're likely to stay up. Nobody really likes to be "sold" anything, but everyone enjoys "buying" things. Therein lies fertile ground for attracting customers to your product or service. Find a way to turn the customer's "fear of losing" into an intense urgency to buy your product or service.

Fad products have made millions based on this principle. Remember the Beanie Baby craze? Or the McDonald's Teenie Beanie Babies craze? The lines stretched around the restaurants well before opening. Customers drove hundreds of miles, visiting dozens of McDonald's restaurants, sometimes buying food they didn't want at the time, all because they were afraid they might miss out on the limited supply of Teenie Beanie Babies.

How did Ty, the manufacturer of both Beanie Babies and Teenie Beanies, create such an overwhelming swell in the market for inexpensive stuffed bears and animals? By capitalizing on two of the strongest human emotions: the fear of loss (translation: "If I don't get one fast, I might be left out"), and the sense of urgency, as each beanie was "retired" after a certain period of time. With a massive, aggressive, multimedia campaign, the company could easily have just saturated the market with stuffed bears. But they knew the result would not have been nearly as effective (translation: profitable.) So instead, they compelled customers to chase down their product by making it somewhat limited.

Find a way to get potential customers worried they might not get the opportunity to own your product or use your service, and you will see a dramatic difference in sales.

Fear of loss and the sense of urgency were also the catalysts for the astounding success of home shopping via television, an incredibly successful method of product distribution. While the spokesperson is hawking the wares, a small box, with a clock counting down the few remaining minutes left in which you can buy that product at that price, is on the screen. In addition, there is another counter showing how quickly the product is being sold and how many are left.

This is a brilliant marketing strategy. First, there are indirect testimonials in the form of the 5,450 other people who liked the product enough to buy it. Second, there is the relentlessly ticking clock letting the customer know that he or she only has two minutes left to buy the product at that price or miss out forever. And finally, there is the fear of loss associated with the customer seeing there are only 50 of these great items left.

So, convince your potential customers that life, as they know it, will cease to exist without your product or service, and that they only have so much time left to get it, and you can reach a level of success you may never have expected.

Now we turn to making your advertisements more effective. With the right message, you can effectively advertise in a variety of ways including television, radio, newspapers, magazines, direct mail, billboards, Internet directories, and the Yellow Pages. Depending upon your particular industry and the product or service you sell, some media will work better than others. In general, however, here are a few things you can do to increase the effectiveness of your advertising campaign.

More Effective Advertising

1. Test your advertisements.
2. Key your advertisements.
3. Track your advertisements.
4. Use photos in any printed medium.
5. Include some kind of money-back guarantee.
6. Offer discounts and coupons.
7. Write in the present tense, using the second-person format.
8. Put the benefits up front.
9. Provide a limited number of free offers.
10. Use testimonials whenever possible.
11. Use a Problem-Solution Approach.
12. Ask questions to which potential customers can answer "yes."
13. Maintain a constant advertising presence.
14. Avoid paying full price for advertising.
15. Avoid the Pied Piper Effect.

Testing

Test different advertisements in different media to determine which venue will work best for you.

Keying

"Key" your ads to determine which are pulling the best. For example, add a different department number on your address or a bogus extension for your phone number to each different advertisement you run. If potential customers are adding that department number or asking for that extension, you will know with certainty which advertisement they saw that prompted them to call.

Tracking

To get the most bang for your advertising buck, keep a written log of each call that comes in and how they heard about you. Then identify the advertisements that are providing the most leads and the most sales compared to the dollars spent on those ads.

Photos

Almost twice as many people will look at a photo as will read an ad. Logically, then, an ad with a photo will attract twice as many potential customers. Also, there is evidence that vertical photos are more effective than horizontal ones, and that doubling the size of your photo usually means that customers will read twice as much of your copy. Go figure.

Guarantees

Sixty percent of people believe advertisements with a money-back guarantee.

Discounts and Coupons

Even Oprah Winfrey appreciates saving a buck here and there! Adding discounts and coupons, even modest ones, can increase the effectiveness of your ad by at least 10 percent.

Always Write in the Present Tense

People are reading your ad now, not later or before. So write it in a NOW format. Also, write in the second person, i.e., YOU, instead of "I" (first person) or "THEY" (the third person). When it comes to advertising, the word "You" is one of the most powerful in the English language.

Benefits Up Front

Put the benefits of your product or service up front. People are likely to quit reading before they get to the end of your ad.

Limited Number of Free Offers

Remember the fear of loss and sense of urgency? Use them by including statements such as "The first 100 customers will receive a free [some type of gift] with their purchase," or "The first 25 callers will receive a free consultation."

Testimonials

As noted earlier, testimonials are more credible to the potential customer. They get to hear others sing the praises of your product or service and the impact it had on their lives.

Problem-Solution Approach

State the problem, then offer the ultimate solution, and you will create a more effective ad. Example: "Do You Have Dry, Itchy Eyes? If So, Try Our New Wet Eyes."

Ask Questions To Which the Customer Can Answer "Yes"

This gives potential customers the feeling that you understand their needs better than your competitors do and helps them see the benefit of contacting you.

Constant Advertising Presence

Okay. Listen up. Don't advertise *ONLY* when you need business. Advertise *CONSTANTLY* so that you *WON'T* need business. Advertising has a cumulative effect on the public, so keep your company uppermost in the public mind. I cannot count (or maybe I don't want to) the number of business owners who have told me: "I can't afford to advertise. I don't have enough business." *Duhhhh?*

Avoid Paying Full Price

Most advertising media build an extra 10 to15 percent into their prices to pay advertising agencies that represent clients. That gives you room to negotiate. Don't take no for an answer and you will usually end up with a better price. It never hurts to ask. Some business owners have started their own "advertising agency" just to recover that 10 to 15 percent!

Avoid the Piped Piper Effect

Have you ever noticed how certain ads tend to show up together on the same pages in a newspaper or how certain companies in the same industries always seem to advertise in the same sections as their competitors? While it's always a good idea to make sure you are seen where your competitors are seen, don't go too far and fall into the trap of following everyone else. That may be the path to failure. Many business owners have never tested their advertisements in different sections of the newspaper or on different pages of those sections. They simply followed the trend, which itself could have been initiated without much experimentation or testing. Your ad may pull better in the Main section of the paper rather than the Sports Section, etc. Bottom line? Advertise in the places that are most effective for *your* business. Don't just follow the piper and end up drowning in the river with everyone else.

Guerilla Marketing

Most businesses advertise through the traditional media venues. But there is non-traditional type of marketing that only a handful of (successful) business owners understand. It's known by many names, including Guerilla Marketing, Grass Roots, Out of the Box, and Viral. Here I'll just call it Guerilla Marketing.

Although it has been around in some form or another for over 20 years, Guerilla Marketing is a fairly new concept in the world of advertising and promotion. A Guerilla-worthy idea must be free or radically low cost (compared to traditional advertising), unconventional, and effective.

Advertising expert, Jay Conrad Levinson, popularized Guerilla Marketing in the early 1980s. Where did the name come from? "Guerrilla" was the rank of an assistant who helped the Duke of Wellington use unusual and unpredictable tactics to push back Napoleon's troops during the Peninsular War. In terms of advertising, Guerrilla Marketing rewards those who are original and who look for and find alternative low-cost methods of getting their message out.

As a rule, the better you target your potential customer base, the more you will sell. Suppose, for example, you put an ad in a newspaper with a circulation of 100,000. Assuming 2.3 people read that paper, you have a potential audience of 230,000 people. But suppose you sell five items from that ad, i.e., only one of every 46,000 people bought your product or service? Suffice it to say, if you targeted that market, you missed!

Stealth Marketing

Here is a Guerilla Marketing strategy that I began using many years ago that may enable you to sell to one out of every 10 people your message reaches.

Next time you go to the library, take a look at all the books specific to your industry. Even if your industry is somewhat obscure, there are still dozens, if not hundreds, of books that would be applicable to your industry. Now, take one of those books off the shelf, insert one of your brochures, and put the book back. Repeat the process with each relevant book. You have just pinpointed your target audience as closely as possible. Anyone who is interested in reading that book will be interested in your service or product. This strategy is extremely low-cost and therefore meets one of the criteria necessary for it to be considered Guerilla Marketing. Of course, most libraries are unlikely to appreciate this activity. To put it another way, you may get kicked off the premises. Officially speaking, it's a good idea to get permission before trying this.

Seminars

Another Guerilla Marketing strategy is conducting free seminars on subjects in your industry. In effect, you now have a captive audience — and a room full of targeted potential customers. Warning: be prepared to share some actual information and don't try to do a lot of selling. Your potential customers are likely to be angry if they think you just got them there to do a commercial for your business. Instead, use this time to establish yourself as the expert in the field. Think of it as planting seeds. You will harvest the crop (i.e., make the sales) later. To make your seminar more effective, include speakers from similar, but non-competitive, fields. Sell them on the idea, and they may help you defray the costs of the seminar. There are industries that generate up to 90 percent of their leads in this manner. Make this work in an industry that has never capitalized on the power of seminars, and you may have found the proverbial pot of gold.

Finally, consider charging a small fee to attend your seminar. I know it sounds odd, but depending on the industry, you may find it actually increases attendance.

Birthday Card Marketing Program‘

Another Guerilla Marketing strategy that I have used successfully is the Birthday Card Marketing Program‘. Many businesses, as a matter of practice, will send birthday cards to their existing customers. My idea took this practice a step farther. I started sending birthday cards to potential customers — people I had never met or even spoke to before.

So where do you get these names, addresses, and birth dates? In most counties, voter registration records are in the public domain. So you can usually go to your local voter registration office and request a list of registered voters. In addition to names and addresses you will typically find they include birth dates.

Choose the names from the age group you are targeting then send those people birthday cards on the actual week of their birth date. Include a birthday gift, in the form of a discount or freebie from your company. Not only are you reaching your target audience, but also they are less likely to think of it as junk mail. After all, it came on their birthday, or at least close to it. It was timely, so they opened it and read it. Even if you don't make a sale right away, they will remember you. When I used this strategy, I got a lot of calls from people who just wanted to thank me — as well as to ask how in the world I knew it was their birthday. I would just say that a little bird told me.

Typo Domains

Here's another effective Guerilla Marketing strategy. This one involves the Internet. Ideally, you would buy the dot.com domain names of words that people would search on to find your product. But since most of the dot.com names were grabbed up long ago, you'll need to take a more creative approach.

When I was marketing my franchise system I advertised on several Internet sites proven to be effective, such as www.franchise.com. People who were interested in the possibility of buying a franchise just went to a web browser and typed in www.franchise.com to see what it would bring up. This site got millions of hits each month. The domain name alone could probably be sold for several million dollars, which explains why it is often impossible to buy certain domain names.

To capitalize on words like "franchise" on the Internet, I needed to think outside the box. I noticed that whenever I searched different sites, I often misspelled the name when I was entering it on a web browser. That gave me an idea. I had 10 people type the word "franchise" 100 times as fast as they could. Then I bought the domain names with the most common typos, and used a free website listing service to mirror my website from those new misspelled domain names. For a total cost of about $8 per year per domain name, I was getting thousands of hits each month.

* * *

Here are 25 other Guerilla Marketing strategies.

1. Mobile billboards on trucks or vans.

2 Unique business cards, such as photo cards or video cards for computers.

3. Aggressive and unique PR and promotional coups. Make news happen.

4. Volunteer for as many speaking engagements as possible.

5. Volunteer to write an "Ask the Expert" column for your local newspaper.

6. On-hold marketing on your telephone.

7. Volunteer to host an "Ask The Expert" radio program for local radio stations.

8. Street marketing by hiring people to get the buzz out on the street about your new product or service. This is also known as undercover marketing.

9. Ask your vendors to pick up all or part of the cost of an advertisement. They are looking for exposure too, so mention that you carry their product line in your advertisement, and they may be willing to pay for all or part of the cost.

10. Hire the local Boy Scouts or a high school band to hang flyers on the doorknobs of homes in your target areas.

11. Develop alliances with other companies.

12. If you have to close your business due to bad weather, get some free PR by contacting the radio and television stations and having them announce it with all the other closings such as schools, government offices, and prescheduled activities.

13. Network within your community.

14. Put magnetic signs on your car and on as many of your employee's cars as you can. *Check with your insurance company or attorney first to be sure this does not create liability concerns.*

15. Create coupons printed on Post-It™ pads and stick them to doors in office buildings, apartments, and condominiums.

16. Develop a free newsletter that is sent to your targeted customer base monthly.

17. Always include one of your brochures when you send invoices and statements to your customers. You never

know when your existing customers may be talking to a friend about your business, so this gives them some extra brochures to distribute. They may also see another product or service you have that they didn't know about.

18. Form an alliance with area companies in like, but non-competitive, industries. Exchange brochures to be included in all the invoices and/or statement mailings of the companies in the alliance.

19. Purchase business card and/or brochure holders that attach to your car window. Leave a supply of cards and/or brochures in these holders when you are shopping at the mall or anywhere else with a busy parking lot.

20. Make certain every one in your sphere of influence — family members, friends, business associates, vendors, acquaintances — knows what business you are in and ask them to keep a lookout for potential customers. This could mean as many as 200 to 300 extra salespeople, in essence, for your organization.

21. Put your business cards and/or brochures on every community bulletin board in your area. There are a lot more than you might think if you're looking for them.

22. Focus your advertising on your most profitable types of customers or clients. Determine which specific types of customers do the most business with you and go after them.

23. Create a DVD or video that features the benefits of your product or service. Then, if it's not possible to schedule a meeting with a potential customer, offer to send them the video.

24. Keep your eyes open for fresh ideas. Look at every TV commercial, listen to every radio commercial, and read every advertisement, billboard, and piece of junk mail you get. If this sounds depressing, that's because it is. But

by evaluating these things you may find some wording or strategy that, with slight modifications, can work for your business. Never copy anything verbatim, of course. This is just a method for stimulating creativity and generating new ideas to attract customers to your company.

25. Get your domain name at the top of the search engine results. While it need not be the first or second listing, it should at least be in the top 10. This is called search engine optimization. It can be a complex process, but it must be ongoing. Different search engines such as Yahoo, Google, MSN, AOL, Ask Jeeves, Overture, and Lycos have different parameters for determining the rank of each listing based on the keywords used to search on these listings. There are hundreds of companies that you can engage to do search engine optimization for your website. Many of them make a lot of promises, but never deliver. To find the reliable companies, try this surefire method, which I developed years ago. I went online to the top search engines and put in the keywords "search engine optimization." Then I hired the company whose name appeared most often at the top of the listings on the search engines I used. If they can get their company to the top, ahead of all their competitors who are also in the search engine optimization business, then they should be able to do the same for you and the keywords applicable to your business.

Now that you understand the basic idea behind Guerilla Marketing, try brainstorming on your own to see if you can come up with some unique ideas. Don't be afraid to experiment. An idea that seems off-the-wall at first may turn out to be the basis of the most successful marketing campaign you ever conceived.

"An idea is salvation by imagination."

Frank Lloyd Wright

FUSION MARKETING, CROSS-SELLING, AND UP-SELLING

Here are three additional methods you can use to attract more customers and increase revenues.

Fusion Marketing *(also called Cooperative Marketing)*

The first time I walked into a gas station/convenience store and noticed that it also housed a Taco Bell, I thought to myself, "Hey, you can get gas twice here!" (Oh, give me a break! Like you never told a corny joke?)

Fusion Marketing is sweeping the nation for the best of all possible reasons: It works. When a fast-food restaurant moves in with a gasoline retailer, many advantages are created. Since each business draws customers from the other, both are likely to see an increase in sales. A person who only came in for a taco may fill up their car as well. Also, in this type of arrangement, both businesses are likely to see a reduction in their high overhead. They may share the costs of the land, building, improvements, utilities, and signage. So, because the two companies are not in direct competition, sales go up for both, expenses are reduced, and profits are likely to soar.

Take some time to think about how you might be able to find Fusion Marketing opportunities in your industry.

Cross-Selling

This strategy is becoming more widely accepted as a means of selling new products to current and/or past customers based on past buying habits.

Banks have been most successful using this approach. For many years, a bank was just a place where you had your savings and checking accounts. Now services available in your bank may also include:

- credit cards,
- investment planning,

- mortgage and refinancing,
- brokerage,
- financial planning,
- credit counseling,
- bill paying,
- student loans,
- IRAs, and more.

Cross-Selling broadens the customer's reliance on a company and thus reduces the likelihood that the customer will go to a competitor to fill his or her needs. Historically, companies have increased revenues using a horizontal approach, i.e., adding more customers to buy more of the narrow line of products or services the company provides. Cross-selling, on the other hand, is characterized by a vertical approach. By adding more products or services, companies are able to penetrate their existing customer base more deeply and profit on additional value-added products or services to the same customers they were already serving.

Up-Selling

Up-Selling is similar to Cross-Selling in that the central tenet is selling more products or services to current customers, but it differs in that it's the process of selling more of the same products or services. One way of creating Up-Selling opportunities is through a volume pricing strategy, i.e., the more you buy, the less expensive each unit of purchase becomes. This is the principle behind warehouse retailers such as Sam's Club or Costco. Nobody really needs 50 gallons of pickles. (I hope.) But the price per pickle may be so low that the customer will buy them anyway.

Any opportunity you can take advantage of by developing and implementing a volume price strategy will provide Up-Selling opportunities and increase your revenues.

The Competition

"I am happy I have competition. It keeps me on my toes all the while and stops me from becoming complacent. So, it works to my advantage."

Amisha Patel

In dealing with competitors, you have three options.

1. Ignore them.
2. Acquire them.
3. Outperform them.

Ignoring the competition is almost never a good idea, except perhaps in the least competitive industries. However, because most industry pies are big enough for everyone to garner a healthy slice, I believe many companies focus too much time and energy on the competition, rather than investing that time and energy in growing their own business. Not withstanding this fact, the best companies still make it a point to know their competitors as well as they know themselves.

A common tactic for big businesses today is to acquire their competitors by buying them out. For giant companies with ocean-deep pockets, buying out a competitor may be easier than competing with them.

Since most companies do not have the kind of resources needed to buy out their competitors, they must develop strategies to outperform them. Outperforming is simply doing a better job of marketing and promoting, providing better-quality products/services, and/or better prices. Before this can be accomplished, however, you must have an intimate knowledge of your competitor.

To understand marketing, it is sometimes useful (albeit perhaps distasteful) to use war as an analogy. In a sense, when you sell your products or services, you are declaring war against your competition, which is what makes this a useful exercise.

If you were to study every major battle and war fought since the beginning of recorded history, one common denominator would emerge. Victory most often belonged not to the largest or strongest armies, but usually to the army whose leaders had the most knowledge of the strengths and weaknesses of the enemy. In business marketing terms, this means you don't have to be the biggest company, or have the most resources, to dominate your competitors. To achieve domination, you simply need to know more about the strengths and weaknesses of your competitors than they know about you, and apply that knowledge to your plan of attack, otherwise known as your marketing plan.

There are a number of ways to gather information about your competitors. These include requesting information and/or interviewing past customers, vendors, or employees. Whatever method you choose, it should be done with care and, above all, with integrity. Although investigating the competition is accepted as good business practice, innocent intelligence gathering can easily turn into unethical and illegal corporate spying and piracy. It is a thin line, and you don't want to cross it.

In October of 1996, the President of the United States signed into law the Economic Espionage Act. The EEA makes stealing or obtaining trade secrets by fraud a Federal crime. Unless you have a signed non-compete or a non-disclosure agreement, obtaining information about your competitors *before* you officially open your own business is generally acceptable. Once you are in business, however, gathering competitive intelligence becomes a much more delicate and sensitive process. Fortunately, everything you need to know about your competitors can be uncovered by legal and ethical means. If there is anything you are unable to find out, use the information you do have to reach an educated conclusion.

Here are a few general guidelines for gathering information about your competitors *without* crossing the line into unethical and/or illegal behaviors.

1. Prior to any interview or meeting, *always disclose your true identity*.
2. Comply with all international, Federal, State, and local laws.
3. Fully honor all requests for confidentiality.

After you have gathered the information about your competitors, evaluate the methods you used. Then plug the identical holes in your own company so that your competitors cannot easily obtain the same information about your company. As is the case in war, it is important to know more about your enemy than they can find out about you.

"Forgive your enemies, but never forget their names."

JOHN F. KENNEDY

To deal with the competition, be sure to establish your marketing strategies early. Decide well in advance how you plan to compete.

There are three elements customers always consider when making a buying decision.

- Price
- Quality
- Service

If you think that your company can provide all three, think again. The fact is that providing all three is virtually impossible. You may have the best quality or the best service, but someone will always have lower prices. You may have the best price, but someone else will offer better quality or better service. At best, you may be able to offer two of the three. So you need to decide which two you want to establish as your competitive advantage.

In general, price is not the best choice. Your margins will be lower, which reduces profitability, customer dissatisfaction will be higher, and you will be under constant pressure to ensure that your prices are always lower than your competitors'.

Think of marketing as a poker game (that's better than the war analogy). Holding a pair — top quality and best service — will always beat a high-card hand of lowest price. Your goal should be to establish a distinctive competency for your business. Starbucks' coffee isn't cheap, but for millions of people it's the best. Nordstrom isn't the most inexpensive retailer, nor is it impossible to find some of the same quality merchandise at other stores for less. But their customer service is the stuff of retail legend. Wal-Mart, due to its outstanding distribution system, has built its empire on its ability to offer the lowest prices.

Some companies may be competent at providing the highest quality, others may provide the best service, and others, the best price. Set your sights on developing a competency for your business in one or two of these areas. Remember: Don't try to be all three. Your efforts are likely to be futile.

An integral part of performing a competitive analysis is identifying the distinctive competencies of your competitors so that you can exploit the areas in which they do not excel. Since so many small businesses will praise their ability to offer all three, you will need to determine in which of the three your competition does not have distinctive competency. Use those areas as your key elements to success — perhaps even as the central focus of your Mission Statement.

A final thought on dealing with competition. It has always been my philosophy to treat my competitors, regardless of the industry, with respect and dignity. I have sent them referrals and thank-you cards, invited them to business meetings, and even had dinner with them. This is an area in which the war analogy does not apply.

> *"Integrity is the essence of everything successful."*
>
> Buckminster Fuller

There is plenty of business to go around, and we can all have our fair share without resorting to rumormongering, cutthroat tactics, and double-dealing. No good can come from this. Evil begets more evil. By being the bigger person, not only will you live a more positive life, but you will also have a much better attitude. You may even turn some of your competitors into friends. While it is easy for a competitor to say some damaging things to potential customers about you if they know you are doing the same thing, it isn't as easy when they know you don't stoop to that level. Some of my best testimonials have come from my competitors. Should potential customers ask about your competition, by all means point out your company's competitive advantages. But always do so in a positive manner and stick like glue to the true facts.

The Power of Publicity

"There is no such thing as bad publicity except your own obituary."

Brendan Behan

Most small businesses overlook publicity as a primary marketing tool. Beyond word-of-mouth, publicity is the best way to gain exposure and attention for your company.

Here's a sobering fact: More than 75 percent of all news is planted. Most of what appears in newspapers comes from press releases sent by businesses, associations, and organizations that felt they had something newsworthy to report. Publicity usually creates more publicity. Sometimes even a bad story can be better than no story at all.

"I only know what I read in the papers."

Will Rogers

Will Rogers was being sarcastic, but in fact a great many people believe that whatever they read in the newspaper is true, otherwise it wouldn't be in the paper! Such is the mystifying power of the press. It confers instant credibility, in addition to the value of the exposure. Stories are read six times more than advertisements.

So you will need to design an aggressive PR campaign, including the specific methods you will use to get as much publicity as possible for your company. Make this part of your overall marketing plan.

If you will be acting as your own publicist, you'll need to assemble a professional PR Press Kit that you can send out. A PR Press Kit usually includes:

- A pitch letter
- Press releases
- Biographies
- Feature stories

- Business card
- Photographs
- Fact sheets
- Testimonials
- Other stories that may have been written about your company.

This information is bundled up in a folder or box and packaged in a way that will get people's attention.

Next, compile a media list, including the names of the editors and journalists from television stations, radio, local and national newspapers, magazines, periodicals, newsletters, and Internet sites. Find out the various policies and procedures for receiving press releases, and follow them to the letter.

There are two keys to effective publicity: timing and angles. Journalists are always searching for great stories or references for stories that are in process. It is important to send out new press releases on a regular basis to those media channels you feel target your potential customer base.

In addition to being timely, press releases should have an angle to get the attention of writers and editors. If the angle is strong enough, even the smallest things can generate a great deal of publicity.

Set aside some time every week to brainstorm on PR. Think about the events that may have happened in your business as well as events in the outside world. Ask yourself how events internal to your business could have an effect on the outside world or vice versa. Then write a press release that shows the connection.

Keep in mind: publicity is not the same as advertising. Make sure your story is newsworthy and provides useful information, even though it is slanted in favor of your business.

After you get their attention, you will be contacted for an interview. Be prepared! If you try to wing it, you're likely to say something that could turn the story against you.

To prepare for the interview, start by compiling a list of possible questions including those that seem too remote to be asked. For each question, compose the best possible answer. Then rehearse those answers over and over again until you know them by heart. A common way of practicing is to write each question and the answer on a 3" × 5" card, and then have someone drill you by asking the questions randomly. If possible, record your practice sessions so that you can hear how your responses sound. Words on paper can be interpreted quite differently when spoken aloud.

When speaking to reporters, remember the yellow traffic light and think: CAUTION! Everything you say can and will be used against you, but in this instance nobody is legally required to remind you of that so you're on your own. Assume that all your responses, even those deemed "off the record," will be used. Regardless of the question, never become defensive. Be the very model — the personification — of professionalism.

Once your story appears, keep several extra copies for marketing purposes. Never let a good story die. Show it to potential customers at every opportunity.

As soon as possible, I recommend hiring a professional publicist for your company. Sustaining a successful PR campaign requires a great deal of energy and the kind of full time attention that you cannot provide, given the mountain of other priorities you will have. True, you know more about your product or service than anyone else and have more enthusiasm for your business. But a professional PR firm can invest 100 percent of its efforts on this activity. In addition, it may be able to help you with any sensitive issues that may arise.

Treat Every Prospect Like Gold

Have you ever walked away from a store where the service was so poor that you were left wondering whether they really wanted your business? Let me rephrase that. *How many times* have you walked away from a store wondering whether they really wanted your business? If you're like me, the answer is, more than you can count. Or suppose you call a company looking for an estimate on a project you are considering?

Weeks go by without a word in response. Of course, it could be that the company has so much business that they really don't need ours. But I wouldn't bet the farm on that.

In the last three months, I have been trying to make two fairly substantial purchases, some remodeling on my home that should be in the $10,000 range, and a large safe that should cost about $2,000.

For the remodeling, I have contacted three different contractors — one, at least three times. But I can't get anyone to come out to my home to even look at the job. It's not a difficult project, and it could be quite profitable for the right contractor. But each time I have scheduled an appointment, nobody showed up.

As to the safe, the first company said they would order the safe and that I would have to pay a shipping charge of approximately $300. Only one problem, the $300 covered shipping to their store. Getting the *seven hundred pound* safe to my home was my problem. Another company said they would be happy to deliver the safe to my home. But I had to get it off the truck myself. Company No. 3 said they would also be happy to sell me the safe and even deliver it, but they would have to call back with the price. One month and three messages later, I'd heard not a word, discouraging or otherwise. In my third message, I mentioned that I had been waiting a month for them to call *and* that this was, in fact, my third message. When the call finally came (hallelujah and the saints be praised), rather than giving me the price of the safe, the gentleman preferred to engage in a debate about how many times I'd called. Ready for the icing on the cake? He also said that he had called me nearly a month ago and had already given me the price. Since I was not home at the time, he had thoughtfully left the information with my 10-year-old son. In short, he saw his duty and he'd done it!

By then of course, I wouldn't have bought the safe from that company if they'd cut the price by 50 percent and had it delivered in a sedan chair supported by seven NFL fullbacks.

The sad truth is that the gentleman with whom I spoke may have actually believed that he had fulfilled his professional responsibility.

Customer service is not rocket science. It is a minor variation on the Golden Rule: treat customers and potential customers the way you would want to be treated. And always remember that good prospects are not easy to find, so never take one for granted.

Another common mistake many businesses make is rolling out the red carpet when the big clients come in, while the small clients are lucky if the carpet has been vacuumed. Again, this is not rocket science. Give your best service to every client, regardless of how much money is spent. Besides, your smallest client could one day become your largest, and vice versa. For example, one of my franchisees brought on a new client that her competitor had turned down because they felt the business was too small to be worth their time. The client initially signed on for only $28 per week's worth of service. Two months later that same client was spending $120,000 annually.

Maintain the same high standards of treatment for every customer and you can't go wrong.

> ***"There is only one boss. The customer. And he can fire everybody in the company from the chairman on down, simply by spending his money somewhere else."***
>
> **SAM WALTON**

Chapter 12

Mastering the Art of Selling

Part I: Break a Leg

"Everyone lives by selling something."

Robert Louis Stevenson

How many business opportunity advertisements have you seen that stated, "No Selling Involved"? Excuse me, am I missing something here? There is no business in which someone is not selling something to someone else. Period. Even if you're not in a business of your own, you're still selling something — maybe yourself or your ideas.

So why do some companies go to great lengths to dissociate themselves from the act of selling?

1. Because most people do not like to be sold anything, and

2. Because a great many others do not like to sell.

I have read countless business books on the subject of starting or growing your own business. Selling as a topic is rarely, if ever, addressed in books concerning business start-ups.

Fact: To be successful in business, you must become an expert in selling.

Even if you intend to recruit salespeople to do the selling, you still must have a proficient understanding of the selling process.

Selling is dreaded and feared by many small business owners. If you are one of them, you will have to get past this fear as quickly as possible. Perhaps you are worried that in the process of selling you will come across as pushy. The good news is that you don't have to be a pushy salesperson to be successful. Maybe you're concerned that some potential customers will not like you and may reject you. The bad news is, you're right, which is why you must continually remind yourself of The Principle of SWSWSWN: "Some Will. Some Won't. So What? Next!"

"Abolish fear and you can accomplish anything you wish."
Dr. C.E. Welch

Two of the greatest ways to overcome the fear of selling are

1. to become an expert on the products or services you are selling, *and*

2. to get enthusiastic about them.

Knowledge and enthusiasm can go a long way in the world of selling. They can build your confidence level and improve your relationship with potential customers, who will listen to you because they believe that you know what you are talking about. Besides, genuine enthusiasm is often contagious.

So why are some people becoming wealthy in the world of sales, while others barely get by?

Pareto's Law
(*a.k.a.* The 80-20 Rule)

You may be familiar with this term. If not, here is a short history.

In 1909, Italian economist Vilfred Pareto discovered a statistical relationship which, to this day, cannot be fully explained, but seems to manifest itself more often than not. Also known as the 80-20 rule, Pareto's Law can be applied to almost any scenario.

In terms of this discussion, 80 percent of the sales are made by 20 percent of the salespeople. Put another way, 20 percent of the salespeople are getting 80 percent of the commissions/revenue generated by their sales, leaving the 80 percent of less successful sales people to share the remaining 20 percent of commissions/revenue.

To be successful, find a way to become part of that top 20 percent.

Sales Presentation

A sales presentation may take many different forms. Depending on the business you plan to start and your target audience, it may be something as simple as a one-on-one presentation with a person in their home or something as formal as a presentation to the Board of Directors of a large corporation using multimedia equipment.

Both presentations will require preparation and will have similarities in terms of outline and purpose. Beyond that, however, it is clear that the two are quite different.

Rule of thumb: know your audience. The CEO of a billion dollar company will likely have different questions than an 85-year old widow. In one-on-one sales presentations, I have found the consultative approach usually works best. Instead of being a salesperson, be a consultant. In the eyes of a potential customer, a salesperson is just trying to sell something, whereas a consultant is trying to help resolve a problem. At bedrock, after all, that is what you are in business to do: help your customers solve problems.

> **Question:** How do you work in a consultative environment vs. making a cold sales pitch?
>
> **Answer:** By asking questions.

That's what consultants do — ask a lot of pertinent questions. A sales pitch is, on the whole, a monologue. A consultation is a *dialogue* where both parties talk more or less equally. For you, it's still a sales process, but it need not feel that way to a potential customer. And if you're the one doing all the talking, you won't hear the customer's needs and determine what you need to do to meet them, i.e., to close the sale.

Even though you have prepared questions to ask throughout the sales presentation, your presentation should still be mapped out concisely. Many salespeople eschew formal sales presentations on the grounds that "canned speeches" or "pitches" make them sound too pushy and over-rehearsed. I disagree. How many times have you found yourself watching a really good movie with really good actors and consciously, for maybe just a brief moment, you forget you are, in fact, watching a movie? You can actually get caught up in the emotions of the scenes. We would never be able to express our own emotions, like crying or getting angry at those scenes if we, at least for a moment, didn't allow the movie to become our reality. Alternatively, when you are watching a poor movie with poor actors, it's a lot easier to remember it's a movie, and a lousy one at that. A sales presentation is really nothing more then a script you rehearse repeatedly until you can deliver it smoothly and naturally. Once you have honed your presentation skills, your delivery will not sound canned or phony.

Another benefit to using a formal sales presentation is that it is consistently more effective. You may be having a bad day, or perhaps you're just in a foul mood, but the moment you begin your presentation those things will disappear (at least for the duration of the presentation). Once you're "on," so to speak, you automatically become more enthusiastic, and you are less likely to forget important points that should be made.

25 Steps for More Effective Sales Presentations

1. Remember the five Ps: Proper Preparation Prevents Poor Performance. Do your homework. Learn as much as you can about your products and services and the needs of your potential customer.

2. Be yourself, because being yourself versus tying to be someone you're not is a lot easier for most of us to pull off.

3. Always call ahead of time to let the potential customer know you are on time and on your way. A great technique when going to a home is to ask if there is anything they would like you to pick up on the way. Whether you can do this will really depend on the type of customer you are serving and the industry you are in. While this may sound corny, done properly, the potential customer will feel you are a thoughtful person, and this can create what is known as a reciprocating effect. They almost feel obliged to repay the favor — hopefully to the extent of placing an order!

4. Arrive on time or up to five minutes early, but no earlier, or the potential customer may not be ready. Worse still, he or she may feel you are pushy and/or rude.

5. Compliment the potential customer on something — their home, office, desk, family pictures, etc. Don't lie. Make it a genuine compliment. Also, build rapport by finding common ground. If you scan the room or office, you can usually find something that you and the potential customer have in common. When you find it, begin talking about it. This is an excellent icebreaker, and it sets a comfortable tone.

6. Take control of the meeting immediately. Begin by getting the potential customer to agree with you about something. It doesn't matter what. Try "Isn't this a beautiful day?" (if it is). Next, direct the potential customer to the room or space where you would like to talk. In a private home, the kitchen table is usually where big decisions are made. If the meeting is in their office, ask permission to bring a chair around to the side of the desk. This implies equal footing, whereas sitting across the desk from them puts you in a submissive position.

7. Ask permission to take notes during the meeting. It will put the client at ease and increase your professional persona.

8. Ask their name, and then use it throughout the presentation — not to the point of becoming annoying, but just often enough to let them know that they are important enough to you that you'll remember it.

"A person's name is to that person the sweetest and most important sound in any language."

Dale Carnegie

9. Use this three-step approach for a more effective sales presentation.
   - **Step One**: Tell them what you're going to tell them.
   - **Step Two**: Tell them what you have to tell them.
   - **Step Three**: Tell them what you've just told them.
10. Smile until it hurts. (A famous actress once said that as a young starlet she used to smear Vaseline across her front teeth to make it easier to smile for long periods of time. That's not a suggestion, of course.) Genuinely laugh at their jokes, provided you do not find them tasteless or crude. If that's the case, try to ignore it.
11. Be enthusiastic. Enthusiasm is contagious. If you are excited about your product or service, it is likely that the potential customer will be, too.
12. Mirror your audience. Try talking at the same speed and level as the person you are talking with. Don't use big words if they don't use big words. If you see their eyes beginning to glaze over, cut back on your material. Don't be afraid to go off your script a little.
13. Never disagree, argue, debate, or use words like "but." If you need to make a point that may not necessarily agree with what the potential customer has said, substitute the word "and." For example, if the potential customer

would say, "Doesn't Acme Co. have a similar widget that costs less?" Instead of saying, "They do, *but* the quality of our widget is higher." You would instead say, "Our widget does cost a little more *and* the quality is much higher." This way you can still make your point without sounding as though you are disagreeing. Also, great advice that I first heard from Tom Hopkins, one of the greatest sales gurus of our time, replace words that make the potential customer feel cautious with softer words.

Yes	No
Paperwork	Contract
"I need your O.K."	"I need your signature."
Invest *or* Investment	Buy, Purchase, *or* Cost
Payment Plan	Financing *or* Loan
Transaction *or* Arrangement	Deal
Customer, Client *or* Future Customer	Potential Customer *or* Prospect*
Expected	Obligation
Challenges *or* Obstacles	Problems
Included Fee for Service	Commission *or* Profit
Meeting *or* Visit	Appointment
Work With *or* Worked With	Sell *or* Sold

Finally, never use profanity, even if the customer does.

14. Go on a fact-finding mission. Ask a lot of open-ended vs. closed-ended questions Closed-ended questions can

*I do use these terms in this book. But never use them when talking to an actual customer.

usually be answered "yes" or "no." Open-ended questions usually require the potential customer to provide more information. Instead of, "Would you like to save more on your heating costs?" Say, "How can I help you save more on your heating costs?"

Be inquisitive. More sales are made with your ears than your mouth. After hundreds of years of retail sales experience, I'm still amazed that so many retail stores still have sales staff greet potential customers with "May I help you?" (British translation: "Are You Being Served?"). That is a standard (make that, substandard) closed-ended question that is bound to garner the standard reply: "No thank you. I'm just looking." An open-ended question would be so much more effective.

During the presentation, periodically ask feedback questions to make sure the potential customer is still engaged in the presentation — questions such as "How does that sound?" or "How does this look?"

15. Tell your story — who you are, how and why you got into business, why your product or service is better. Stories sell, and a good story will draw in a potential customer. So develop your story and practice telling it until you can do so with ease and enthusiasm. Then share it with every potential customer.

16. Use a formal sales presentation book or a laptop computer with presentation software such as Microsoft PowerPoint. Which one you choose will depend on your audience. The point is that a prepared presentation will keep you on track.

17. Turn intangibles into tangibles. For example, you do not sell "insurance." You sell "peace of mind, safety, and security." Use pictures to turn these intangibles into tangibles or be descriptive. Paint the pictures into their mind with your words.

18. Assume the sale throughout the presentation. They have asked or at least allowed you to be there, so they have some level of interest in what you're selling.

19. If you are ever stumped, answer a question with a question. Politicians do this all the time (I didn't say it was right, but it works). For example, suppose your potential customer asks, "Which feature of your product will provide the best solution for our problem?" Of course, if you've done your homework, this kind of question should not stump you, but let's say that it does. One possible reply would be "That is a great question. What do you feel that it is?" Find a way to pass the conversational ball back to them; then listen to what they say. More than likely they will fill in the blanks themselves. Then all you have to do is agree with them.

20. For a complicated question, just answer "yes" or "no." Don't expand any further. In addition to keeping you out of uncharted territory, a short answer has a confident ring to it.

21. Be truthful. Lying or exaggerating will catch up with you, and you will lose all credibility.

22. Focus on their "pain" or "hot button." Ask questions to pinpoint their problem, then show them how your product or service can resolve it.

23. Base the start of your presentation on logic and the close on emotion.

24. Remember the ABC's of selling: Always Be Closing. Be ready at any moment in your presentation to close the transaction. When you sense that the potential customer is ready to buy, stop and close. Don't get so caught up in the wonders of your presentation — "Wait. You can't buy yet. I've got some more great things to tell you!" — that you literally "talk" your way out of a sale.

25. At the end of every sales presentation, regardless of the outcome, go back to the office and debrief yourself. Identify the things you did right and put them in future presentations. Learn from your mistakes. Ask yourself at what point the sale was really made or lost.

Listen, Listen, and Listen

"Listening is a magnetic and strange thing, a creative force. The friends who listen to us are the ones we move toward. When we are listened to, it creates us, makes us unfold and expand."

Karl A. Menninger

Are you a good listener? Most people don't realize that there is tremendous difference between "hearing" and "listening." In the absence of a physical malfunction, we can all hear. But listening is a conscious choice. If, while someone else is talking, you are thinking about what you will say when he or she finishes, or what you need to pick up from the grocery store, you are *not* listening. Listening requires concentration and the ability to clear your mind of extraneous thoughts so you can focus on what the other person is saying. Listening is a skill, and it is not always easy to learn. But, as with so many other things, recognizing the problem is the first step toward solving it.

I'm not a good listener. (Just ask my wife.) I have been working on this for years, and there is still a lot of room for improvement. Here are a few tips I have been using to improve my listening skills. Maybe some of them can help you as well.

Become a Better Listener

- Maintain eye contact with the person you are talking to. This keeps you focused on the conversation.

- Be attentive, but relaxed.

- Don't ask questions while the other person is speaking. Be patient. Perhaps the answers are forthcoming.

  Exception: You may interrupt with a question *if* the goal is to clarify something you did not understand.

- Pay close attention to body language. It speaks louder than words. In fact, body language accounts for more than 90 percent of the message. Consider doing some research in this area. Learn how to interpret nonverbal cues. This information can be of tremendous value.
- Avoid getting too emotionally involved with content. Try instead to think logically about what is being said.
- Put yourself in their shoes and try to feel what they may be feeling.
- Make listening a mental challenge for yourself.
- Ask yourself questions during the conversation to make sure you understand what is being said. Try to fill in the Who, What, Where, When, Why, and How. The answers to these questions will give you a much better understanding of what is being said as opposed to what you think you heard.
- Pay attention to the content. Try to avoid any distractions that may be happening around you.
- Keep an open mind.

These tips or mental exercises can help you fill the gap between your rate of thought and the rate at which a person is speaking. You think faster than they can talk. By slowing down the mind, these exercises are constructive to the overall listening process. Effective listeners give a positive impression and earn respect.

Chapter 13

Mastering the Art of Selling

PART II: I Object

> *"Every sale has five basic obstacles: no need, no money, no hurry, no desire, no trust."*
>
> Zig Ziglar

Objections are a natural part of the selling process. If you're not hearing any objections, there is a good chance that you're not making many sales. The trick is not to be discouraged. Objections are necessary steps the potential customer must go through to communicate where they are at in the sales process. An objection lets you know you are on the right track toward making a sale.

Potential customers raise objections for several reasons. Perhaps they have become frightened by their own interest in the product or service. ("Oh no, I might buy something, so I better find some holes in it quick"). Then again, objections may stem from legitimate concerns that the potential customer must address before they are prepared to buy.

The point is: Objections can sometimes be smokescreens. Whatever the basis, if you can identify and address the concerns behind the objections, there is a good chance that you can turn a potential customer into an actual customer.

Ideally, you should try to identify and eliminate objections before they arise. In other words, be the first one to bring them up. If you are hearing the same objection often at various sales calls, then clear the air by incorporating a modified rebuttal into your presentation. For example, if potential customers always balk at your price, you might say: "Our product is not the cheapest, but it is the most affordable for this level of quality." Say something to this effect three or four times during the presentation and the potential customer is unlikely to raise the issue later on.

Objections can come at any time during the sales process. Handle them as soon as they arise. Never tell the potential customer that you will deal with their objection later. This is likely to cause a negative reaction. The answer to an objection is called a rebuttal.

To effectively address an objection, you must turn negatives into positives. Put another way, "boomerang" the objection by turning it into a reason to buy.

The Four-Step Process for Handling Objections

1. Listen! Make sure you have a precise understanding of the potential customer's objection. Don't interrupt or anticipate what you believe they are going to say. This is a great temptation, but you must resist it. Let them finish. First, interrupting them would be rude. Second, you may discover that they weren't going to say what you thought anyway. The risk of making this mistake is particularly high if you have heard the same objection many times before. Regardless, never interrupt the potential customer who is voicing an objection. It may turn out to be something you haven't heard before.

2. Clear communication is essential to handling objections. If you aren't sure what the potential customer meant,

politely ask them to clarify. ("How do you mean?") If you are still not sure, repeat the question back to them (" I think I understand. So what you are saying is . . ."). Sometimes it is helpful to ask the potential customer to explain further before you answer the objection ("Very interesting. I'm curious. Why do you feel that way?").

3. Isolate and probe. "Is it just (insert problem)? So if it weren't for (insert problem), you would move forward?" Once they confirm, you can move on to your rebuttal.

4. To address objections concisely and professionally (as you must), memorize rebuttals for as many objections as you can think of *before* they come up. If necessary, you can slightly modify your prepared rebuttal to suit a particular objection. Once you have addressed it, find out if the potential customer is satisfied with your response ("Does that make sense?"). If they are, then close the sale. One final tip: *Always* attempt to close after resolving an objection.

Feel, Felt, Found Format

Zig Ziglar, one of my favorite sales and motivational gurus, suggests another method of handling objections: the Feel, Felt, Found Format.

I have used this for many years, and it is one of the most effective ways of handling almost any objection. Here's how it works.

Whatever objection the potential customer raises, once you have completed steps one through three of the four-step process, begin step four with "I understand how you feel. Many of my customers felt the same way and what they found is . . ." Then go on with your prepared rebuttal.

In one statement, you have accomplished many things. You've taken an agreeable and positive approach ("I understand how you feel") rather than disagreeing with them. You have let them know that their concern is normal — possibly even perceptive ("Many of my customers felt the same way"). Finally, and most important, you have provided a rebuttal that has the feel of a third-party testimonial (". . . and what they found is . . .") from other satisfied customers.

The Feel, Felt, Found Format is a powerful and highly effective technique for rebutting objections. Learn to use it.

The 10 Most Common Types of Objections

Now let's discuss the 10 most common objections and the corresponding rebuttals. Keep in mind that you may encounter specific objections that are unique to your industry and therefore require unique rebuttals. However, any of these rebuttals can be modified to deal with unique objections. To make these 10 types of objections easy to remember, I assigned each of the 10 to a letter in the word OBJECTIONS.

THE 10 MOST COMMON TYPES OF OBJECTIONS

Open and Sincere Objections
Buried and Hidden Objections
Justified Quality Objections
Expenditure or Price Objections
Competitive Objections
Trust Objections
Insincere Objections
Order and Priority Objections
Need Objections
Stall Objections

I have provided examples of each of these objections and the corresponding rebuttal. For purposes of this discussion, let's assume you are in the business of selling computers. (modify your answers for your particular industry).

Open and Sincere Objections

In an open and sincere objection, the potential customer feels that his or her concerns are valid. Whether that is true is irrelevant. It's how they feel.

> **Potential Customer:** "I'm just not sure I will be able to learn how to use a computer."
>
> **You:** "I understand how you feel, many of my customers have felt the same way, but what they found is that, with our training software, which they received free when they invested in one of our computers, they were able to become proficient on their computers in a short period of time. How does that sound?"

Buried and Hidden Objections

A potential customer may have objections that they are not sharing with you. To make the sale, you must get those objections out in the open. Body language is often a good indication of hidden objections. Here are a few signs:

- Crossed arms
- Hand covering their mouth
- Lack of attention
- Negative facial expressions
- Change in the tone or pitch of their voice

To uncover hidden objections, you must ask probing questions.

> **You:** "Is there anything about this that you are uncertain about or don't like?"

If they give you a real objection, you can now deal with it.

Justified Quality Objections

These objections arise when the potential client has a justified reason to be concerned about a problem with the quality of your product or service.

Potential Customer: "My friend bought a computer from you folks and he has had problems with it."

You: "I'm sorry to hear that. We pride ourselves on having one of the highest-quality products on the market. I'm sure my company has been working to resolve any problems your friend has been having with his computer, haven't they?"

Potential Customer: "He didn't say."

You: "I'm sure that is the case, but as soon as I get back to the office I'm going to check into it just to be safe. I hate to hear when something like that happens, but I'm sure you will agree there isn't a computer on the market that may not have some type of problem at some time, wouldn't you agree?"

Potential customer: "I guess."

You: "What really is important is not necessarily the possibility that you could have a problem, but instead how the company handles that situation if you do."

Potential Customer: "That's probably true."

You: "This is one reason why investing in our equipment makes perfect sense. Not only do you get an unsurpassed written guarantee, but you also have the advantage of our technical department being local, instead of having to box your system up and ship it across the country." (Then close using an assumptive close.)

Expenditure or Price Objections

This is the granddaddy of them all. If you have been in sales for at least 15 minutes, you have already heard a price objection from a potential customer. Price objections are by far the most common you will encounter, and no matter how low your price is, you may still get a few.

Here are a few of the most common Expenditure or Price Objections that will be raised.

- "Your price is too high."
- "I can't afford it."
- "(Competitor) is a lot cheaper."
- "It's not in my budget."
- "You need to sharpen your pencil."
- "You'll have to do better than that."

The first step in handling this kind of objection is to find out exactly what the potential customer means. For example, "Your price is too high" can mean

- Too high compared to the competition
- Too high compared to what the potential customer can afford or has available to spend
- Higher than expected, even though they may not have anything on which to base that opinion
- Concerns about whether the price is reasonable for the value of the product or service
- A negotiating tactic to get a better price.

You have to determine what their anchor is. Are they comparing apples to apples? One of the best ways to determine this is simply by asking.

Potential Customer: "Your price is too high."

You: "When you say that I'm curious, too high compared to . . . ?"

or

You: "What price did you have in mind? How did you arrive at that price?"

or

You: "Is it a question of the price, or of the funds not being accessible at this time?"

Their answer will give you the information you need to decide which rebuttal will be most effective.

Rebuttals For Price Objections

As there will always be someone who can provide your product or service at a lower price, you have to brush up on your rebuttals to price objections. You will need them. Zig Ziglar proposed one of the most effective price rebuttals I have ever used.

Price Rebuttal #1: Apologize for Price

Potential Customer: "I can get a computer from ACME Computers cheaper than that."

You: (Lower your voice and look the potential customer in the eye.) "You know, interestingly enough, when I founded this company, I started it with one basic philosophy when it comes to pricing. It's easier to apologize for price one time than it would be to apologize for poor quality and poor service forever. And I'll bet you're glad I made that decision, aren't you?"

This rebuttal takes a great deal of practice, but when you can do it right, there is nothing more powerful.

Price Rebuttal #2: Reduction to the Ridiculous

Potential Customer: "I can't afford that."

You: "I am glad you mentioned price. That's one of the great things about working with our company. We'll put the purchase price into small installment payments, so your actual investment is only $24 per month. That certainly falls within your budget, doesn't it?"

Price Rebuttal #3: Deal Only With The Difference

You: "Your total investment comes to $1,250."

Potential Customer: "That's just too high."

You: "What price did you have in mind, and how did you arrive at it?"

Potential Customer: "ACME Computer gave me a price of $1,050."

You: "Do you have the specifications available for the system they were quoting so that we can better analyze the $200 difference?"

Now that you know the difference, don't even mention the $1,250 price again. Sell the added benefits they are getting for that $200 difference. You don't have to convince them on the first $1,050 of their purchase anymore — just on the last $200. It is a much easier proposition.

Price Rebuttal #4: Price Versus Cost

You: "Your total investment comes to $1,250."

Potential Customer: "That's just too high."

You: "What price did you have in mind, and how did you arrive at it?"

Potential Customer: "Another company gave me a price of $1,050."

You: "Just so I understand, are you more concerned about price or cost?"

Potential Customer: "Is there a difference?"

You: "Absolutely. Price is what you pay initially, and cost is what you end up paying in the long run. Where my price may be only $200 higher initially, chances are in the long run it can turn out to be a much lower cost. For example, the hard drive I included is 250GB, compared to theirs, which is only 120GB. That extra 130GB's may become important to you in the future; as software programs get more complicated you will need additional storage. So if you buy theirs, you may need to upgrade in the near future, and a 250GB hard drive costs about $300. Also, the printer they included uses a $100 color cartridge for about every 1,000 pages printed. My printer, which produces the same quality, uses a $50 color cartridge for the same 1,000 pages printed. That means my printer will save you over $150 per year if you print an average of 3,000 pages. Just factoring those two elements into the equation would mean that their price of $1,050 would ultimately cost you an additional $300 for the upgraded hard drive. Plus, your extra operating costs would be an extra $150 per year. So three years from now, your true COST for their system could end up being $1,800 compared to the price of my system, which is only $1,250. When would you like to take delivery?"

Competitive Objections

Many competitive objections are just camouflaged expenditure or price objections. When voicing a competitive objection, the potential customer may not necessarily focus on price, but on some other reason for choosing one of your competitors.

If they have had a good relationship with another company, convincing them to switch their business to you will be difficult. People (customers or business owners) only make changes for one of two major reasons: pain or profit. If the potential customer is having problems in their relationship with your competitor, you can focus on that as their "pain," or your company may be able to fulfill their needs either for less money or in a way that creates more value than they are currently getting ("profit"). A soft-sell approach that can be effective is to present your company as an alternative instead of a replacement.

Potential Customer: "I already have a company that serves my computer needs and I have been happy with them, so I don't really want to change."

You: "I completely understand and, under the circumstances, I would never be so bold to ask you to stop doing business with them and start doing business with us. You would agree though, it is prudent to have a back-up in place should something happen that changes your relationship so that you don't find yourself between a rock and a hard place, don't you?"

Potential Customer: "I guess."

You: "Well that's really all I'm asking for. I don't mind being your second choice. I would love to be your first choice some day, but I don't mind being your back-up for the time being. We just want you to know we are here if you need us. Should a situation ever arise where they can't deliver on something you need in the time you need it, or if you feel they are getting too complacent in their relationship with you and it's reflected in their prices, why don't you give us a try. Eventually, if we do what it takes to earn your business, you may decide that we should be your first choice?"

Potential Customer: "I suppose I could do that."

You: "Great. Just to give me an idea, what priorities are you trying to achieve? May I ask how much are you currently paying for (X). How long does it typically take them to deliver on (X), (etc)?"

This allows the customer to open up, and you can begin making a list of your competitive advantages versus your competitor's. You will either leave with a sale or, at a minimum, with proper follow-up, you will keep the door open for a future sale. Another benefit to this method is that the potential customer will be watching everything their current vendor does, and may be much quicker to switch if there is a problem.

Trust Objections

Trust objections can occur for various reasons. Maybe your company is relatively new, or you are relatively new to the industry. Maybe you said something that has given the potential customer reason to believe you are not being honest. Perhaps they heard through the grapevine about problems your company had in the past. Whatever the reason or reasons, trust objections must be handled completely — and with finesse — if there is to be any chance of a sale.

To build trust you need to establish rapport with the potential customer. Maintain eye contact, be aware of your body language, and have an encyclopedic knowledge of your product or service.

Trust objections are best handled if you raise the issue *before* the potential customer does. If you even suspect that trust is an issue for them, cover it in your presentation, which should include information that reinforces your credibility, for example:

- Proof of insurance and bonding
- Testimonials
- Proof of any required licensure, certification, or training
- Guarantees or warranties
- Favorable articles about your company.

Whatever the issue, bring it out in the open, and tactfully set the record straight. *Never argue or disagree with the customer or the source of their information.*

Insincere Objections

Insincere objections are excuses that the potential customer knows are not true. Just before voicing an insincere objection, they may go off on a tangent. If it seems as though their objection has no merit, ask questions to uncover the real objection, such as: "How do you mean?" or "May I ask why you feel that way?" Find out what their true objection is, and then resolve it.

Order or Priority Objections

Sometimes the potential customer has an interest, but the timing for a purchase is not right because of higher priorities. Overcoming this objection can be difficult. This is a case where taking the time to qualify a potential client pays off in that you will already have determined whether there is truly a need for your product or service at this time.

With this objection, the potential customer is essentially putting a higher priority on spending their money on something else. If possible, you have to make your product or service their priority. This means giving them valid reasons for working with you now.

- Why not start saving money/time now?
- If I leave now before you can take advantage of (X), then your problem will still exist.
- Deadlines on your offer.
- Prices may be going up (only if that is true).
- Limited supply and we will sell out.

Need Objections

In this case, the potential customer doesn't know whether they need your product or service. Unless this was a "cold call," where you dropped in unannounced, there must have been some level of interest that got you to this meeting. So what is the basis for these objections? Perhaps, during your presentation, you did not fully demonstrate the value of your product or service. Go back and highlight the strongest benefits they will obtain from working with you. Remember: Sell the sizzle, not the steak.

Another possibility is that they just do not like making decisions. Perhaps they feel that no decision at all is better than the possibility of making a bad one. In this case, focus on their "hot button" or "pain," i.e., the problem that your product or service will reduce or eliminate for them. If possible, close with a statement such as, "What do you have to lose? There's a money- back guarantee. Why don't you give it a try?"

Stall Objections

If price objections are the most common, stall objections are a close second. Stall objections are easy to recognize, and include statements such as:

- "I need to think about it."
- "I want to talk it over with (X)."
- "I'll get back to you."
- "Let me mull it over."
- "I'll let you know."
- "I need to sleep on it."

There are a number of reasons for stall objections. The potential customer may be stalling to camouflage the real reason for not making a purchase. They may be trying to avoid making a decision. Perhaps you haven't sold them yet. Perhaps the person you are speaking with is not the decision-maker, or they feel that someone else should approve the purchase before a final decision is made.

No matter what kind of stall you are getting, the first rule of thumb is: stay on their side. Novice salespeople often run into problems at this point. Everything seems to be going well, and then suddenly the potential customer says they want to think about it — rather than buy it. A tennis match erupts, with the salesperson and the potential customer spiking the ball back and forth, creating tension that didn't exist before. Don't let this happen. Instead show them that you understand their hesitation.

Potential Customer: "I want to think about it."

You: "I understand that this is a big decision and one that shouldn't be rushed."

With this approach, the potential customer is less likely to put up their defenses, which would eliminate any opportunity to further explore the objection.

If the potential customer says "I want to talk it over with (X)" or something similar, you may not have set up the initial meeting correctly. This is called a "one-legged" presentation, i.e., all decision-makers are not present for the meeting. To avoid this type of stall objection, you need to address it when you are setting up the meeting. Tactfully ask the potential customer to be sure that any advisors, family, or friends on whom he or she may rely for a final decision are present at the initial meeting. If all the decision-making parties are there, this type of stall objection is unlikely to arise.

Another way that stalls can be addressed is to ignore them altogether. While this is a bold step, it can be effective under some circumstances. Just proceed by moving into the close.

Objection/Rebuttal Journal

Keep an Objection/Rebuttal Journal. For the most part, you will hear the same objections — or variations on the same objections — from many different potential customers. However, once in a while you will encounter a new objection. When this happens, be sure to record it in your Journal. If you felt the rebuttal you used was effective, record that as well. If your rebuttal was not effective, make some modifications to improve it. Then test it a few times. If the revised rebuttal seems to work, make it a permanent part of your repertoire.

Finally, once you are back at the office, review your sales presentation. Think about what objections came up, how you handled those objections, and what, if anything, you should do differently the next time that objection is raised.

> *"So many objections may be made to everything, that nothing can overcome them but the necessity of doing something."*
>
> Samuel Johnson

Chapter 14

Mastering the Art of Selling

Part III: Close It!

The close can be the most important step of the entire sales process. Everything you have done and said up to this point boils down to this one moment. Closing is the conclusion of the sales process. It brings the customer to a decision. The most successful close will always be a great presentation because if you have done everything correctly up to this point, the close can be simple, particularly for smaller transaction sales. The larger the sale, the more resistance you are likely to get from the potential customer. Large transactions mean larger commitments. Think of it this way: if a homeless person asked a stranger for $100, the commitment level is pretty high and it is unlikely he would get even one out of 1,000 people to oblige. On the other hand, if he asked for a quarter, the commitment level is low, and he may be successful as often as 50 percent of the time.

We tend to think of the close as what happens at the end of a sales presentation, but the truth is that you are closing from the first time you meet the potential customer and throughout the presentation. This is accomplished through the use of trial closes.

Trial closes accomplish many things. They build momentum towards the final close. They test the waters to give you an indication of the potential customer's level of interest. They are a good indicator of how imminent you may be getting to the final close. Finally, they help you get the potential customer to begin agreeing with you in small, non-committal steps.

How does a trial close work? A trial close is an affirmative question. So, every time you make a point about the benefits of your product or service, you ask a question, such as

- "Wouldn't this be helpful to you?"
- "Can you see how beneficial this will be?"
- "Wouldn't that be nice?"
- "How many are you considering?"
- "That's pretty fantastic, isn't it?"
- "In your opinion, would you say…?"
- "Are you more interested in (x) or in (y)?"

With each trial close, nod your head a bit — almost unnoticeably. It's a small gesture, but it helps to keep the potential customer moving in a positive direction. Soon agreeing with what you have just said begins to feel natural.

Although you can use trial closes almost anytime during the sales presentation, there are certain times when the use of a trial close is critical. Always use a trial close when:

- You have successfully rebutted an objection.
- The potential customer asks to take a second look at your product or samples.
- It appears that the customer may be on the fence, but leaning in the right direction.
- You want to test the waters to get feedback on where you stand in your presentation.

- You conclude a product demonstration.
- The potential customer gives you buying signals.

Buying signals are visual or verbal cues indicating that the potential customer is almost ready to make a purchase. Here are a few buying signals.

- The potential customer begins asking "Buy-Like" questions, such as, "How long is the wait?", "Do you have financing?", "How long before it would come in?", "How much does it cost?", or "Do you have any sales going on right now?"
- The potential customer makes positive comments about the product or service.
- The potential customer appears to have become more relaxed and comfortable with you.

In general, trial closes have four inherent elements.

1. The answer requires a minimum amount of thinking from the potential customer.
2. They are concentrated toward the "big picture" rather than specific details.
3. They are low-commitment questions. You are not asking them to buy, only to agree on that one point.
4. They are usually closed-end questions requiring only "yes" or "no" answers. Trial closes are generally the only time you will ask closed-end questions during your presentation.

How many trial closes should you use during a sales presentation? The answer depends a lot on whom you ask. Some experts say three. Others say as many as 10 or more. My personal opinion is don't try to nail it down to any particular number. Every presentation will be different. Decide how many trial closes to use based on the situation and the potential customer. If the customer says, "Where do I sign?" as soon as you walk in, you don't need a trial close at all! Get the signature, and then fill them in on the details. On the other hand, if you have been presenting to a potential customer for three or more hours and they still seem interested, you may end up using two dozen trial closes.

Wrap It Up: The Final Close

Okay. You've set the stage with trial closes. You've built momentum, and your potential customer is responding in the affirmative. You've generated enthusiasm and excitement about your product or service. You've stimulated their emotional desire for the benefits of your product or service and justified that desire with logic.

Now it's time to wrap it up with your final close.

Seven P's of Purchasing

There are seven basic emotional reasons behind a decision to buy your product or service. We will call them the *Seven P's of Purchasing*.

1. **Profit** — Your solution decreases expenses or increases their income or both.
2. **Pain** — Your solution resolves a conflict in their business or personal life.
3. **Pride** — Your solution may be something they have worked long and hard to deserve.
4. **Pleasure** — Your solution will give them enjoyment or comfort.
5. **Panic** — They fear they will lose the opportunity to have your solution.

6. **Prestige** — Your solution will stroke their ego.

7. **Passion** — Your solution may put more love into their life.

During the presentation, use consultative questioning to tactfully identify which of the *Seven P's of Purchasing* the customer is seeking to fulfill. It may be more than one. Then use that information as the basis for the close.

Rule of thumb: Persistence overcomes resistance. That said, however, there is an enormous difference between hard selling (i.e., being pushy) and being persistent. Never try to pressure anyone into a sale. You do need to ask for it, though, often several times.

Many people do not like making decisions. They spend a lot of time "on the fence." Average salespeople may only attempt one close. If they are not successful, the customer doesn't buy. Above-average salespeople know their product and service well, and they know that owning their product or service would be in the best interest of the potential customer. So when it looks as though the potential customer is on the way to making a "No-Decision Decision," the above-average salespeople know how to give them the push they need to get off the fence.

There are hundreds of different closing techniques from which to choose. Which one is best for you depends on the type of potential customer you are dealing with, how well the presentation is going, the type of product or service you are selling, your personality, and finally, your integrity. In this chapter, we will cover the most popular and effective closing techniques. You may be more comfortable and effective with some than with others. Some may not fit your personality or your industry. Experiment until you find the best ones for you. Although, as a rule, you should have a minimum of five different closing techniques that you have polished to perfection, in general, the more closing techniques you know, the more prepared and successful you will be.

When it comes to closes, experts are divided into two camps. Some shy away from prepared closes, which they feel sound too much like canned speeches and make the salesperson seem cheesy and slick. To some extent I agree. But what is the alternative to proven closing techniques? No prepared closes at all? I have yet to hear an expert recommend that approach! Besides, the same salespeople who argue against prepared closings use them (or variations on them), though they may not realize it. I've even heard a few of them use some of these closing techniques when they were trying to convince people not to use closing techniques!

I can only say that I have successfully used these types of closes both in direct selling and in working with employees, negotiating with vendors, and resolving customer complaints. Closing is nothing more than summarizing the things covered in your presentation with a question or statement that you feel best relates to the potential customer. Practice these closes, in your own voice and words, without high-pressure hard selling, and you may find them to be very effective. The more you practice, the less "canned" they will sound. It may take years of experimenting to perfect your closing techniques, but in the end you will close more sales, which is what it's all about.

There is a cardinal rule of closing: The last person who talks takes the product or service home with them. Once you've closed, be quiet and patient. Let the customer talk. The urge to break the uncomfortable silence after the close has caused many salespeople to talk their way out of sales. The only exclusion to this rule is if you find yourself presenting to a potential customer who is also a salesman. The close has been delivered, and the ensuing silence is deafening. Since you both probably know the cardinal rule (*He who talks first goes home with the product*), this could go on for quite some time. So, rather than sitting there indefinitely, after a minute or so break the silence with, "Are you shaking your head back and forth or up and down?" Make sure you deliver this line with a big smile on your face so that the other party knows it is meant to be a joke. This will usually break the tension and get the potential customer talking again.

Don't get caught up in the fancy titles of these closes. Study them and analyze the possible effect on the potential customer. There will be some closes you don't like. Don't use them. Remember, you need only a minimum of five closes that you have perfected to the point where you can deliver them on a moment's notice.

It's also important to remember that the type of close that is most effective will vary from industry to industry. A close that is acceptable in one industry may be too high-pressure in another. Your particular product or service, your audience, and your venue will have a tremendous impact on what types of closes work best for you.

The 10 Most Popular and Effective Closes in Selling

1. Affirmative No Close

(*Alias: Deductive-Reasoning Close, Clear-the-Smoke Close*)

Sometimes it is difficult to close a customer who has not yet divulged the true reason for their objection(s). It is almost impossible to close without first rebutting objections.

This close will help you to unearth the real objection(s). Ask specific questions about their reasons for not buying (each time waiting for their answer) until you come across the true reason. Save the price (or money) issue for last because nine times out of 10 it will be a money issue. For example:

> "Mr. Smith, many times when someone tells me they want to think about it, there is something specific about the investment that concerns them. Just to make sure I am able to clearly answer any questions you still have may have, why is it that you're not investing today? Is the concern about my employees? My company? Our reputation? The size or color? Is it me? (*Smile when you say this.*) Could it be the money?"

Through deductive reasoning you will either identify the true objection, which you can then address, or you will show the potential customer that there really is no reason not to make the purchase.

> ***"How often have I said that when you have eliminated the impossible, whatever remains, however improbable, must be the truth."***
>
> Sir Arthur Conan Doyle

2. Assumptive Close

(Alias: Assumption Close, John-Hancock Close, Signature Close, Order Blank, Physical Action Close)

Assume the sale throughout the presentation. Act as though it is perfectly natural for all of your customers to buy. You pull out your order from and start filling it out while asking the potential customer basic questions. "What is the spelling of your last name?" "What is your address?" "Your phone number?" Just keep filling out the form and asking questions. If they don't stop the process, they have decided to make the purchase. When you have completed the form, slide it over to them and say, "All I need is your okay here." If they do begin to balk, uncover the true reasons and resolve their objections. If the potential client has been giving you buying signals throughout the presentation and talking socially as you filled out the form(s), you may not have to say anything to close. Just slide the form over, hand them your pen, point to where they need to sign and continue talking socially.

Note: The most successful sales people use this close the majority of the time.

3. Ben Franklin Close

(Alias: Pro-versus-Con Close, Decision-Making Close, T-Account Close, and Balance-Sheet Close)

List all the pros and cons of making the purchase. Begin by saying, "Well we could always do what Ben Franklin used to do. Ben Franklin became famous for being a scientist, an inventor, a statesman, a printer, a philosopher, a musician, and an economist, as well as America's first self-made millionaire, but he was also one of the greatest decision-makers in our country's history. Whenever he was faced with an important decision he was said to use this process to reach his conclusion. He would take a sheet of paper and draw a line down the middle (*you do the same*). On the left side of the line he would write "FOR" and on the right side he would write "AGAINST" (*you do the same*). Then, he'd consider all the reasons why he should decide to do something and all the reasons he should not decide to do something and write them down under the applicable columns. Then he would total up both sides and make his decision based on which side had the most reasons. Let's give this a try and see how it comes out."

Next, give your potential customer your pen and help them with all the reasons why they should buy today. When it comes time to list the "AGAINST" items, state the obvious "AGAINST" items, if any. Then let them come up with any additional reasons on their own. In most cases, if the purchase is truly in their best interest, it will be difficult for them to come up with more "AGAINST" items. If they do, it's because they truly don't want or need what you're selling. This is your cue to make a polite exit.

The other 95 percent of the time, when you have more "FOR" items than "AGAINST" items, go directly into an assumptive close.

4. Buying Criteria Close

(*Alias: Need-Benefit Close*)

Summarize the ways in which your product or service satisfies the needs the customer has already identified. For example, suppose you are selling copiers.

> **You**: "You mentioned you wanted to be able to make at least 25 copies a minute, correct?"
>
> **Potential Customer**: "Yes."
>
> **You**: "And you wanted it to be able to collate and staple, is that right?"
>
> **Potential Customer**: "Yes, I did."
>
> **You**: "With the ability to also use the same machine to send faxes?"
>
> **Potential Customer**: "That is what I was hoping for."

After you have covered all of the customer's requirements, then wrap up the sale using the Alternative Choice Close.

"Great! It sounds like this machine meets your specifications perfectly. I guess all I need to know now is whether you want it delivered this week, or would the first of next week be better?"

5. Compliment Close

(*Alias: Flattery Close, Ego Close, Vanity Close*)

If the potential customer seems to have an overactive ego, this may be a good close to consider. Begin by paying them genuine compliments when they add things throughout your presentation. Egocentric people will want you to know that they know everything about what you are selling, so finding times when a compliment is in order should not be too difficult. Respond to each of their comments (while maintaining eye contact, smiling, and looking somewhat awed) with statements such as "I'm impressed. You really know a lot about (*whatever they are commenting on*)." "Wow. Most people I speak with don't know that about (*whatever they are commenting on*)."

You get the idea. Then ask for the sale. If it seems this technique is working better than usual, you might even attempt the close by saying something to the effect of,

> **You:** "Well, as educated as you are about (*your product or service*), then you know how good this really is."
>
> **Potential Customer:** "Yes, it sounds good."
>
> **You:** "Great. All I need is your okay here."

6. Exit Close

(*Alias: Doorknob Close, Columbo Close*)

Remember the old television show *Columbo*? He had a standard technique. He would ask a series of minor questions, seemingly unrelated to the murder, then close his notepad, say good-bye, and start to walk away. Then, just as the suspect began to relax, Columbo would raise his hand, twirl around, and say, "Just one more thing . . ." Caught 'em off guard every time.

This close is similar to Lieutenant Columbo's technique. Let's assume you have unsuccessfully attempted several trial closes, and the meeting is about to end. As you are packing up and preparing to leaving, or if the potential customer is at your establishment, as they are beginning to leave, say, "I'm curious. What was the reason you didn't buy today?" Feeling that the meeting has concluded, the potential customer may open up and tell you the real reason. You then say, "Oh, I feel foolish. I'm sorry I didn't explain to you that . . ."

Then address their concern and close again.

7. Impending Event Close

(*Alias: Urgency Close, Help-Me-To-Help-You Close, Guillotine Close*)

If the customer gives you a time frame in which they need to own your product or start using your service, this may be the right close. Use that time frame as the reason they need to buy now, provided that is truly the case. "You mentioned that you needed to have this by (*their stated time frame*). In order for me to make that possible, I need to get the ball rolling now because we need to. . ." Then go through the things that need to be done to meet their stated time frame.

There may be other ways to add an element of urgency to the sale. If, for example, your product or service is on sale at a significant savings, but the sale ends the following day, then you can honestly say, "I'm afraid this price is only good today. Tomorrow the (*product or service*) will be at regular price."

Use this close only when the urgency is valid. Most potential customers will be suspicious of any offer that mysteriously disappears, and they will consider it to be a hard-selling technique. If you cannot reasonably back up your claim of urgency, this close will blow up in your face.

8. Instant Reverse Close

(*Alias: Boomerang Close, Objection Close*)

Whatever objection the customer gives for not wanting to buy, reverse it into the exact reason why they should.

> **Potential Customer:** "I think your price may be a little too high."
>
> **You:** "That is exactly the reason why you should own this. (*Expect a glazed look in response to this.*) Because our price is a little higher than our competitors' price, it should be a signal of the quality and value of our product. You should have less downtime due to repairs, and with our lifetime warranty, you will never have to worry about spending another penny later on this equipment. By investing a little more now, you'll end up spending a lot less later."

9. Major/Minor Close

(*Alias: Minor-Points Close, Secondary Close, Little-Decision Close, Incremental Close*)

Use this close to assist the potential customer in making the big decision (the actual buying decision) by having them make a small decision instead (something much less relevant), but which still implies the bigger decision. It could be as simply as saying, "I need your okay right here. Do you need to use my pen?" There are hundreds of variations you could use with this close. Customize it to your particular industry. For instance, let's say the potential customer is at your store and is considering a product that is fairly large in size. You could say, "Do you have a way to get it home, or would you prefer we deliver it to you?"

The Major/Minor Close is one of the most commonly used closes, and it can be very effective. If you have young children, it has been used on you many times. "Mommy, can I have the yo-yo or should I get the bouncing ball instead." You're not being asked to make the major decision, i.e., whether they are allowed to buy something. Instead, they are assuming you will let them buy something, so the only remaining question is what it will be, which is a much smaller decision.

My children have mastered this closing technique.

10. Puppy Dog Close

(*Alias: Trial-Order Close*)

This close is based on an old pet store technique. One Friday afternoon, you bring the family into the pet store to "just look" at the new puppies in the window. You might get a dog some day, but you're just looking today. The kids spot a particular puppy, and the pleading begins. "Oh please can we have it?" Then the storeowner comes up with a great idea. "If you're not sure this is the puppy for you, why don't we do this. Take the puppy home for the weekend with no commitments. If everything works out, great. If not, just bring the puppy back on Monday for a full refund." The kids' eyes light up. "Oh can we, please, daddy?" "Well, I suppose, it can't hurt," you say, caving in. Forty-eight hours later, and the puppy has a name, has slept in the kids' bed, and is now a part of the family. You couldn't give it back now if you wanted to.

If you can't get a commitment initially and you have the luxury of letting your potential customer try before they buy, this can be an effective method of closing. What's the first thing the car dealer wants to get you to do? Slap that dealer plate on and take it for a test drive.

They sell a lot of cars this way.

Closing Ratio

To continually evaluate how well you are doing, track your closing ratio. This is relatively simple. Divide the number of sales you make by the number of presentations you have given. For example, if you made eight presentations in a week and you closed three of the eight, then your closing ratio would be approximately 38 percent for the week.

It is difficult to state in general terms what a good, bad, or average closing ratio is, because the ratio varies by industry. Based on my research,

I can say with some level of confidence that the average national closing rate is 20 percent, without regard to industry. Top salespeople in many industries consistently achieve 85 percent or higher closing ratios.

Tracking your own ratio (or that of your sales force) allows you to analyze different aspects of your selling skills to achieve an increase. If possible, find the average closing ratio for your industry. This will give you a standard against which to measure your progress.

The more sales you can close within the same number of leads will maximize your advertising dollars, increase your revenues, and grow your profits exponentially. So it is important to keep score.

In virtually all competitive sports, athletes keep and monitor individual stats on their performance so that they can continue to improve.

It works in the world of sales, too.

Indifference Sells

"Back in the day," when I was selling home improvement products, I noticed that my closing ratio was much higher at the end of the year than at the beginning, even though I was selling the same products with the same presentation. Why was I closing more sales at the end of the year? Elementary, my dear Watson! With a little deductive reasoning, I figured it out.

Our business virtually shut down over the winter months and I was working on straight commission, which meant that for most of the winter I had no income. When spring came, I was selling and selling hard. I really needed the sales. By the end of year, I was breaking records and, therefore, was more financially secure. Besides that, I usually had a number of home improvement jobs that had to be completed before winter, so I wasn't nearly as aggressive in sales.

Even though my presentations were identical year round, the potential customer could sense a difference. At the beginning of the year, I probably seemed more desperate for the sale, which made them a little skeptical and more resistant. On the other hand, by the end of the year, they probably sensed indifference. By then I didn't *need* their business; I just *wanted* it. This impression may have created a fear of loss on the part of the potential customer. Perhaps they felt that, since I wasn't trying too hard to sell them my services, my business must be booming and I didn't really need the sale. In effect, my closing ratio was going up during the times when I wasn't trying as hard. Once I recognized the psychology behind this, I used that slight feeling of indifference at the beginning of the year, and my closing ratio rose to the pre-winter level.

Moral: Never seem desperate to make a sale. Certainly, you *want* every sale, but there is an enormous difference between wanting and needing, and a customer can sense that far better than you may think.

Fear of loss is one of the most powerful motivators. I was once on a flight heading east, and the flight attendants were handing out small bags of mini-pretzels. A lady sitting across the aisle from me was engrossed in a book and did not notice, until she looked up, that the flight attendant hadn't given her a bag of pretzels. A look of sheer desperation came to her face as she realized that the flight attendant was now several rows further down the aisle. "She forgot my pretzels!" the lady said to me. For the next few minutes, she tried without success to get the flight attendant's attention. When the flight attendant finished the pretzel run and started back up the aisle, the near frantic lady stopped her. "Miss, you forgot my pretzels!" she said. The flight attendant replied, "I'm sorry. Let me see if we have any more left. I know we were getting low." The flight attendant went back up front and the pretzel-less lady began talking to herself and to anyone who would listen. On and on she went wondering how they could have forgotten her pretzels and how upset she would be if there were none left. A few moments later the flight attendant returned with a bag of pretzels. The relief on this lady's face was almost palpable. (The rest of us were pretty relieved, too.) Altogether it was a ridiculous and childish display. To cap it off, the lady never even opened the bag of pretzels. In fact, she left them on the plane in the seat pocket. The pretzels were only important when she thought she wasn't going to get any. Once she had them, she lost interest.

The point is: If the fear of loss can produce this kind of reaction over a small bag of stale pretzels, imagine how powerful it can be for something that has real importance.

Sell With Integrity

If you want to be a great closer, then abide by this simple rule: If you honestly feel that the product or service you represent cannot resolve the customer's need and/or would not be in their best interest, walk away from the sale. Period. Sure, it might be possible to sell them anyway, but you will never be a great closer if you do.

> *"Prefer a loss to a dishonest gain; the one brings pain at the moment, the other for all time."*
>
> Chilon (One of the Seven Sages of Ancient Greece)

Chapter 15

Thinking Outside the Box

"Obstacles are those frightful things you see when you take your eyes off your goal."

Henry Ford

I recently did an Internet search on the phrase "Thinking Outside the Box," using a popular search engine. I found more than 122,000 references for a phrase that has obviously become quite clichéd over the last few decades. There are a myriad of definitions. Here is mine.

Thinking Outside the Box is solving problems through brainstorming techniques and creative thinking, while, at least initially, resisting the urge to eliminate any possible solution no matter how far-fetched it may seem.

Putting aside all the hype, there is actual science behind the idea of Thinking Outside the Box. Done properly, it can increase your creative thinking abilities and help you become a more effective problem-solver. Problem-solving is the essence of business. Your product or service must solve some type of problem or no one would buy it. Selling is also problem-solving, as is managing operations. Everything we do in business is problem-solving in one form or another. Thus, the people who can solve problems more effectively and efficiently will be the most successful in their industries.

Before you can become a more effective problem-solver, you must change your view of problems in general.

> *"The problem is not that there are problems. The problem is expecting otherwise and thinking that having problems is a problem."*
>
> Theodore Isaac Rubin

Most of us do not look forward to problems. For one thing, they are apt to take us out of our comfort zone. They cause aggravation and stress and loss of focus — if you let them.

But when you begin to think of problems as opportunities, a whole new realm of possibilities opens up. For instance, most customers expect a few problems with a new purchase. In general, they will be less bothered by the problem itself than by how you handle it. So when a customer has a problem, use that as an opportunity to show them that your product, your service, and your business were the right choice.

When a problem becomes an opportunity, you can attack it with greater enthusiasm and clarity.

Here is my six-step process for resolving problems by Thinking Outside The Box.

Six-Step Process for Thinking Outside the Box

1. Define
2. Compare
3. Create
4. Evaluate
5. Solve
6. Implement

Define

First, identify the true problem. To do that, you have to find its root. Otherwise, it is too easy to get sidetracked into resolving the *effects* of the problem, rather than the problem itself. If a building catches fire and firefighters only attempt to extinguish the flames coming out of the building, rather than locating and eliminating the source, the fire is unlikely to be put out and will probably devastate everything inside the building.

To define a problem, conduct a root cause analysis. Keep in mind that a single problem may have more than one root cause. For example, let's say you have a dissatisfied customer who says that the product they just purchased was installed incorrectly and does not work. It is easy to jump to the conclusion that the employee who installed the product made a mistake. However, many other factors could have been at play. Perhaps the employee was improperly trained or was given the wrong information. Perhaps the salesperson gave the customer incorrect information. Perhaps the product itself is defective. In that case, even if was correctly installed, it still would not work. Perhaps the product works and the customer is not operating it correctly. Perhaps the problem is a combination of some of these possibilities. The point is: don't pass judgment too quickly. Evaluate all the potential root causes before reaching any conclusions.

Compare

Ask yourself: Have you had a similar problem in the past? What did you do to resolve it? Would that work in this case?

Create

There is almost always more than one way to solve a problem. Once we have identified one solution, we have a tendency to fixate on that. We stop thinking about other alternatives.

This step in the problem-solving process can be the most enjoyable and rewarding. On a piece of paper, list every possible way you can think of to solve the problem. Don't worry if a particular solution may lead to other problems. Jot it down anyway. If possible and when time allows, do this exercise in a group that includes people who are close to the problem and others who may not be. It can sometimes be more difficult to solve problems you are close to. Outsiders bring a fresh perspective and clear mind to the task, both of which can be effective in solving problems. Never condemn any idea at this stage of the process. Let everything flow out as quickly as possible. This is a brainstorming session. No logic allowed! You are not trying to determine what will work, what won't work or all the details behind a particular idea. The issue in this step is quantity — not quality. So anything goes. If you are conducting a group session, make sure everyone understands this. People tend to hold back ideas until they think they have come up with a great one or because they think the idea they have is dumb. Make it clear that all ideas — from the scientific to the just plain goofy — will be welcomed as equals. Also, don't be too quick to select an idea and thus prematurely stop the process. And never allow arguments or finger pointing to break out among the participants. In a true team environment, everyone, including the boss, should accept equal blame for the problem whether they like it or not. Also, a little bit of humor can stimulate more creativity. Have lunch brought in for these meetings and, if possible, make it a casual day. Finally, make certain no one passes judgment or criticizes the ideas generated in the brainstorming session. Productive things can happen in a well-run brainstorming session.

> *"Thinking isn't agreeing or disagreeing. That's voting."*
>
> Robert Frost

Evaluate

Evaluate likely results and/or the consequences of each of the solutions identified during the brainstorming session. Use cause-and-effect strategies to predict all possible outcomes from each idea. Which solutions produce the greatest net effect without causing as much damage in other areas? Prioritize the problems to determine which should be resolved first. Finally, does the solution stay within the People First Philosophy? Make this a litmus test for any solution you decide to use.

Solve

Solve the problem using the most effective solution that comes out of your evaluation. Keep in mind that this is usually not a make-or-break situation. If the results of Plan A do not fully address the problem, go to Plan B, which you should have as an alternative or backup solution.

One of the mottos of the U.S. Marines is: Adapt, Improvise, and Overcome. This is particularly applicable in problem-solving.

Implement

After you have solved the problem, implement strategies to eliminate or at least minimize its chances of coming up again.

So what does all this have to do with "Thinking Outside the Box? For many people the most challenging part of solving a problem is Step Three, the creation phase. Most of us are not as creative as we would like to be. As a child you may have spent hours playing with action figures or Barbie Dolls. You dreamed up entire scenarios in which you could go anywhere and do anything. Your imagination was boundless. How many pictures did you draw or color? Children are curious and creative. "Why" is often the first question they ask, regardless of the topic. I laugh out loud when I think back on some of the truly creative things my own children have done or said over the years. Anyone who has children has had the same experience. Here's a story I heard Zig Ziglar tell many years ago.

One evening a man was at home feverishly working on an important project for which the deadline was fast approaching. He couldn't concentrate, however, because of constant interruptions from his five-year-old son who wanted to play. "If I could just buy 20 to 30 minutes of time with no interruptions, then I could take a break and spend some time with my son," the man thought to himself. Then on the table he spotted a magazine opened to a page with an intricate picture of the globe. Sensing an opportunity, he ripped out the page, tore it into small pieces, and handed them to his son. "I'll play with you just as soon as you put the picture of the world back together again," he said. The little boy left the room and sat down on the floor with his new "puzzle," and the father went back to work, secure in the knowledge that he had bought himself the uninterrupted time he needed. After all, five-year-olds don't know enough about the continents to put them together very quickly, especially in the form of the globe. You can imagine his astonishment when, just a few minutes later, the little boy returned the picture with every piece of the globe taped perfectly in place. "How did you do that so fast?" he asked. The little boy replied, "Daddy, the other side had a picture of a man on it. When I put the man back together the world came together." The father immediately put his work aside to spend time with his son.

I love that story. It shows that children do not always think like adults. When adults have a problem, we use our advanced knowledge and cognitive skills to solve it. At the same time, though, we have a tendency to overcomplicate things. Children, in their innocence, will solve a problem in the easiest way possible.

> *Hey Diddle, Diddle, the Cat and the Fiddle*
> *was a lie like all the rest.*
> *The astronauts killed the man in the moon and*
> *growing up took care of the rest.*
>
> Unknown

We are born into this world without many rules. Almost immediately we begin to learn the rules, many of which are essential to our survival. Still, it's been said that by the age of five a child has heard the word "no" at least 40,000 times. The rules begin to play a major role in our lives. At school we learn that you can only add or subtract in a certain way, and that your "T's" have to look like this and your "A's" have to look like that, and so on and so forth. If this sounds as though I am supporting the advent of chaos, nothing could be further from the truth. I am a strong supporter of education. My concern is that one possible consequence of education is a concurrent decrease in creativity. It has been said that our creativity decreases as much as 90 percent between the ages of five and seven. Almost of necessity, we rely on the logical part of our brain to get us through school as well as college. The higher the educational level we attain, the more analytical we become in our thinking.

Certainly there are times when creativity must take a back seat to logic. If you were facing brain surgery, you'd want your surgeon to be a highly educated, analytic, and logical thinker, not someone who decides that your brain is a good place to begin experimenting with untried techniques! Nor am I suggesting in any way that intelligent people cannot be creative or that having no formal education is preferable simply because formal education may curb creativity.

I raise this issue only to engage your thinking about the possibility that as we become more educated we may become less creative. Name some of the most creative and successful people in history — Thomas Edison, Alexander Graham Bell, Orville and Wilbur Wright, John D. Rockefeller, Henry Ford, and Walt Disney (who, as a young man, was once fired by a newspaper editor who said he "lacked imagination").

Question: What does this interesting mix of inventors and successful business people have in common?

Answer: None of them had a college degree, and most of them didn't graduate from high school.

Most were either self-taught or home-schooled, an environment in which the rules of learning were more relaxed. Note also that these names go back many years. In their time, many people never finished high school, let alone went to college. Is there any validity to this today, you may ask, in light of how much education has changed? Well, let's see. There's

- Steve Jobs, Apple Computer
- Ted Turner, media mogul extraordinaire
- Michael Dell, Dell Computer
- H. Wayne Huizenga, entrepreneur and former owner of Blockbuster Video
- Daniel S. Abraham, founder of Slim-Fast
- David Geffen, cofounder of Dreamworks SKG

- Larry Ellison, Oracle Computer
- Herbert Wexner, founder of The Limited, which also owns Victoria's Secret,
- Bath & Body Works, and Limited
- Ty Warner, of Beanie Babies fame and, last but for heaven's sake not least,
- Bill Gates, founder of . . .what was the name of that company again? Oh, yes. Microsoft.

All of these people have at least four things in common.

1. They are self-made.
2. They each have a net worth in excess of $1 billion dollars.
3. They are all in the Top 100 of *Forbes 400 Richest Americans*.
4. All of them either dropped out of college or never went.

Before you say anything... No, I am not making a case for dropping out of school. The majority of successful business people and entrepreneurs have had comprehensive education. But the fact remains that some of the most creative and successful people in the world have not.

We are all born with creativity. Some people learn how to harness it, while others either ignore it or let it wither away.

Left Brain and Right Brain

So what can you do to become more creative? Exercise your mind! Like every muscle in the human body, the brain, too, atrophies if it is not used. Put another way, mental fitness requires mental exercise.

The human brain consists of tissue, which is composed of nerve cells, gray and white matter, and supporting tissue made up of glial cells. It is estimated that we have more than 100 billion nerve cells or neurons in our brain (or slightly more than twice the net worth of Bill Gates in dollars). These neurons regulate everything we think and do. The neurons emit neurotransmitters — chemical messengers that run between the neurons.

The study of the Left Brain/Right Brain phenomenon dates back to Hippocrates. But it wasn't until the 1960s that scientists began experimenting with certain aspects of the brain to provide evidence for the theory, which holds that the two different sides of the brain — the Left Brain and the Right Brain — control different methods of thinking. The Left Brain controls logical, rational, and analytical thinking. In general, schools accommodate Left Brain thinking since studies will focus primarily on logic, accuracy, and analysis. This is the basis for my claim that the higher a person moves through the education system, the more Left Brained (i.e., logical and analytical) they become. We get our intuitiveness, creativity, and visual awareness from the Right Brain. In school, subjects such as art and music may stimulate the creative mind, although the major emphasis remains Left Brain thinking.

People usually have a definite preference for one or the other style of thinking. Due, in part, to our education, there are more Left Brain than Right Brain thinkers. However, some people are considered to be Whole-Brain thinkers: they are equally proficient at using both sides of their brain. Ideally, this should be our goal.

To be more creative, we must increase our ability to tap into our Right Brain, which should be in the forefront for the creation phase (Step 3) of the problem-solving process. The Left Brain comes into play in Step 4, the Evaluation phase.

Because a lifetime of discipline and education has fortified our Left Brain thinking, we must devise ways to get the neurons on the right side of the brain firing more often and thus get both sides communicating more effectively. Do this and you will find that your creative thinking and logic skills will become more effective and efficient.

Visual brainteasers that combine logical thinking with visual clues are an excellent tool for getting the Left Brain and the Right Brain to work together. Each side must communicate with the other to solve these types of problems. If you are even moderately educated, your

Left Brain will initially attempt to dominate the process. But over time and with practice, you will develop a better grasp of Whole-Brain thinking and thus strengthen your problem-solving abilities.

Here are a few visual brainteasers that are helpful to this process. The answers are provided at the back of the book, but don't look at them until you have at least given yourself a fair chance to actually solve the problems. Otherwise you're just cheating yourself out of the benefits of the exercise.

Look at the image below. Quickly count the number of squares. How many do you see?

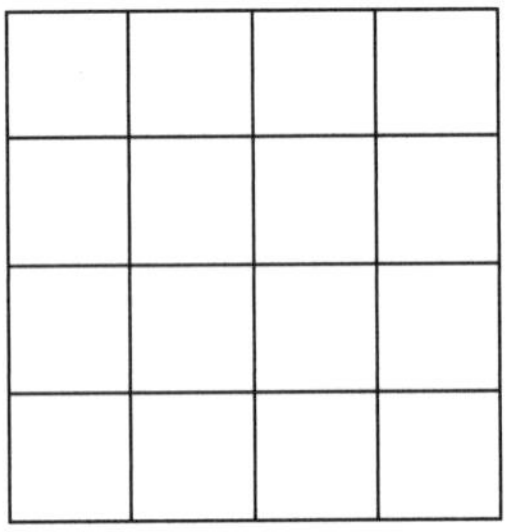

Here are nine dots arranged in a square matrix. Can you draw four straight lines that connect all nine dots without lifting your pencil from the paper?

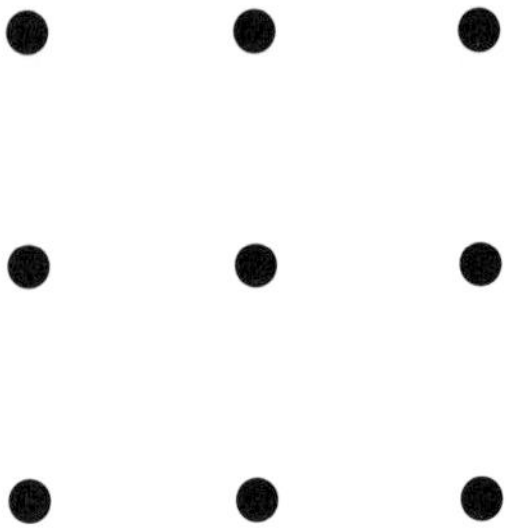

A farmer owns 1,000 acres of land. He is getting on in age and has decided to give his farm to his five children. He has one son, and he would like his son to continue to farm. He realizes that to do so, his son will need a minimum of 250 acres. He also has four daughters. His daughters have always been critical about their father's fairness to them. He knows that to make them all happy he will need to give each of his daughters equal shares of the 750 acres that remain. They understand and accept the fact that their brother will get a larger parcel than they will to keep the farm running. The farmer also knows that to avoid other complaints among his daughters, each of their parcels will have to be exactly the same shape. Determine how many acres each of his daughters will get and draw out exactly how the parcels need to be divided up so that each of the four parcels of the remaining 750 acres are exactly the same size and shape.

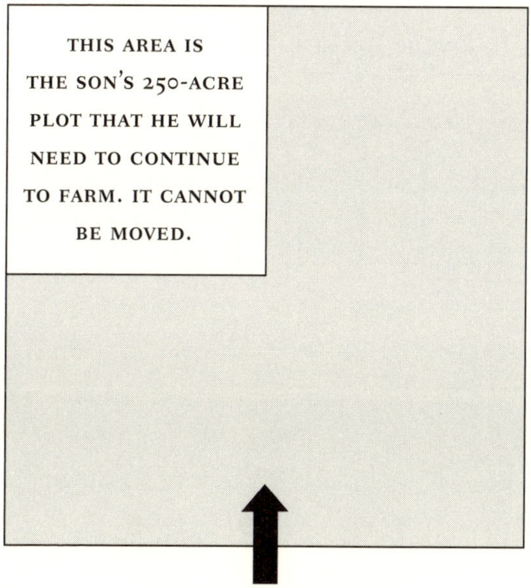

THE REMAINING AREA NEEDS TO BE DIVIDED UP INTO PARCELS EXACTLY THE SAME SIZE AND SHAPE FOR EACH OF THE FARMER'S DAUGHTERS.

How many cubes do you see? How many cubes would you say are entirely hidden? How many cubes are there in all?

There are six lines shown below. Add five more lines and come up with nine.

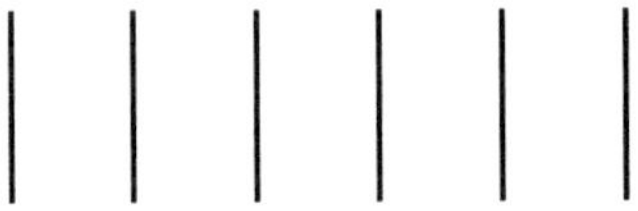

Count the objects in the picture below. How many objects do you see? Describe the objects you see.

There are dozens, if not hundreds, of books and magazines that contain brainteasers similar to these. Buy some of these publications and practice solving a few problems each day. Make sure you look for brainteasers that will require the use of both your visual and intuitive Right Brain and your logical and analytical Left Brain. Over time, you may find that your Left Brain and Right Brain begin to work together better, and problem-solving may become a little easier.

Besides, brainteasers can be a lot of fun!

Chapter 16

Building Your Team

"The speed of the boss is the speed of the team."

Lee Iacocca

Andrew Carnegie was once asked, "Which element is the most important for the success of a business: labor, capital or brains?" His reply was in a form of a question: "Which leg of a three-legged stool is most important?" What a thought-provoking answer.

You can have all the money and the intelligence in the world, but unless you recruit and retain the best employees, your stool will topple over. The best companies have the best people. Period.

New business owners have somewhat different challenges than established companies when it comes to hiring new people. Some of these challenges include:

- Not filling new positions early enough
- Working for your business rather than working on your business
- Trying to keep the overhead lower by recruiting less-qualified candidates

- Not attracting the most marketable candidates
- Not hiring the right talent with the right skills.

Not Filling New Positions Early Enough

This is the proverbial Catch-22 for new business owners. It is also a vicious circle from which it can be difficult to break free. New business owners find themselves so busy they cannot maintain or grow their business any further. The only way to grow their business is to hire additional staff to handle the growth; however, they don't have the time to look for additional staff because they are too busy running the day-to-day duties of their business. To further complicate matters, this problem is usually coupled with a second Catch-22. They find themselves too busy to grow their business and need to hire additional staff; however, they don't think they can afford to pay additional staff until the business grows further.

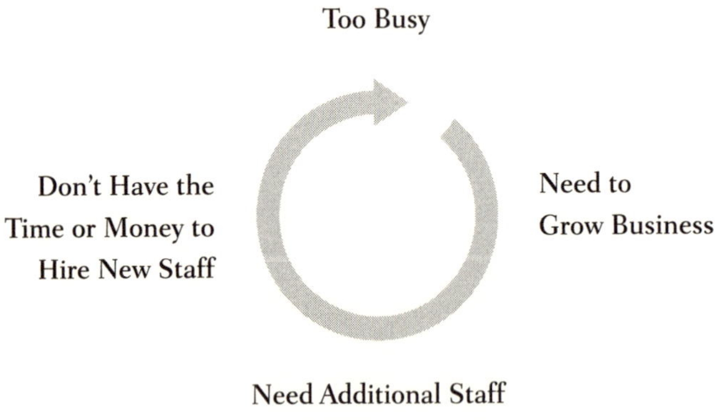

The solution to this problem is: don't get caught in it in the first place. In Chapter 8, we discussed the necessity of writing a Business Plan that includes your staffing requirements along the way. Ideally, if your initial estimates were fairly accurate, you may never have to face this problem because you hired the people you needed before you needed them. In reality, this is not usually the case. You're usually better off overestimating your need for staff requirements and building more working capital into your initial budget to cover the cost.

The key to managing your staffing needs is to be proactive rather than reactive. New business owners often take a wait-and-see approach before hiring additional staff, only to find that they have waited until it was too late. This is an easy mistake to make because the biggest problem for most new businesses is cash flow. When cash is tight, a deliberate decision to increase your overhead by bringing on additional staff may seem, at best, foolhardy.

But the question is not whether you can afford to bring someone on right now, but whether you can afford *not* to.

Question: What is the likely outcome if you don't hire someone?

Answer: You may never be able to grow the business to the point where you feel you can afford to hire someone.

Worst case, you may end up burning yourself out and closing the business altogether.

> ***"The definition of insanity is, doing the same thing over and over again and expecting different results."***
>
> Benjamin Franklin

So don't wait until it's too late. Sometimes you have to step out of your comfort zone and bring on the needed staff before you feel you can afford it. *Note:* The key word here is "feel." If you *know* you can't afford to hire someone because you don't have the money, then you shouldn't hire someone until you have secured additional working capital. Quite often, however, it is not so much the fact that the money is not there as it is the fear of going further into debt. "Feeling" you can't afford to bring on additional staff may mean you won't be able to pay yourself much of a salary, if any. I know only too well how this feels.

About three years from the point of start-up, my business reached a critical mass, and I knew we were getting close to a turning point. It would either continue to thrive and grow or it could flounder and die. I was bogged down doing most of the day-to-day operational issues, fighting fire after fire, and putting in upwards of 70+ hours per week. While we did have competent and hard-working staff, their time was already taxed to the limit. I have always believed in the principle of promoting from within. But we needed to fill some high-level, key positions for which no one on my staff was sufficiently experienced. And we needed to do it, like yesterday! I decided it was time to bring on some heavy-hitters.

I needed a President to take over the day-to-day operational responsibilities so that I could refocus my time on growth strategies. And I found an excellent candidate. But the compensation package we negotiated ended up being more than five times what I had been paying myself as CEO. Was I concerned about whether we could afford him? You bet I was! Was it initially hard for me to pay someone else exponentially more than I was paying myself in a business that I owned? You bet it was. But I had confidence in my strategy and I was comfortable that this decision was best for the company. It was an investment in both my future and the company's. I relived that same experience several times along the way, bringing on additional people at higher salaries than I had been paying myself. In personal finances, the rule of thumb is: Pay yourself first. But if you want to start and build a successful business, be prepared to: Pay yourself last! The good news is that, in the long run, you have a much better chance of paying yourself more than you ever imagined when those investments start paying dividends.

Go to Work *on* Your Business, Rather than *in* Your Business

This concept, discussed by Michael Gerber in *The E-Myth Revisited*, is one of the most common traps for new business owners. Rather than breaking off portions of their responsibilities and hiring the right people to assume them, they continue to take on more and more responsibilities on their own.

The true entrepreneurial spirit can be a double-edged sword. On the one hand, you have total confidence in yourself and your ability to make your business succeed. On the other hand, that same confidence can cause you to become an entrepreneurial one-man-band who thinks he or she can handle everything by themselves until it's too late — until you realize that you waited too long to get help.

Moral: Always remember, you are *not* an employee. You are the employer.

Have you ever watched a plate-spinner perform, perhaps on the street or at a circus? If you are "of a certain age," you probably remember seeing one or two such acts on *The Ed Sullivan Show*. Plate-spinning dates back thousands of years, to the time of the Chinese Emperors. I first saw plate-spinning at the circus almost 30 years ago, and I still remember it vividly. I was captivated. I just could not figure how this guy was able to get so many plates balanced and spinning on all these little wooden rods. (Being a child, I had to try it when I got home. I broke two of my mom's good plates — something she probably never knew until this day.) The circus performer started by placing a china plate on top of a long hardwood rod. He then set the plate spinning. A combination of gravity and momentum seemed to keep it balanced. Soon the plate began to lose its momentum and started to wobble and the spinning slowed. Just when you were sure that the plate was doomed to crash to the floor, the guy grabbed the rod and with a slight shake rebuilt the momentum of the plate. And so on he went with more rods and more plates and repeating the same actions over and over. Pretty soon he had six plates spinning, and the pace became more and more frantic as he ran back and forth spinning new plates and, in the nick of time, keeping the others from falling. Before long he had at least 12 plates spinning. The more plates he had spinning, the more frantic he became, running back and forth at warp speed. Suddenly, there were 15 plates. Things were getting hairier by the second. Then, after he had about 20 plates rotating, he began pulling the plates down one at a time, leaving only one plate remaining, nonchalantly taking his bow as though he'd forgotten that last wobbling plate. The crowd went wild, screaming for him to notice the last plate, and at the last possible second, he ran back and grabbed the plate just before it fell off the rod.

At the circus, it's great fun to watch. But too many small business owners run their operations in a similar manner, and they're usually just one wobble away from a crash. They've got too many plates in the air, and they keep adding more, piling more responsibilities on themselves. Unlike the circus act, which always ended crash-free, there are only three possible outcomes for this business scenario.

1. They end up making big mistakes and "dropping a lot of plates."
2. They get tired and burned out, and finally they close down. Forget the plates. Nothing left but broken china.
3. They stop working harder and start working smarter. They hire more people. With an unlimited supply of professional plate spinners, you can keep an unlimited number of plates in the air.

Hire the right people, before you need them. Chip away your responsibilities so you can concentrate on the business as a whole, instead of individual business operations. Your business will grow and flourish, and you get to keep your sanity and your good health long enough to enjoy it.

I know many business owners who have been overworking and overstressing themselves for years. For whatever reason, they have been unable to hire the right staff and reduce their own responsibilities to the point where they can begin to enjoy their business. In the beginning, you may have no choice but to do the majority of the work yourself. But keep in mind that your goal is to work yourself out of a job. Trust me. There is no better feeling than owning a business that not only earns you a great living, but also allows you to live your life.

I am fortunate to have hired the right people. At least 10 times a year Kris and I take trips and do the things that we enjoy doing. This is only possible because we have the right people in place in our businesses. We are totally confident that should anything come up, it will be handled correctly and professionally. If we wake up feeling under the weather, we're confident the business will survive the day without us.

Don't be a plate-spinner; instead, hire the best plate-spinners.

"No man will make a great leader who wants to do it all himself, or to get all the credit for doing it."

Andrew Carnegie

Trying to Keep the Overhead Lower by Recruiting Lesser-Qualified Candidates

New business owners generally must make substantial investments of time and money in their companies to make them work. Many of them do everything right up to a point, and then they start cutting corners in the most important areas to save money. For example, they may get the best office space, create the best sales literature, buy the best equipment, and do everything else necessary to get that phone to start ringing. Then they hire someone who will work for minimum wage to handle incoming calls from potential customers, and to top it off, they don't train that person properly.

Cardinal Rule: A company is not the building, the equipment, the furniture, the website, the phone number, the literature, or even the trademark. A company is the people. Make your investments in the areas that will give you the greatest payoff. That means your first priority should always be your people.

Not Attracting the Most Marketable Candidates

Most companies, small, medium, or large, are not nearly as effective as they could be when it comes to recruiting the best candidates.

I'll never forget when I first took a job in the recruiting industry. I have always been confident in my ability to sell, but I knew I had to have confidence in any product or service I sold before I could ever be successful. Quite frankly, when I first started in recruiting, I was a little concerned about why these HR managers who had specialized in recruiting for many years would be willing to pay me recruiting fees that normally ranged between $15,000 and $30,000 to find them someone. Especially when I didn't have any experience in recruiting. It didn't take me long to realize why they were interested. The methods they were using to locate potential candidates were not nearly as effective as the methods I learned as part of my training to become a retained recruiter.

Just pick up any newspaper and scan the help-wanted advertisements placed by many companies. The common theme in these ads speaks volumes about addressing the core differences between recruiting styles. The ads will be similar to the mock-ad I have provided here. For purposes of illustration, I used an Engineering position in the Electronic Systems industry. But the theme of the message mirrors advertisements in virtually all industries.

ELECTRONIC SYSTEMS ENGINEER

We are seeking highly skilled and experienced candidates to be responsible for troubleshooting and monitoring our equipment. The successful candidate will be required to have the following:

- Must have a min. of five years experience specifically working in the print technology industry
- Strong understanding of software programs, including Siemens, GE Fanuc, Allen Bradley, Texas Instruments and or EAE (FPS)
- Bachelor's Degree in Engineering required
- Must be a team player
- Must have strong organizational skills
- Must be willing to work some weekends
- Must have extensive knowledge of the installation, programming, and debugging of all PLC's and AC & DC controllers.

We offer competitive salary and benefits. For consideration, send your resume to:

Employee Relations
Attn: ES Engineer
P.O. Box 1234
Anywhere, USA 54321

Now, let's analyze this ad. What actual information does it provide about the job or the company? There is little about the job itself. The most marketable candidates will want to know what they will be doing on a day-to-day basis. Will it be more challenging and rewarding than what they are doing now? We all have a selfish side. This is what programs us to strive for our own survival and success. Typically, then, we analyze almost everything first for how the outcome will affect us, and second, for how it will affect others. So you can see why ads like this one are not effective. The ad lists the requirements of the job, but provides no information on what the candidate will actually be doing.

In all the marketing I do, whether it is advertising my products or services or in my recruitment advertising, I use the What's In it For Me (WIFM) principle. Each time you create an ad, think about this principle and try to look at your ad from the perspective of the reader. Ask yourself the same questions a reader may ask. Why do I want to respond? Does this look interesting to me?

In our sample advertisement, there is little if any evidence of the WIFM principle. The focus of the ad is what the company wants. Ads like this often have an effect that is quite the opposite of what the company intended. The goal is usually to screen out those who may not be qualified and attract only the most qualified candidates. But qualified candidates need to be sold on the benefits of taking a job with your company. So the company usually ends up getting nothing but shotgun resumes from people who respond to any and all ads that are even vaguely related to their field.

> ***"If you want to catch a trout, don't go fishing in a herring barrel."***
>
> Ann Landers

That is the core difference between highly paid retained recruiters and the way most companies recruit. Companies may look for ways to reduce the time required in the hiring process by treating the initial phase of recruiting as a screening process. They only want those who are definitely qualified to respond, whereas professional retained recruiters understand that recruiting is nothing more than a marketing process.

Too much screening in the initial phase of recruiting contradicts marketing, as it reduces the number of people you will be able to talk to. You are narrowly defining and restricting whom you are willing to speak to.

Think of the hiring process as a funnel. You put candidates into the top, and based on the information gleaned once they've gone through a series of interviews, employment testing, background checks, and character references, you decide which candidate you want to hire. But suppose you attracted only 10 potential candidates? Because of your hiring criteria, that number may be reduced to one or two, if any, from which to make a selection.

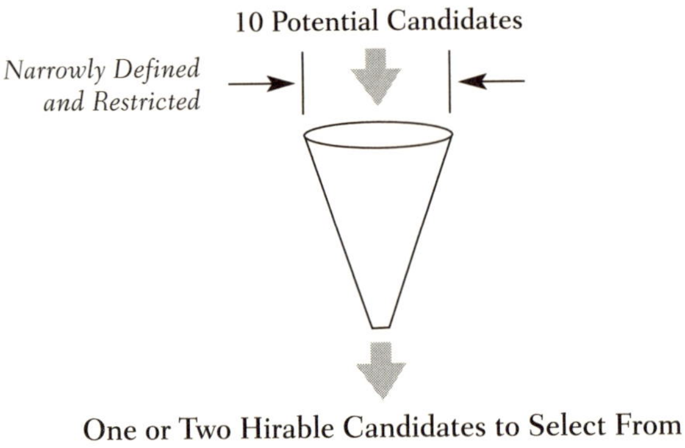

Now let's see what could happen by treating the recruiting process as a form of marketing. Just as a company markets their products or services, they should market vacant positions to attract the best candidates. Marketing is selling, and, as the old adage goes, selling is just a numbers game: the more people you speak to, the more sales you will make. Be less restrictive in terms of the applicants you will talk to and you may generate 10 times more potential candidates. Put another way, you open the top of the funnel wider to accommodate more people. The more people you talk to, the greater the number of hirable candidates you should have to select from after they have come through the additional steps of your hiring process.

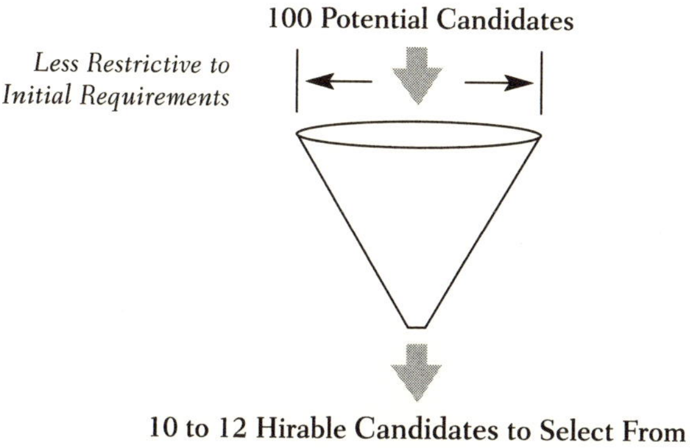

If you want to catch more fish, cast a wider net!

Now let's reconstruct our mock advertisement using the WIFM principle: instead of telling the candidate what the company wants, tell the candidate what's in it for them.

ELECTRONIC SYSTEMS ENGINEER

Are you ready for a change? Are you ready to actually start doing what you wanted to do when you got into engineering in the first place? Our company may be a great match for you!

We need your problem-solving and troubleshooting skills to head up our systems trouble-shooting team. Use your experience and training to help us remain one of the top companies in the industry.

We Offer:

- The most competitive salary around
- Paid Health and Dental Insurance
- Some flexibility on schedule
- Outstanding 401K Plan

- 18 days paid time off even the 1st yr
- Casual dress permitted

If you are ready for a more challenging and rewarding career, join our team of appreciated and respected employees at:

ABC Engineering, Inc.

Just give us a call at 555-1234 and ask for John Smith for an immediate tour of our facility. We'll respect your confidentiality.

Equal Opportunity Employer

Do you see the difference between the first ad and this one? If you were an engineer, which ad would attract you most? The second advertisement is based on marketing the position rather than screening out candidates. It is written from the perspective and psychology of the reader. It spells out all the position's advantages, tangible and intangible. Rather than providing a list of requirements, this ad says enough about the job to allow the candidate to begin visualizing what they would be doing.

Note also that the ad doesn't require the candidate to go through a lot of hoops to respond. They just have to pick up the phone. Compare this to the first ad, which requires the candidate to update and print their resume and mail it to a P.O. box. The most marketable candidates, who may be coveted by many employers, may not want to jump through hoops to express interest in a position.

Another advantage to the second advertisement is that the company name was clearly stated. The first ad had an air of anonymity. The candidate may wonder why the company would not show their name and why resumes must be sent to a P.O. box. Any number of reasons could cross their minds. "It must be such a poor to company to work for that they feel by putting their name in the advertisement it might stop people from applying." "Are they firing someone and looking for a replacement? If so, could this be me six months or so in the future?" "What are they hiding?" "What if this is really that company I can't stand?" "What if it's the company owned by Mr. Smith, who's a good friend of my boss? I don't want him to know I'm looking." "What if I'm answering an ad that was put in by my own company?"

Finally, the second ad addresses any concern a potential candidate may have about initiating contact with the company. "We'll respect your confidentiality" allays any fears about your contacting the candidate's present employer who may not be aware that they are looking for another job.

Again, put on your WIFM hat when you write an advertisement and think about it from the perspective of the candidate — the kind of candidate you want to hire. Would they even bother to submit an application to your company based on this ad?

If the answer is no, your ad needs work before you run it.

Not Hiring the Right Talent with the Right Skills

Hiring additional staff members should be a well thought-out process. But too often it is treated haphazardly. A new business owner may know they need help, but not know what type of help. So they take a quick scan of the organization, do a fast inventory of some of the jobs that have been piling up, throw an ad together, and run it. They need warm bodies, and they need them fast.

Rule of thumb: Hiring incorrectly can cause more problems than not hiring anyone at all. How? Two ways.

1. Recruiting for the wrong positions to fill, i.e., hiring people to do one thing, when there is something far more important that needs doing and for which you need to find the right person.

2. Recruiting the wrong candidates to fill positions.

To determine what positions need to be filled, what responsibilities you will want to assign to those positions, and who would be the best fit for those positions, you need to do three things — a Needs Analysis, a Job Analysis, and a Job Description.

Needs Analysis

First, evaluate the strengths and weaknesses of your organization. Look at all aspects of your company's business functions and activities. There are six key functions in any business.

1. **Management:** Coordinates all the functions of the business's resources to achieve the company's goals
2. **Finance and Accounting:** Accounts receivable, accounts payable, budgeting, asset management, financial reporting, and capital acquisition
3. **Production and Operations:** Includes all functions of converting resources into goods or services
4. **Information Systems:** Systems to keep all the other functions working together
5. **Marketing:** Sales, advertising, public relations, and marketing strategies
6. **Human Resources:** Recruiting, training, payroll, time and attendance, record keeping, and compliance with Federal, state, and local laws that concern employees and employers.

Look at each of these areas. Which, if any, are being underserved? The Needs Analysis doesn't have to be based on negative factors. A Needs Analysis can be part of your strategic thinking for expanding your business in new areas.

For the Needs Analysis you will need to visualize what your organization should look like based on your Business Plan.

Job Analysis

Once you have determined your needs, you can begin determining the requirements and duties of the position(s) you need to fill. Here are a few things to consider.

- Why does this position need to be filled?
- How does this position relate to other positions in the company?
- What are the mental and physical requirements of the position?
- What should the qualifications for this position be (i.e., skill sets, educational level, amount of experience, training and personality that would best fit)?

The Job Analysis can be difficult. If you hit a snag, compare your company to other companies to see how they have handled it.

Job Description

Use your Job Analysis to build a Job Description, which will identify the position's major duties, responsibilities, and tasks. It should also show the methods that will be used to complete those tasks, the person to whom the new person will report, how the position may relate to other positions in the company, and the qualifications required for the position. Be realistic when developing a Job Description. Here are some things to keep in mind.

- Have you given this person too many tasks? Is it realistic to expect someone to be able to accomplish all of the tasks you are including in the amount of time you are allotting for the position?
- Have you kept the general theme of the position consistent? Meaning, how many of the six business functions are you pulling from when assigning tasks to this position?

- Based on the tasks you are assigning, is it reasonable to expect that candidates are available who possess the varied skills?

- Have you budgeted enough to be able to pay someone what will be needed for those skills?

- Don't become too inflexible with any Job Description you may develop. Every company faces change every now and again, and you will need some room to accommodate that change as well as being able to give your new employee the opportunity and latitude to grow within your company. You may later find that they have some hidden talents that you would like to incorporate into their job.

"Never tell people how to do things. Tell them what to do and they will surprise you with their ingenuity."

George S. Patton

At a *minimum*, the Job Description should include the following information.

- **Job Title:** The official title this person will hold.

- **Purpose Statement:** This statement gives the reader an overall idea of the position's broad function and scope.

- **List of Duties and Tasks Performed:** Although this list should include every major duty and task that is to be performed by the person who holds this position, it generally only comprises those tasks that represent five percent or more of the person's time.

- **Problem-solving and Decision Making:** This should explain the degree and level of the person's role in making decisions.

- **Interaction:** Describe the working relationships in which this person is likely to be involved. Will they hold a supervisory role? If so, what positions within the company would report to this person? To whom will this person report?

- **Job Specifications and Requirements:** What are the minimum qualifications the person must have to perform the position's major required functions (e.g., education, experience, knowledge, and skills)? Depending on the job, the qualifications may also include the ideal personality fit, communication and interpersonal skills (e.g., patience, motivation, or being a self-starter).
- **Location:** Where will the work be performed?
- **Machinery or Equipment:** What machinery or equipment will the person be using to perform the essential functions of the job? Depending on the position, this could be anything from office equipment and computers to specialized assembly line machines.
- **Projected Salary Range:** Initial pay range for the position. Also, show any other bonuses or commissions that may be earned.

Once completed, use the Job Description to create your recruitment material and help-wanted advertising, orienting your new employee to the position, training, and conducting employee performance appraisals.

The Interviewing Process

Effective interviewing is an art. Business owners often make the mistake of talking to several candidates and then making a decision based on gut instinct. No matter how good you are at reading people, this is not a scientific approach to hiring. For one thing, it ignores the fact that some people are very good at being interviewed. They may not be able to walk the walk, but they can talk the talk. Rather than a job, what they may deserve is an Oscar!

Do not cut corners in your interview process. Investigate the applicant's background and speak with their former employers. Personally,

I will always hire attitude over experience, if I can't have both. You can always train people and increase their experience. Changing a poor attitude may be impossible, and even if it can be done it may take too much time.

The most valuable candidate should be determined by the interview process — not by whom you like the best. Most of us like people who are like ourselves. It's a natural preference. But a staff of people who are just like you does not make for a balanced and effective team. Of course, you have to recruit people who fit your company's culture and avoid those who are likely to create personality conflicts. But that doesn't mean you cannot hire people who have different likes and dislikes, different personalities, strengths, and weaknesses. (I do not, however, recommend hiring U of M football fans in conjunction with OSU fans, unless they will be working on different continents.)

Each of us has what I refer to as a "dumb switch." It's a mental on-off switch that we subconsciously flip as soon as we make a decision. This can cause you to make up your mind about a person even before you've gotten very far into the interview process. Program your brain to avoid flipping the "dumb switch" prematurely. This way you will make hiring decisions based primarily on the facts. Your instincts will be an important part of the interview process, of course, but they should not be the only part, and they should be secondary.

Not flipping your "dumb switch" can be difficult. After interviewing hundreds of candidates over the years, I am still amazed at how some applicants present themselves for an interview. One of the most extreme cases I recall (vividly!) happened about five years ago.

I had an interview scheduled for 10:00 a.m. The candidate arrived at 10:20.

A Disclaimer: *Before I go any further, I wish to go on record as stating that I am not biased against those who are, for whatever reasons, calorically-challenged. So if, dear reader, you happen to be a little zaftig, please do not take this personally.*

To continue . . . When the interviewee entered my office, I was taken aback. She had curlers in her hair. She was dressed in ragged cut-off jean shorts and a tank top that was roughly three sizes too small, thus clearly revealing the fact that she had nothing on beneath it. Did I mention that she must have weighed at least 350 pounds? To maintain my professional composure, to say nothing of not flipping my "dumb switch," I summoned the strength of Goliath. It was clear that she did not want the job. If this is how she presented herself in an interview setting, one only knows how she would have dressed for my customers. Suffice it to say, it is an image that will be forever burned into my retina.

My final thought on recruiting is to never let your ego stand in your way. Don't be afraid to hire people who may have strengths superior to your own in some areas. If anything, make an effort to find those people and hire them. Who cares if you don't always get the credit? You own the company. In the end, the mantle for success or failure will fall on you.

> ***"First-rate people hire first-rate people; second-rate people hire third-rate people."***
>
> Leo Rosten

Retention

Now that you have found them, you need to keep them. If you follow the People First Philosophy (See Chapter 6), you're already about 90 percent of the way toward achieving a good retention rate of your employees. Remember the order of priorities:

1. Employees
2. Customers
3. Profitability

Beyond this guiding philosophy, there are a multitude of things you can do to reduce turnover within your organization. But first, let's discuss the top reasons employees leave.

According to research conducted by the *Harvard Business Review*, the top reasons, in order of priority, that people leave their jobs are:

1. Job content
2. Level of responsibility

3. Company culture (i.e., they feel underappreciated)
4. Caliber of colleagues
5. Salary

Not surprisingly, of the hundreds of people I have asked, the majority believes that money is the number one reason people leave their jobs. Yet in almost every survey, money ranks fourth or fifth down the list.

One of the best retention methods is to evaluate each of the top reasons and proactively take steps to address these concerns before they arise. Let's further define each of the top five reasons shown in the *Harvard Business Review* research results.

Job Content

The job may no longer be interesting to the employee or, at the other end of the spectrum perhaps it has become too stressful and difficult. Employees need to have enough to keep them busy, but not so much they constantly feel overwhelmed and stressed out. Is the work challenging and rewarding? If it isn't, burnout can occur quickly. Are there opportunities for the employee to learn new things? Does the job involve a great many monotonous tasks? If so, are there ways to break up that monotony?

Level of Responsibility

Are you demanding too much or too little from the employee based on their level of experience or skill? Are they ready for more responsibilities, or have you already given them too many? Don't fall victim of the Peter Principle.

Introduced by author Laurence Peter, the Peter Principle characterizes the Catch-22 of bureaucratic organizations. In essence, people tend to be promoted up to their level of incompetence. A new employee starting at the lower ranks of an organization who proves they can handle the tasks assigned to them continually gets promoted up the ranks until they reach a level where they are no longer effective. There is a fine line between giving too much and just enough responsibility to your employees. If you have not given them enough, they may find their work boring and no longer challenging or rewarding. If you have given them too much, they might find themselves in over their heads. Either way, they may be inclined to leave.

Company Culture

This is where our People First Philosophy comes in. If your company culture is pro-employee, your employees will feel they are respected and appreciated.

Create an effective employee recognition program. Celebrate the major holidays with them, recognize employment anniversary dates, and show them how much they are appreciated, especially for work above and beyond the call. Get involved in their lives. If you can, help them with their problems — personal or work-related. Show them you are interested in them and that you will always be available to help in any way you can.

Many owners and managers are apprehensive about doing this. Many feel they already have enough problems of their own. Having to deal with their employees' personal problems as well would take the meaning of aggravation to a whole new level. What they don't realize is that, one way or another, they will be dealing with those problems because unresolved personal issues almost always integrate themselves into the employee's work life.

I remember an employee who came to me after only six weeks on the job. She was part-time and earning less than $150 per week. Timidly, she walked into my office and said she needed to talk to me. She was in a predicament that involved her home, and the only way out was going to cost her $800, which she did not have. She was embarrassed that she had come to me, but she had no place else to turn. Without the $800 she was going to lose her house. I should mention that she had been with the company only for a short time and the advance she needed was large compared to her average weekly earnings. I should also mention that our company had only been open for a year and a half, and money was still tight. Moreover, the problem with payroll advances is that an employee could take the advance and hit the road, and if that happens, you can generally kiss your money good-bye. I knew it would be a tremendous gamble, especially on an employee who had been with the firm for such a short time. But I wanted to find a way to help, even though, as I explained to her, it was company policy not to give employee advances during the first 90-day introductory period. We discussed the possibility of collateral, and as it turns out, she had a late-model van that was paid off. She brought the title in for me to hold and I wrote her a check for $800. Four months later, she had paid every penny of it back. She turned out to be one of the hardest-working and most loyal employees we have ever had. Again, don't be like so many employers and demand respect from your employees because you'll never get it that way. Instead, earn it!

Another thing that will create a team environment and establish a positive culture in your company is to give your employees a feeling of ownership in the company. This doesn't mean you have to give every employee an equity interest in the company. It means making sure they feel as much a part of the team as anyone else — including you, as the owner.

Have an open-book philosophy when it comes to your financial situation. Any employee who wants to see the company's financial statements should always be more than welcome to do so. Any big decisions our company needs to make are first discussed with our employees. In addition, we are always asking for employee feedback on how well we are doing. Evaluations should be a two-way street. We also have something called the Bright Idea form. We pay employees a bonus for any ideas they submit that we ultimately use. The bottom line is, we have created an environment where our employees feel as if they work *with* us rather than *for* us.

Just look around the world: even the way countries are governed has changed dramatically over the past hundred years. Dictatorships continually fall throughout the world, and democracies replace them. The walls are literally coming down, yet managers at thousands of companies still cling to a dictatorial, authoritarian or autocratic style, which creates an "us vs. them" mentality that is not as conducive to teamwork. Managers who take this approach may feel their subordinates obey them out of respect, when in fact it's usually out of fear. A democratic management style promotes growth and teamwork. This does not mean that situations may not arise when a more autocratic style is necessary. A true leader takes on that style when decisive actions must be taken quickly to ensure that everyone pulls together in the same direction.

One final comment: Make sure the loyalty your employees show to you and the company is mutual. As your company grows more successful and you have more cash to work with, you may be tempted to replace lower-skilled employees with those with higher skills. Think long and hard about this decision. Evaluate all the ways under which you can keep all of your employees. Analyze their strengths. There may be other places in the company where an employee could work, perhaps in a different capacity, which allows both the employee and the company to continue growing.

In short, "Dance with the girl [or boy] that brung ya!"

> ***"You can make more friends in two months by becoming interested in other people than you can in two years by trying to get other people interested in you."***
>
> Dale Carnegie

Caliber of Colleagues

Being part of a winning team is very important to winners. The best employees want to be around other great employees. The worst working environment for a motivated, positive go-getter is to be stuck in a lackluster group. They don't put up with it for very long. Hire right every time, and you will substantially reduce the possibility of anyone leaving due to the caliber of his or her colleagues.

Salary

If your employees' salaries are competitive with what is dictated by the rest of the market, then most salary concerns will be based more on perception than reality. Both the owner and the employee need to perceive the exchange of time for money as an equitable transaction. These perceptions can be created by many factors, most of which are internal: i.e., employees comparing their pay to that of other employees within the organization.

While I prefer a base salary to ensure that employees have some stability in their lives, I have always tried to combine it with bonuses or other forms of compensation and to somehow tie all or part of those bonuses to both individual performance and overall profitability of the company. Let's compare a straight salary to a compensation package that includes bonuses for individual performance. If you paid two employees who have similar positions in the company a similar salary even though one of the two employees always seemed to go the extra mile, that employee might become discouraged and question why they work so much harder than the fellow employee. By establishing a compensation package that factors in individual performance, you will reward those employees who put in the extra effort, and, hopefully, motivate the others who always seem to do the minimum work required. However, you must be very fair about how you evaluate this individual performance. If it becomes standard operating procedure that everyone gets the bonus, then there is no point in having the bonus. You're still not rewarding the best employees above and beyond the rest of the staff. Finally, by adding the element of company profitability, this will, in effect, put the employee in the same boat with you. Let them experience some of the same pleasure — and pain — as the owner. When things are going well, they make more money. When things are not going as well, they don't earn as much. This will also help keep down unnecessary expenses, as employees will begin to relate expenses that may be under their control to their own earnings.

To summarize, the best way to resolve a problem is to avoid it in the first place. By evaluating the reasons people usually leave companies and then proactively addressing those areas ahead of time, you should enjoy a much higher than normal employee retention rate. Be realistic in your expectations. No matter how well you treat your employees, some of them may still leave — on good terms or bad. There is no way to completely avoid this, but you can learn from it.

"If you pay peanuts, you get monkeys."

James Goldsmith

Exit Interviews

There can be many advantages to Exit Interviews. If there are downsides to them, I don't know what they would be. Yet, if structured Exit Interviews are one of your standard operating procedures for every employee who leaves, your company is in the minority. Most small business owners do not conduct Exit Interviews.

Here are just a few of the advantages.

- You may find you can resolve whatever problem the employee has and ultimately retain them.
- You may discover problems that you have not addressed and reduce the possibility of losing future employees for the same reason or reasons.
- You may rectify a potential litigation that could have resulted had you not discussed the issue with the employee before he or she left.
- You may be alerted to problems that you did not know existed, particularly problems with other employees.
- You may be able to repair any damage that would have caused the employee to leave with the proverbial "bad taste in their mouth," which, in turn, may have caused them to speak disparagingly about your company in the future.

To create an open and trusting environment during the Exit Interview, the employee must know that you agree to hold in confidence any information they disclose to you. This is particularly important with regard to not sharing what is said during an Exit Interview with other employees. Also, you must not disagree or place any blame on them. Make it clear that what you want is an honest and candid perspective. Although it will be difficult, you must remain objective. If, after uncovering the facts, you feel you would still like to retain the employee, then tell them you hate to see them leave and ask them to stay. Be the bigger person. Apologize whenever you can. Explain that you will be committed to making an effort to resolve their concerns. Then ask them to reconsider.

On many surveys, one of the more popular reasons employees list for leaving a company is, "Nobody asked me to stay."

Now there's food for thought.

Chapter 17

Dialing in Your Business

"It takes only one individual to provide vision, but it takes a team effort to achieve it."

Jeff Gordon

I am a big NASCAR fan. Fortunately, Kris and my children enjoy it, too, so four or five times a year we make a beeline for wherever a race is being held that weekend.

I recently tried the Richard Petty Driving Experience. If you have never heard of this and you enjoy racing, you are missing out on an experience of a lifetime. When you arrive, they put you in a uniform. After about an hour of training and a drivers' meeting, they strap you into a NASCAR Nextel Cup stock car for a total of 30 exciting laps. Is it a real stock car you might ask? I did. The cars that you drive are virtually identical to those you see each weekend, except for the engine. The difference is revving up a 600 HP engine compared to the 750 HP of those in the actual NASCAR series. Don't worry, though, 600 HP is more than enough to scare the wits out of most people. You then fly out of the pits ready to take your first 10 laps. There is no one in the car with you — it is just you and the car. You follow a professional race driver in a car that seems to be no more than 10 to 15 yards in front of you. Given the speeds at which you are traveling, this is enough to get your heart pounding. After 10 laps, they bring you back in for another drivers' meeting to go over areas that you can improve. Then they send you out to the track again for 10 more laps. You're allowed to increase your lap speeds with each 10-lap segment provided it looks as though you have been following all of their directions. The final 10 laps are the most exhilarating, as you reach your fastest lap speeds. After everyone is done they bring you back in for the Closing Ceremony, where you receive your lap-time sheet and graduation certificate. My fastest average lap speed was just a little over 158 mph, which means that in the straightaways I was probably reaching top speeds of close to 170 to 175 mph. Talk about exciting! As they were handing out the lap-time sheets to all the other drivers, they left the top four or five fastest drivers until the end. I could feel my ego building, as the last few names were being called and I had not yet heard my name. For a minute, it looked as though I was going to be the Number 1 or 2 fastest of the day. Sure enough, I got my certificate as the second fastest.

Then it was time to call up the king of the day — the driver with the fastest average lap speed. The name was called, and up walked a petite teenage girl. She was deemed the fastest of the day and got a certificate to prove it. One could almost hear the "macho" wafting from the room. And, once again, I was reminded of the truth in that old adage: Never judge a book by its cover.

In recent years, auto racing has become as much a science as it is an art and a skill. This is particularly true in NASCAR, which has undergone dramatic changes over the past two or three decades.

There are four major components to an auto racing team.

1. The Driver
2. The Car
3. The Pit Crew
4. The Team Owner

If any one component is not doing their job, it can mean the difference between winning or picking up the twisted wreckage that would be left over. Many times the members of the pit crew are the unsung heroes of a race. Any NASCAR driver will tell you that there is no way they will get a top-five finish without a top-notch pit crew. Each pit crew has their own "tricks of the trade" for dialing in a car. Dialing in a car refers to the driver and crew communicating what is happening on the track, after which the crew makes slight setup adjustments to achieve the car's optimum handling characteristics. The pit crew also has the job of getting the car out of the pits as fast as humanly possible. The difference of only tenths of a second can mean that a driver gains or loses up to three or four positions on the track. The pit crew will play a major role in winning or losing a race, and it usually comes down to the most minor adjustments they made in dialing in the car and the few tenths of a second they saved in the pits.

> *"Racing is a team sport. . . . I like to talk about our 'team IQ' — because none of us is as smart as all of us."*
>
> Ray Evernham

So what does all this have to do with your business? Regardless whether you are talking about a successful racing team or a successful management team for your business, both need to have the best people working in conjunction with everyone else on the team. Any weak areas in the team will drag the entire team down to that level.

1. The Driver = The Salespeople. The people who drive the revenues of the business.
2. The Car = The Business. The vehicle in which you generate revenues and profit.
3. The Pit Crew = The Operational Staff. Those who maintain and grow the business.
4. Team Owner = The Business Owner. The person who keeps each component working together and ensures that they have everything they need to move the business forward.

We've spent a good deal of this book talking about "The Car" — the actual business itself — and "The Driver" — the sales and marketing component of your business. We also talked about the "Team Owner," which would be you, the business owner. What we have not discussed in as much detail yet is "The Crew," the operational side of the business. Unfortunately, to get too involved in that subject would be a book in its self. So instead, I will dedicate this chapter to what I will refer to as the "tricks of the trade." These are things I have discovered over the years and have applied to my own business. Most of these tricks of the trade focus on the operational side of the business. Many of these tricks might be considered minor points to some business owners and certainly not revolutionary thinking, but I'm not trying to convince you that you need to revolutionize how businesses are operated. Instead, by just applying these little tricks of the trade, making slight adjustments and "dialing in" your business, you may be surprised just how much faster and more effectively you'll be driving your business and the number of positions you will gain against your competition.

> ***"Sometimes when I consider what tremendous consequences come from little things, I am tempted to think there are no little things."***
>
> Bruce Barton

Pricing

Don't be afraid of asking the right price. You may be surprised to learn that a large percentage of new business owners are afraid of the prices they have established for their products or services. Usually they feel they have priced themselves too high. Not only can this trickle down subconsciously to potential customers, who then also become concerned about your pricing, it also can be devastating to your business's profitability. You have to decide whether you want to be the cheapest or the best. You can't be both. Being the best doesn't necessarily mean that you have to also be the most expensive. Ideally, if you can price yourself just below the highest competitor in the market, you will have a competitive advantage. The majority of people don't like to buy the cheapest or the most expensive; instead, they like to buy from the companies that are priced somewhere in the middle. Now, don't get me wrong. There are people who will only buy the cheapest, and there are those who will always buy the most expensive, even when the most expensive is not the best. Many people have a tendency to distinguish the most expensive as the highest quality, and that is not always true. To set prices for any given product or service, I prefer to use a cost-based pricing formula whenever possible. There are several benefits to cost-based pricing.

1. It's an easy way to price products and services.
2. It's fair and equitable to both the customer and the business.
3. It's easy to consistently recheck your pricing to verify that you are maintaining the desirable profit margin.
4. It gives your company more stability than other pricing methods.
5. It guarantees a specific level of profitability, provided you stay within your budget.

While cost-based pricing is one of the simplest pricing strategies, it is still far too complex and dull to address in this book. I would recommend consulting with a competent accountant to assist you in developing the pricing for your particular product or service.

OPM

What do people like Donald Trump and Bill Gates have in common, outside of being wealthy? They understand the principle of OPM, which stands for Other People's Money or otherwise known as Leverage. Smart businesspeople who seem to have all the money in the world rarely ever use much of their own money to do business deals. They understand that no matter how much they are worth, it is still much less than the pool of money and resources they can amass by involving large groups of other people. While OPM in the form of venture capital or even bank financing is more often used for generating additional working capital to further grow your business, there may be other ways you can creatively use OPM. For instance, when I started my company I looked long and hard at how I could benefit my business through the principle of OPM. My solution? I designed my billing policy around having the customers pay for the service in advance of the service being performed. This way I could use their funds to cover most of my expenses even before I had incurred them, rather than the traditional method of getting paid after the services were performed. If I had done the latter, it would have required a much larger amount of working capital to float the expenses until the customer finally paid me. While there were a few minor disadvantages of setting up my company in this fashion, the advantages far out weighed the disadvantages. Keep in mind that it may not always be possible to do it this way. I was fortunate enough to be entering an industry in its infancy, and standards or generally accepted practices of that industry had not yet been formed in the minds of potential customers. So when I said that payment needed to be made prior to the service being performed, I was essentially setting the standard, and it did not send up red flags to potential customers because they had little to compare us to. Most competitors that entered the industry at a later time followed suit and asked for payment in advance of the service being performed. It would not be as easy to enter an industry that is highly competitive and well-established and go against the grain and ask for advance payment when all of your competitors allow it to be made afterwards. Keep in mind though that I only said "not as easy." I did not say impossible. Many years ago, when I was in the home improvement business, I would give cash discounts for payment in full prior to the job's even being started. I would back up the work with a comprehensive guarantee and had built enough trust with the customer that often they would pay for the entire job before it was ever started, or at least would provide a substantial down payment, which was not typical of the industry. The home improvement business is well established and I was going completely against the grain, but many times it boils down to trust. Establish enough of it and people will go outside the set standards. Keep in mind, however, that when someone has put that much trust in you, you better not blow it. It is even more imperative that you make them ecstatic about their purchase throughout the entire process.

Proactive vs. Reactive

If you have heard the word "proactive" once in the business world you have heard it a thousand times. The word "proactive" has become a cliché. Everyone seems to throw it around an awful lot, even when they aren't actually doing it. To be proactive simply means to strategically plan and act in advance of an expected problem or difficulty in an effort to diffuse the problem or eliminate it altogether. Alternatively, a reactive approach would be one of dealing with problems or difficulties after they occur. Many small business owners, unfortunately, take the reactive approach, usually not by choice; it just seems that things turn out that way. Lack of time is the most popular excuse. They may say they don't have enough time to permanently fix the problem, so they go day in and day out fighting fires. The best way to resolve problems is not to have them in the first place. Keep your eyes and ears open for areas that are likely to cause problems in the near future and make it a point to deal with them before they actually turn into problems. It is infinitely easier and less aggravating to resolve a potential problem than it is to resolve an actual one.

> ***"When it comes to fighting fires in business, sometimes you just have to put the hose down and instead go take the matches away from the guy who is starting all the fires."***
>
> Jerry L. Clum, Jr.

To-Do Lists

"The key is not to prioritize what's on your schedule, but to schedule your priorities."

STEPHEN R. COVEY

By nature, I am a disorganized person. Most people, other than Kris, would probably not say I am so disorganized. I have to work hard to at least appear organized. I have found that the best method is to use a To-Do List. It doesn't have to be fancy. You don't even need to use one of those high-tech PDA's (Personal Data Assistants). Quite frankly, a piece of ruled paper and a pen is all I have ever used. Anytime something comes up that I need to remember to do it goes on my To-Do List. I also have a system of prioritizing the list to ensure that the hottest issues get done first. In one day I may cross off 30 items and add 50 more, but chances are if I didn't use the list I would certainly forget at least one of those 50 things that had come up. Don't clutter your mind with a lot of useless information. Keep your mind free to think instead of having to remember all the dozens of things that have to get done. Albert Einstein was once asked what his telephone number was, and instead of rattling it off from memory, he simply walked over, picked up a phone book and looked it up. The man who asked him was astonished that one of the most intelligent people on earth didn't even know his own phone number. When questioned, Mr. Einstein simply said, "I never bother to clutter my mind by memorizing things that can instead easily be looked up." While this example may be a little extreme, the idea still sounds pretty reasonable to me. You will feel a lot less stressed and at least appear to be more organized by using a daily To-Do List.

Focus

In a previous chapter, I credited burnout as one of the top four reasons that businesses fail. A loss of focus would at least make it in the top five. Many times burnout itself will be the cause for a loss of focus. An owner gets tired and burned out working endless hours as they are trying to grow a successful business, and their mind begins to wander to all the easier ways they might be able to make a living. They may remember the great business opportunity they saw on an infomercial the night before, when they weren't able to sleep, and they start visualizing themselves being successful in that new business. People sometimes have a way of talking themselves out of success rather than into it. I'm sure you must know at least one person who, every time you see them, is babbling on about the next new big thing they are getting into. This next new big thing may be number 248 on the list of business opportunities they have tried. The problem is, all they ever do is just try — not hard, and certainly not for long. Don't find yourself getting caught up in this vicious circle. If you travel in circles you will always end up back where you started. Once you have lost focus, you will find yourself just going through the motions, and the enthusiasm, positive attitude, and motivation you once had will be gone. If you do not regain that focus and get your spark back, your ship will sink fast. It is unfortunate when this happens to people, because it usually happens just before their business would have taken off and they would finally have started to realize the rewards for all their hard work.

> *"Most people give up just when they're about to achieve success. They quit on the one-yard line. They give up at the last minute of the game one foot from a winning touchdown."*
>
> H. Ross Perot

You cannot afford to lose focus in your business. If you find yourself having an all-around bad day, and even though you are "there" you aren't really "there," you're usually much better off to leave for the rest of the day and clear your head. Do whatever you have to do so that you can start thinking straight again. When you make a commitment to start a business, don't shortchange yourself, follow it through to the end, whether it be bitter or sweet. There are thousands of business success stories each year that never get told because the owner rewrote the ending by losing focus in their business.

KISS

Human beings are the most intelligent creatures on earth, but there is a drawback. Because we are so smart, we have a tendency to overthink, overanalyze, and overcomplicate almost everything. You certainly have heard of the old KISS principle, which stands for KEEP IT SIMPLE, STUPID, or another variation, KEEP IT SHORT AND SIMPLE. The KISS principle is taught in virtually all structured organizations, including the military, police, government agencies, and hospitals. I almost took the time to define the principle for you — but talk about an oxymoron: if I had spent the time to define it, I would not be following the principle. Another similar condition that may affect some small business owners is what we will refer to as "Analysis-Paralysis." This happens when you spend so much time analyzing a particular situation that you never implement the solution. Results only occur from action, not analyzing. When all else fails, sometimes you have to go with your gut.

> *"Follow your instincts. That's where true wisdom manifests itself."*
>
> Oprah Winfrey

Just don't overcomplicate your business. A great book that describes this principle excellently is entitled *Who Moved My Cheese*, by Spencer Johnson. It is a quick and delightful read, and it really drives the point home.

Partnerships

You may have considered going into business with another person or even a small group of people. Unfortunately, I have seen too many partnerships such as this just not work out, especially if that person is a good friend or family member (excluding your spouse). Partnerships always start with the best intentions. You may identify your strengths and weaknesses and contemplate the benefits of bringing in someone who has strengths where you have weaknesses. You rationalize that by giving them an equal share of the company, you may not have to pay them much, if anything, when you first get started. It sounds logical and well thought-out. However, whether this is a person you just met, your best friend, or a family member, the chance of the partnership surviving over the long haul is slim. Don't get me wrong: I have seen some partnerships work, but the odds are drastically stacked against you. At some point in time, one or both of the partners may begin to feel that there are inequities in the arrangement. One may feel that they are doing more of the work, or another may feel that they are bearing too much of the financial burden. Ultimately, it puts a strain on the relationship. I would encourage you to avoid partnerships at all costs. Here is one way to think about it. More than half of all marriages in the Untied States end in divorce. This is a relationship built on love and trust. In business partnerships, the relationship is built on time and money. When money is the relationship's primary bond, odds are that successful business partnerships will be even less likely to survive than marriages. There are only two exceptions I would usually make to this rule. The first would be in well-established companies. In bigger companies, you should be better-staffed and more financially independent, so many of the reasons that partnerships erode in small start-up companies have been eliminated by then. The second is when it comes to husband-and-wife teams. You already have a relationship in place that should have far more importance than the business relationship, and the money being used to start and maintain the business would be coming from the same pot. However, if you are considering starting a business with your spouse, you need to be certain that your relationship is rock-solid. If you already have problems in your marriage, then starting a business together may just be adding fuel to the fire.

Business Cycles to Avoid

Some business owners, especially those running small businesses, find themselves operating their business in focused cycles. They may bounce around from one business procedure to another. This week they feel business is low, so they focus on their marketing. The next week they see problems with their staffing levels, so they switch to hiring and interviewing. Then maybe the next week it's scheduling and payroll where they invest their time. Maybe they overhired and now they need more business, so they switch back to marketing. Operating your business in cycles such as this is a reactive approach to growing a business. You are waiting for the problem before you take the action necessary to resolve it. A proactive approach would be more balanced and consistent. You do less of everything, but do it more often. You are always marketing, always recruiting, always thinking ahead on your scheduling, etc. Break down each of your business activities by day, instead of by the week or month. You are marketing even when you don't need business, so you'll never "need" business. You are recruiting when you don't need employees, so you never need employees. Eventually, you will want to bring on the staff necessary and make these separate functions their full-time jobs.

Don't Put All Your Eggs in One Basket

Allowing any one customer to become the majority share of your business can have serious negative consequences. I have seen several businesses actually go out of business for this reason alone. Besides the fact that it is a huge risk to your business's success, you give the customer too much leverage. Ultimately, you may find yourself stuck in a corner having to make further bad business decisions to retain the customer. Ideally, you should never allow one customer, client, or entity to become more than one-third of your business book. This can become a challenging problem you'll have to deal with, but it does need to be dealt with sooner rather than later.

Serve Your Customers

"The purpose of business is to create and keep a customer."
Peter Drucker

Serve your customers well, or your competition will. It amazes me how much we hear about customer service, yet when push comes to shove, we rarely see outstanding customer service in the majority of our own purchases. Untrained employees, undertrained employees, lack of appreciation, policies that seem to be anti-customer, careless attitudes, bad attitudes, voice mail and automated phone menus that make you feel as though you have fallen into a black hole. Does anyone care anymore? The worst part to all of this is that providing good customer service can be one of the easy parts of the entire sales process. Want to be ahead of 90 percent of your competition? Simply keep your promises and return calls quickly, and it is likely you will be. According to a Nielsen study, there are six reasons that you will lose customers:

- 68 percent are dissatisfied with the attitude of one of your employees
- 14 percent are dissatisfied with the quality of merchandise
- 9 percent say your prices are too high
- 5 percent make other business contacts
- 3 percent move
- 1 percent of customers die

The biggest reason companies lose existing customers is because of the attitude of one employee. Yet we have a tendency to put so much focus on our prices or our quality. It is your employees and, of course, you, the owner, who sets the tone for everyone else.

It amazes me how much emphasis many companies put on finding new customers compared to how much they focus on retaining the ones they already have. Generally, it costs six times more to win a new customer than it does to retain an existing one. The most successful business owners understand this, and they do everything in their power to keep their existing customers. On the other hand, even some of the largest companies haven't seemed to fully recognize this fact. For example, years ago my business was a customer of a large long distance telephone company. To protect their anonymity, we'll just call them AD&D — I certainly wouldn't want anyone to know whom I was talking about. I was fairly happy with my service, but just like everyone else, I would get several calls each month from their competitors offering me every new plan under the sun. Usually, I would ignore these solicitations just because I didn't like the hassle of having to switch, but on one occasion I received a call from Sprint, and their offer was just too good to refuse. The rate they offered was less than half the rate that AD&D was charging me, so I decided it was time to make the switch. Remember, business people usually only make decisions to change suppliers or vendors based on one of two major reasons, pain or profit. Either they are having a great deal of problems with their current supplier or vendor, or they discover that they will save enough that it is worthwhile to change. In my case, the savings were going to translate into about $5,000 a year in long distance charges, so my decision was strictly based on profit. After only a few weeks with Sprint, I began receiving an enormous number of marketing calls from AD&D asking me to come back. In addition, they would send checks for me to sign and cash, which would automatically flip my service back over to AD&D. The bribery didn't work, nor did the calls. On one such call the representative asked how much Sprint was charging me. I told them it was less than half what they had been charging me. The representative went on to say they would be willing to beat that rate. An interesting discussion pursued after that disclosure. Here is roughly how our conversation went:

AD&D Rep: "Mr. Clum, we really want your business back. We would be willing to beat Sprint's rate and come down to X cents per minute."

Me: "So, do I understand you correctly? You can actually drop your rate by that much, give me the same service as before, and beat Sprint's price?"

AD&D Rep: "We certainly can. We want to do whatever we can to retain our customers and give them the best-quality service in the industry."

Me: "So, if I understand you correctly, what you are telling me is that you can provide the same service I was getting, at less than half the cost, and the amazing thing is that you think by telling me you have essentially been ripping me off and over-charging me by more than double what you had to over the last three years, that is supposed to make me happy and make me want to come back to do more business?"

That was pretty much the end of our conversation. His computer screen that contained scripted rebuttals to customers' objections must not have listed that objection. It amazes me how some companies do business. For three years, not only was I a customer, but obviously a very profitable one, since they were charging me more than double what they needed to. In all that time, I never received one phone call asking me how I liked their service or whether there was anything they could do for me, but almost instantaneously when I left them as a customer, the phone calls and letters started arriving to get me back. Had this company put more emphasis on customer relations and retention, I wonder how much better off they would have been. For instance, at any time during that three-year period, had they simply called and said, "Mr. Clum, I believe we have a program that could save you 35 percent compared to what you are currently paying, and we would like to put you on that program," it is doubtful that I later would have switched to another carrier even if they were able to offer a little more in savings. For one reason, I would know that AD&D was truly looking out for my best interest by voluntarily reducing their rates when they could.

I'm sure that you run into examples like this every day. Most business owners are guilty of doing this at some time. There is a certain level of excitement you experience when getting a new customer, and that has a tendency to skew your thinking. For example, when you come back into your office and see that you have five messages, four of them are from existing customers and one is from a potential new customer. The tendency is to pick up the phone and immediately call that new potential customer, because we want more business. While it may feel logical, let me give you a better method of doing business. Call the existing customers back first and take care of their needs. I'm not saying you should put the potential new customer off indefinitely; instead, simply adjust your priorities a bit. If you take care of your existing customers better than anyone else would, you will never have to worry about getting new customers because your company's name will be gold. Everyone will want to do business with you.

Sam Walton of Wal-Mart fame certainly understood the importance of customer service. Mr. Walton opened his first store in 1962. A little more than 40 years later, the company has more than 3,500 Stores, Supercenters and Sam's Clubs worldwide. They have become the number-one retailer in the world, with annual net sales of almost a quarter of a trillion dollars! That is almost too hard to comprehend. We're talking about almost $250 billion dollars in annual sales! That is equal to nearly $1,000 in sales for every man, woman and child in America. Obviously, they are doing something right. Sam Walton had a simple list of rules when it came to customer service:

CUSTOMER SERVICE RULES

Rule #1: The customer is always right!

Rule #2: If the customer happens to be wrong, refer to Rule # 1.

Top 25 Suggestions for the Best Customer Service

If you want to get an edge on your competition and maybe even dominate them, then implement as many of these top 25 suggestions as possible into your business. If you are successful at making these suggestions a part of your company's culture, your business will likely grow beyond your wildest dreams.

1. Your telephone should always be answered by a (live) person who is capable of answering questions or at least efficient at putting customers in contact with someone else who can. (*Note:* I am not holding my breath waiting for this to be reintroduced as standard business practice, but there is an ancient Russian Proverb: Hope Dies Last.) Voice mails should only be used in the worst-case scenario and during times outside normal business hours. Callers should not have to go through the endless black hole of automated menus or be passed off to voice mail as the standard operating procedure.

2. You have to have a passion for customer service. It has to be part of the culture you set up for your company and for every employee in your company.

3. Open earlier and close later than your competition.

4. Always return calls within the same day, or the next business day if the message was left on a weekend, holiday, or evening. Just making the commitment to do this will make your company better than 90 percent of your competition.

5. Under-promise and over-deliver. I'm sure you have heard this before, but if you live by it you will be well ahead of your competition.

6. Tell it like it is. Don't be deceptive. Honesty really is the best policy.

7. Take a customer's concerns seriously, no matter how trivial they may sound. Do whatever it takes to ensure their satisfaction, even if it means taking a loss. The only exception to this is when a customer is demanding something that far exceeds reality.

8. Never tell a customer that something is company policy. There are certainly better ways to tactfully explain things,

but the average person cares less what your policy is; they just want their problem resolved.

9. You should never be too busy to talk to a customer, nor should you even look, act, or imply that you are too busy. The whole point to being in business in the first place is to serve the customer, so no one should ever be too busy to help the customer. If a customer feels as though they are bothering you or one of your employees, something is not right.

10. Train, retrain, and then train your employees again when it comes to their jobs and the importance of the customer. There should be little customer contact until the employee understands their job completely. Even then, when something comes up that they are uncertain about, they need to physically accompany the customer, whenever possible, to a person with the answer.

11. Hire the right employees in the first place. A thorough screening and interviewing process is critical. Competent employees will do more to bolster great customer service than anything else.

12. Offer solutions instead of excuses. There is nothing worse than having to rehash the problem over and over again and hear another person trying to make excuse after excuse. Does anyone really want to hear these excuses? Does it make anyone feel better other than maybe the person making the excuses? Take responsibility and ensure that you will resolve the concern. "I'm sorry we haven't taken care of your needs, please allow me the opportunity to resolve this for you. What can we do to try and make this a better experience for you?" Those two sentences can change an upset customer almost instantly.

13. Pay attention to the details. They will make your company stand out from everyone else.

14. Thank your customers every chance you get. You can never thank your customers enough. This is one of Kris's biggest pet peeves. Every morning for nearly a year, Kris would stop by the drive-thru of a fast-food restaurant to pick up her morning caffeine. Every morning the same employee would take her money and give her the change and hand her the drink. My wife would take the drink and say "Thank you." Without a word uttered by the employee, the drive-thru window would close. Every day Kris would get more annoyed that this person would barely acknowledge her existence, let alone do something as easy as thanking her for her business. Kris made it her personal crusade to impress the importance of good customer service upon this fast-food employee. Every morning the same ritual would take place, but now just before the employee closed the window, Kris would say, "You're welcome." She continued this each and every day, only varying the volume at which she said the words, "You're welcome." After several weeks, and at the point that she was almost screaming the words, "You're welcome!" the employee handed out the drink, looked at Kris and in a soft-spoken, but clear voice said, "Thank you." It has been more than a year later, and the employee never forgets to say thank you to every customer who comes through the drive-thru. Don't allow your business ever to get to the point that your customers have to be the ones who train your employees on customer service.

15. Empower every employee with the responsibility and power to serve the customer. No one should ever say to a customer, "I'm sorry, that's not my job."

16. Ensure that the necessary systems are in place to exceed the expectations of the customer — not *meet* their expectations, but *exceed* them. You go to a restaurant and the manager comes out and says to you, "Is everything okay?" Is that good customer service? Well, since it

happens so rarely, you might be apt to say that it is, but if you analyze that question you might think differently. "Okay" really only refers to the minimum level of acceptability. Do we really want to know that we met only their minimum level? Strive to exceed it.

17. Learn from your past mistakes and continue to improve on your customer service program.

"Your most unhappy customers are your greatest source of learning."

Bill Gates

18. Create a Mission Statement that supports your customer service expectations, and then fulfill that mission.
19. Have a legitimate customer survey program that uses customer comment cards, surveys or toll-free feedback lines. Ensure that the results cannot be skewed. To make improvements, you have to know the facts, not just what you want to hear.
20. Realize and expect that most customers are a little cynical these days. Quite frankly, as customers, we expect we are going to have problems because that is what we are use to. By understanding this, you can empathize with the customer and not be so quick to defend yourself. Impress them with action instead of with words.
21. Repairs and service calls should be met with a strong sense of urgency. Exact times need to be given to customers whenever possible, and those times should be met.
22. Create the best guarantees or warranties in the industry then stand behind them.
23. Make it easy for people to do business with you. Eliminate the stress and as much paperwork as possible.

24. Create customer service guidelines and make them a vital part of your Operations Manual, Employee Manuals, and employee training. Have clear-cut penalties in place for those employees who fall below your customer service guidelines. Alternatively, have rewards and incentives in place for those who go above and beyond your guidelines for excellent customer service.

25. When you have to deliver bad news it may be possible to defuse the situation through the use of humor, but be careful, as it can backfire. Delivering bad news is never fun, but if you have one of those personalities that can usually get away with more than most people can, using a little humor can break up the tension. Not long ago, I was sitting at an airport waiting for my flight to board. At the gate next to me, the people waiting were growing weary. They had incurred three delays for their Delta flight to Atlanta due to weather, and they were already more than fours hours delayed at this point. The captain for their flight came out and went up to the counter to make an announcement. He said, "I have some good news and some bad news. First the bad news. We are being notified that our flight will be delayed by another 45 minutes." Amidst the grumbles and growls of everyone waiting, he continued, "Unfortunately, the weather is just not cooperating with us, and we are doing everything we can to get this flight off as soon as possible. Now for the good news: I just saved a bunch of money on my car insurance." At the precise moment he said that, the entire room went from scowling to laughing. The tension on everyone's faces just seemed to vanish. Of course, they certainly weren't happy about their fourth delay, but that captain turned bad news into something that immediately made the mood of the room more positive.

It seems as though true customer service is hard to find these days. Implement these suggestions, make customer service one of the major priorities of your business, and you will have a competitive advantage that will be difficult to beat.

> *"A business absolutely devoted to service will have only one worry about profits. They will be embarrassingly large."*
>
> Henry Ford

Chapter 18

Business Blackjack

I like to think that I have few vices. I sometimes enjoy unhealthy foods, I like a cold beer on a hot day, and I love to play blackjack. Over the past 15 years I have been to Las Vegas 18 times, Windsor, Canada, four times, Monte Carlo once, cruise ship casinos four times, various river boats about nine times, and Indian reservation casinos twice. That comes to 38 times. Am I a glutton for punishment, you might ask? Fortunately, I have had good luck at the casinos, more specifically at the blackjack tables, which is the only game I play. I have come home a winner 28 of those 38 times, a real big winner six times, and a real big loser only twice, knock on wood. I've tried every system in existence, but have found that a combination of several systems has worked the best for me. Again, there is no one magic bullet, but instead a good recipe for success. I recently had a conversation with a Casino Host at one of the well-known Las Vegas casinos. I was not surprised to hear her say that a large percentage of her biggest clients are entrepreneurs. What is the correlation? Are all entrepreneurs inherently gamblers? Not really. That is probably one of the biggest myths today about entrepreneurs. Sure, they take risks, and those risks may be larger than many people are willing to take. They might have everything they own on the line, but most entrepreneurs will only take calculated risks in their businesses. In many cases, their confidence level is so high they won't even admit they are taking much of a risk.

An interesting story I heard years ago was about a man named Fred, who started a business in the early 1970s. Even though it was a great concept based entirely on filling a niche where major supply and demand problems existed, and even though Fred was able to raise the largest amount of venture capital money in history at the time, the company still floundered near bankruptcy. Within the first two years it had gotten to the point where Fred had used up just about every bit of credit he could get his hands on. The end was drawing near for his company when his payroll was coming due and he did not have the cash to cover it. Fred took what was probably his last $200 and flew to Las Vegas. After many hours on the blackjack tables he parlayed that $200 into more than $26,000, flew back to his office, and made his payroll. While this may seem like a risky thing to do, Fred probably felt he didn't have much to lose at that point, and frankly, he was not one to leave any stone unturned. You probably have heard of ol' Fred, but if you haven't, I'm certain you have heard of his company. Fred Smith is the founder of that little company known as FedEx.

In the process of writing this book, I happened to visit a casino in Kansas City, actually twice over a two-day period, both times profiting fairly decently. On the way back to the hotel the second night I had an epiphany: running a successful business is a lot like winning at blackjack. How close are they, really? Compare my seven rules for winning at blackjack to my seven rules for starting and running a successful business. As you will see, they have some close similarities.

JERRY'S 7 RULES OF BLACKJACK

1. Don't play at all if you can't afford to lose. Blackjack can be a very enjoyable game provided you don't lose your perspective, but it is a *game*, and no one has any business gambling away next month's mortgage payment.

2. Pick the right casino, table, and chair. Only play at those casinos that stand on all 17s, including soft 17s. Those that pay 3:2 on blackjacks. Those that allow doubling down after splits. In other words, those casinos that allow blackjack to be played like blackjack and have not stolen all of the advantages from the players. I prefer to play at the third-base position, the last player to act on his/her hand before the dealer. If the table seems rather hot, raise your average bet a little. If it seems impossible to win, go to a different table. If there are others at the table playing amateurishly, for instance, they are splitting 10s or are not hitting 16s when the dealer's up card is a 10, find a new table.

JERRY'S 7 RULES OF BUSINESS

1. Understand that your new business may fail; however, you don't have to take it lying down. You should always give it your all, but realize it's not going to be a cakewalk. If you're not willing to give it 110 percent, then don't start your own business.

2. Pick the right business. Find a business that is not saturated with competition. Do a competitive analysis to make this determination. Perform a market feasibility study to determine whether your business concept will have a good probability of success, and whenever possible, do test marketing before getting in too deep with your new concept. Evaluate the supply and demand trends and pick the niche that is right for you, your market, and the future trends. Use the 15 Item Acid Test to evaluate each of the businesses you have an interest in. Finally, do something you can have a passion for. Remember, it is easy to have passion for something you are passionate about.

Jerry's 7 Rules of Blackjack

3. Ensure that you have the bankroll to play the average bet you intend to make. Use a factor of 40 multiplied by your average bet to determine the necessary bankroll. If your average bet is $10, you should have 40 times this average bet available to play: in other words, $400. This should get you through most of the peaks and valleys of one session.

4. Always use a basic strategy card until you have memorized every possible play. A basic strategy card will tell you exactly when to split and double down, when to hit and when to stand, depending on what the dealer's up card is. For the most part, always stick to the strategy card, but don't be afraid to deviate from it infrequently if you really feel you have a big hunch.

5. Use a card-counting system. While counting cards is not usually considered illegal, most casinos reserve the right to throw you out. Use them at your own

Jerry's 7 Rules of Business

3. Make sure you have the capital necessary to start the business you are considering. This includes initial start-up funds, furniture, equipment and supplies, as well as the on-going working capital necessary to get you through break-even. Don't forget about your own living expenses that you will have to pay until your business starts turning a profit.

4. Have a well-written and comprehensive business and marketing plan to avoid flying by the seat of your pants. Think this plan through and try to come up with as many obstacles as you feel you could run into and the solutions for those obstacles. If you fail to plan, then plan to fail. Stick to your business plan, but be prepared to modify it should it become necessary.

5. Take every advantage you can get. Learn the strengths and weaknesses of your competitors, implement the People First Philosophy, hire the best staff

risk. The most popular is called Hi-Lo. It works like this. All twos, threes, fours, fives, and sixes are counted as a positive one point. Sevens, eights, and nines count as zero. Tens, face cards and aces are negative one point. At the beginning of a new shoe, watch every card that is dealt. Keep a running total in your head by adding or subtracting one point based on each card that is played. This total will either be positive or negative or zero. The more positive it is the more favorable the remainder of the shoe is to you. Raise your bets accordingly; however, never raise more than four times your average bet or you will begin to raise eyebrows from the pit bosses. Start all over again once there is a reshuffle.

available, even if it means paying them more than you may be comfortable paying, maintain a Positive Mental Attitude, create a powerful USP, think outside the box, be chased versus doing the chasing, have a powerful presentation, remember that problems are really opportunities, pay yourself last and plow your profits back into the business, keep your promises, and serve your customers well or your competition will.

---

6. Money management is important. You should know exactly how much you have in front of you at all times. You should never place a bet if you don't have at least four times the amount of that bet on-hand in case you need to double down or split or both.

6. Keep good books. You should always know just exactly how much cash you have on hand and how much you will need in the future. You should be able to quote your current profit margin at any given time, and do not be afraid of pricing your products or services to their true value.

Jerry's 7 Rules of Blackjack

7. Above all, know when to quit. I get up and take a break any time I have lost my original buy-in. I never go back to the wallet during a session and throw good money after bad. I also get up as soon as I have doubled my buy-in. If I'm only off a few dollars from doubling my buy-in, I still get up rather than playing one more hand. Once I have cooled down and I'm no longer as emotional about the money I lost or won, only then will I sit back down at a different table. This is the area that breaks many blackjack players. I've seen tens of thousands of dollars of profits lost back because a player felt they were on an unbreakable winning streak and became greedy.
At some point in time in each session, you'll likely be down, and at other points you'll likely be up. If you always get up when you're ahead, you'll always walk away a winner.

Jerry's 7 Rules of Business

7. Have well-defined and written goals you are working toward. Finally, have an exit strategy. Not only is timing important when it comes to starting a business, it is equally important when it comes to exiting the same business. Remember, he who hesitates is not only lost, but usually miles away from the next exit ramp. All too often, business owners sell for the wrong reasons: sales are down, they lost key people, the competition is getting too strong, markets are getting saturated, they become ill, they are past the point of burn out, they have lost focus in the business, and so on and so forth. Exit when your business is at its peak, not when it becomes a turnaround opportunity. When you go out on top you will definitely go out as a winner.

This is very important! Please do not run off to the nearest casino in an attempt to use my Seven Rules of Blackjack to win the initial start-up capital that you need to begin your business. I included my Seven Rules of Blackjack ONLY to show that having systems and processes is much better than not having them and to draw an interesting comparison to building a business. I do not in any way advocate gambling. I play blackjack for entertainment value. I *never* ever gamble more than I can afford to lose, and I certainly would *never* try to do it to supplement my income in this fashion. Multi-billion dollar casinos are born because of the losers — not the winners! Unless you are already a millionaire and have plenty of cash available to invest in your business, *I suggest you stay out of casinos entirely*. Once your business is fully and completely viable and you're able to enjoy the rewards of your efforts, then you can decide how you like to spend your free time. Until then, I can only make this guarantee. An extra $1,000 properly invested in your business versus being laid down on any gaming table in the world has a much higher probability of a better return on your investment.

> ***"The gambling known as business looks with austere disfavor upon the business known as gambling."***
>
> Ambrose Bierce

Chapter 19

The Sky is the Limit

After you have turned your start-up into a growing business, what now? How do you take your business to the next level? What is the next level? That really depends on two things: where you are currently and where you want to be in the near future. One of the greatest things about growing a business is there really isn't a ceiling to your growth. The sky is the limit. You can become as large and successful as you desire. Maybe you want to open multiple locations around your city, or maybe you have considered expanding nationally. Before we can rule the world and turn that business into an empire, we need to make sure you have totally maximized your business. Benjamin Franklin once said, "A penny saved is a penny earned." When it comes to profitability in business, a penny saved actually translates into more like five pennies earned. For example, if your designed profit margin is 20 percent, then it means that for every $5 worth of revenue you bring in you would net $1 worth of profit. Conversely, every $1 you can save in expenses would be equal to $5 worth of revenues. There may be many things that still can be done to increase your revenues and profitability further before you take your business to the next level.

20 Tips for Increasing Profitability

1. Make it easy for people to do business with you. Accept every payment method that is possible: cash, check, and every credit card you can. If your average sale is a bigger ticket item, you should negotiate with local lenders to arrange a financing program for your potential customers. Get the best possible rates you can, while at the same time, see if you can gain an incentive from the financing company or bank for sending them the business. Many banks and financing companies offer dealer participation programs where you can earn additional profits on the financing portion of the transaction. However, if you participate in such a program, you need to make sure that the overall rate to the customer is extremely competitive compared to what they may be able to arrange on their own. Affordability and convenience should be your goal.

2. Make sure your product or service is priced correctly. You need to remain competitive in the marketplace, but at the same time be certain that your prices truly cover your expenses and overhead while earning a fair and equitable profit. Don't undercut yourself, but on the other hand, don't gouge the customer even if you don't have competition in the marketplace. Sometimes it makes sense to experiment with different price points to see what effect they have on sales. Many times, increasing your price can even increase your sales volume.

3. Stay open longer. It may be possible to spread your staff schedules out over a longer period of the day, giving your business more opportunities to touch potential customers.

4. Initiate a profit-sharing program. By setting aside a percentage of your profitability and using it to reward your

employees, you will allow them to share in the same pain or pleasure of business ownership that you experience. When it comes to maximizing profits, the devil is in the details. Every few pennies you can save can add up to a much higher percentage of profitability, and getting your employees personally aware of this fact can go a long way to increasing your overall profitability.

5. Use up-selling and cross-selling opportunities. Your current customers can be your best new customers. Design programs that will increase your average transaction value, while at the same time giving your customers more value for their money. Sell them more of what you sell and look for other products or services you may be able to sell that will complement your original line. You need to go back to your customers more often and encourage them to do business with you again. This might be accomplished through actions like sending thank you cards, having special events only for past customers, or some sort of customer appreciation program that offers your best customers additional discounts or special offers. It can also be accomplished by initiating a program that rewards your employees a larger commission on those types of transactions where they are able to up-sell or cross-sell additional products or services to the same customers.

6. Create competitive advantages over your competition. This may be in the form of better guarantees, higher quality, and/or more value. You might also consider creating specialty products or services your competitors do not offer.

7. Have someone else look over your numbers. Turn to one of your trusted advisors and have them look over your financials. Something that may be hidden to you could jump off the page for them.

8. Lower the costs of the transaction. Negotiate better prices and terms from your vendors, and make this negotiation and bartering a continued effort, especially as your volume increases. As I said in an earlier chapter, when it comes to negotiating, if you don't hear the word "No" on your first offer, you made the wrong first offer.

9. Create better advertising to get more bang for your buck.

10. Control the amount of overtime you are paying. In most cases, if you are staffed correctly and do a good job with your scheduling, you will be able to reduce your overtime to negligible levels.

11. Find high-volume products or services you can market that will bring in more customers, which in turn will give you more opportunities to sell your higher-margin products and services.

12. Initiate tighter inventory control.

13. Double-check all bills and invoices you receive. It is common to find errors, and more often than not, these errors are not in your favor. Do not get into the habit of just paying invoices without looking them over.

14. Improve your collections. Receivables that are 30, 60, or more days out can wipe out a huge percentage of your profits.

15. Constantly shop your insurance costs. Insurance premiums can vary greatly over time from one vendor to the next. Make it a point to at least shop your rates annually.

16. Analyze each step of your sales and operational process. Determine whether other strategies could be implemented or modified to reduce the costs or increase the sales revenue. Remember the KISS principle, and simplify the process.

17. Train your people well. The more assistance they can provide to customers, the more they will directly increase

the perceived value of your product or service. You will sell more, period.

18. Take a close look at your employees. You may find that some are not being used to their fullest, others may not be working in the area of their strengths, and a few might just be deadweight.

19. Form strategic alliances with other companies and organizations. Not only will this increase the number of customers you can come in contact with, it will provide the perception that you are a more reputable and credible company to do business with.

20. Implement an effective Customer Referral Program.

"Profit in business comes from repeat customers, customers that boast about your product or service, and that bring friends with them."

W. Edwards Deming

Customer Referral Program

Let's expand on that last tip. Generating referrals from existing customers can mean the difference between being super-successful in your business and just being average. Someone who is referred to your business is up to 15 times more likely to do business with you than a cold prospect. Referrals or word-of-mouth advertising, as it is sometimes called, is the least expensive and most productive advertising you can get. Think back over the last couple of dozen buying transactions you have had as a consumer. How many of those salespeople asked you for referrals — a couple of them, at least one of them, or none at all? One of the top skills that separate the master salespeople from the average ones is their ability to generate referrals. The master salespeople successfully get referrals from existing customers. They'll even get referrals from people they presented to but didn't sell to and sometimes from complete strangers. What's their big secret? They ask for them! That may seem a little simplistic, but by simply asking for referrals on a consistent basis you are likely to get 10 times as many referrals as those salespeople who rarely ask. Of course, with an effective Customer Referral Program in place you may be able to double or even triple your success rate. Word of mouth can be the best advertising you will ever get. It can come automatically, without much influence on your part if you are providing a great product or service with a high level of customer service. However, by implementing a strategy and putting together an effective Customer Referral Program, you can actually stimulate that word-of-mouth advertising. One of the best methods of stimulating referrals comes in the form of thank-you cards. Thank-you cards once were a lot more popular than they seem to be now. I guess a lot of business people must feel they are too busy to send them out. A few years back, I ran out of thank-you cards. Normally I have my cards printed up professionally and customized for my business. The printer wasn't going to be able to get me the cards for about a week, so I decided in the interim I would just go buy some generic cards and use them. My logic was that any thank-you card would be better than none at all. I went to one of those big office stores in my area and searched through their aisles. I was surprised to see that they didn't have any thank-you cards. I jumped into my car and went to the second office store, another large chain; again, no cards. I then drove about 30 miles away to yet another large office store where I at least found some individual thank-you cards, but I wasn't able to find them in bulk. I knew they would probably have some at the big discount stores like Wal-Mart, but I was hoping to get a theme that was a little more business related. At first, I was a little angry. How could these stores call themselves office stores? Weren't they supposed to be in the business of selling supplies that you use in your day-to-day business? They had every form of generic invoice and billing statement you could ever want, but no thank-you cards? I even considered writing their corporate offices to let them know how ridiculous it was that they wouldn't sell thank-you cards or at least sell them in boxed bulk quantities, but then I started thinking it through a little bit. I finally convinced myself, if they didn't think it was a big enough seller for them to keep them on their shelves, I'm not going to be the one who complains about it. Why make it any easier for my competitors to use this strategy?

> *"Develop an attitude of gratitude, and give thanks for everything that happens to you, knowing that every step forward is a step toward achieving something bigger and better than your current situation."*
>
> Brian Tracy

It certainly isn't revolutionary thinking to send thank-you cards, but the program I'm recommending to you may be a little more sophisticated than the way most businesses use thank-you cards. Many people assume that thank-you cards are a cliché because everyone sends them. Actually, few businesses send out thank-you cards, and those that do rarely send them out on a regular basis. Generally, the businesses that do send out thank-you cards will send them out to customers once the sale has been consummated, and that will be the only time they send them. I recommend sending them at a much greater frequency, and send them not only to customers but also to vendors, employees, other businesses, or anyone else who helps you along the way.

Seven Events for Sending Out Thank-you Cards

1. Immediately after making the sale.
2. Immediately after delivering the product or service.
3. Anytime a customer compliments you, your staff, your product or service, or your company.
4. Anytime you have followed up with a customer.
5. Anytime you have resolved a problem to a customer's satisfaction.
6. Anytime a customer sends you a referral.
7. Anytime and to anyone who has helped you in any way or to those who went the extra mile for you.

These cards should be relatively small, usually not more than 5" × 4". Keep them simple but elegant. It is better to use cards that are blank on the inside and include a handwritten and short personalized message, no more than three or four lines. It is important to ensure that your message is genuine. Never ask for anything from the recipient in your thank-you card. A card should be sent immediately following one of the Seven Events, no more than 24 hours from when the event took place. I always like to put both the date and the time of day on the note, and I'll use a unique closing rather than "Sincerely" or "Best Regards." This closing would be something that has some common ground with the recipient. When I send thank-you cards or letters to my franchisees, I might use, "Good Selling" as the close. If you keep yourself alert for genuine reasons to send thank-you cards, you will find dozens of opportunities to do so every month. Make it one of your goals to send at least three thank-you cards each week (not necessarily to the same person, but at least three total). How does sending thank-you cards translate into referrals, you might ask? There are two extremely important things one must understand when it comes to getting referrals.

1. Qualified referrals will only come when the person making them feels that you deserve them. If you have done everything else right during the transaction, by being thoughtful enough to take the time to express your appreciation and thanks to that person you will set your company apart not only from your competition, but also from almost any other businesses that person does business with.

2. Qualified referrals will only come after a foundation of trust has been established. Giving people unexpected but due appreciation will go a long way in establishing that trust.

"Make it a habit to tell people thank you. To express your appreciation, sincerely and without the expectation of anything in return. Truly appreciate those around you, and

you'll soon find many others around you. Truly appreciate life, and you'll find that you have more of it."

Ralph Marston

Generating Referrals from Your Customers

Once you have established a foundation of trust, delivered on your promises, and earned the right to ask for referrals, you should follow a prescribed pattern to effectively generate them. There are certain times when asking for a referral will seem more natural. These times are essentially the first five of the Seven Events for Sending Out Thank-you Cards. These five events are times when it is likely the customer is in the correct frame of mind. They are thinking how happy they are about their purchase and how wonderful a job you have done for them.

When to Ask for Referrals

- As soon as the sale has been made.
- As soon as a customer has received the product or service and you are certain they are satisfied with it.
- Anytime a customer compliments you, your staff, your product or service, or your company.
- Anytime you have followed up with a customer to ensure their continued satisfaction.
- Anytime you have resolved a problem to a customer's satisfaction.

You should wait until you know the customer has had a chance to receive your thank-you card and then follow up with them. The only exception to this would be at the time of the sale, when you would ask for a referral even prior to sending the thank-you card.

How to Ask For Referrals

The secret to generating more referrals really comes down to how you ask for them. The most common way people will usually ask for referrals, if they ask at all, sounds something like this: "Do you know anyone else who might be interested in . . . ?" Many things might go through a person's mind when he or she is asked a question like this. They might be afraid of siccing a salesperson on one of their friends, or they might overqualify their friends and acquaintances and eliminate people who really could use the product or service. The most likely thing is that no one will instantly come to their mind. You have put them on the spot, and the uncomfortable silence after the question usually leads to the knee-jerk answer, "No, I can't think of anyone." The best way to ask for referrals is to customize the question to the specific benefit(s) of your product or service. What problem has your product or service just solved for the customer? Then, instead of asking a closed-ended question that can be answered with only a yes or no, it will be more effective to ask a more assumptive question like, "Who do you know that . . . ?" Instead of asking them "if they know someone," we are assuming that "they indeed know someone" who can use your product or service. Now let's look at an example that combines these two elements into a question.

Let's say you are the owner of Larry's Lawn Care, and your client has just told you that you are doing a wonderful job for them. Here is one way to properly ask for a referral.

> Thank you for that compliment. Your satisfaction is very important to us. Actually, we have brought on a few more employees recently and we have room for a couple of new clients. I know how much you appreciate not wasting away your weekends by having to take care of your yard. Who do you know who might also enjoy some extra quality time with the family? I'd love to drop off a brochure so they will know we are available should they ever need us.

Several things are accomplished by asking in this fashion. First, you thanked them for their compliment. Second, asking them just after they have complimented you, it is unlikely they will have the concern that they are siccing a salesperson on their friend. Third, basing the referral request on the benefits of your product or service rather than the product or service itself, they will feel more as though they are helping their friend. Finally, by closing your question on a soft note such as "so they will know we are available should they ever need us," you will further reduce their worry that you may go out and hard-sell their friends. This makes the referral a low commitment. If they are able to provide some names, always thank them and always ask them permission to use their name when you contact the person they referred. You may say, "Do you mind if I let them know I'm doing work for you?" If they aren't able to come up with some names, then you may need to help them a little by dropping some hints. "Maybe one of your neighbors?" or "How about someone you work with?" or "Possibly someone who attends your church?" If you drop enough hints, it might stimulate their thinking, and someone may pop into their head.

By asking the right people at the right time with the right question and asking enough of them, you can generate an enormous number of referrals. If you find it necessary, you might even consider making your Customer Referral Program more formal by offering some form of incentive to customers who refer new customers to you. Generally, if you do everything right and do everything well, you won't need the extra incentives.

Getting Referrals from Other Businesses

The secret to getting referrals from other businesses is simple. To get referrals you have to give referrals. Be alert for opportunities that may exist where you can provide a referral to another business. Let's say one of your friends just told you they are looking into buying a new computer, and you bought one recently and had a good experience. Rather than just telling your friend where you bought it, volunteer to call the company and let them know he or she might be interested and have the expert you worked with call him or her directly. This way you will get "credit" for the referral. Do this enough and the favor will eventually get repaid, especially if you tactfully remind them what it is that you do and that you, too, are always seeking new customers. You may also look into referral groups in your local area. These groups are sometimes referred to as networking groups. Business owners from various industries periodically meet, rub shoulders, and exchange leads. Depending on the industry you serve and the quality of the group, you may find this to be a low-cost but productive method of generating leads.

My final thought on providing referrals to businesses revolves around your competitors. I have made numerous referrals to my own competitors over the years. I recommend this technique, because it works. Usually when I say that, I'll get a few raised eyebrows. This is a technique I learned many years ago when I was in the home improvement business. I was in an extremely cutthroat industry. The backstabbing and price-slashing that went on was shameful. Everyone seemed to badmouth everyone else. I made it a point not to participate in such activities, but I noticed that even though I didn't, my company was still getting its fair share of badmouthing from the competitors. One day I received a call from a potential customer who had an interest in a project that I was just not going to be able to help them with. I told them that one of my competitors specialized in those types of projects and that I would pass along their name and number to them right away. I picked up the phone and contacted the competitor. I could hear the uncertainty in his voice when I gave him the lead. Several weeks later he called to thank me for the lead. I noticed that not long after, whenever a potential customer would ask representatives of their company what they felt about the competition, they would still rant and rave about everybody else, but when my company was brought up they would either give us a satisfactory rating or not say anything at all. From that point on, anytime I had a lead that I was not able to assist on for whatever reason, whether it was because I was too backed up or because the customer wanted something outside our normal product line, I would make it a point to refer it to one of my top five competitors. Pretty soon we were not being badmouthed. It is an amazing thing when garbage seems to be thrown around everywhere, but none of it ever lands in your yard. In a few years, our reputation was considered the finest in the community, and even our competitors were being nice to us.

Taking Your Business to the Next Level

Once you have established a growing and successful business and you have taken the steps necessary to maximize your profitability, where do you go from there? If your business is a franchised business, maybe it's time to begin investing in multiple locations. If you analyze franchise systems, you will find that the top performers are usually those that own multiple locations. However, they may not have begun their franchise endeavor by initially investing in multiple locations. Instead, they became successful in their first location and then bought out neighboring franchisees and duplicated their success. Some of the biggest franchisees in the country may own more than a hundred franchised locations they have acquired over many years of using this duplication process. In many franchise systems, one franchise can usually provide a comfortable living once you finally mature it, but if you want to secure your future and become a multi-millionaire, it will usually take time and more than just one unit. You may also consider diversifying yourself into other types of franchised or possibly non-franchised businesses. The key to doing this is to make sure you do not forget what you are good at, or you may find yourself getting mixed up in something you had no business getting into. Failing endeavors can be a big draw on your time and resources, and pretty soon you may find your original, once-successful business is also paying a big price.

If your business is a non-franchised one, you may consider expanding nationally. There are many methods of doing this, whether it is done privately through company-owned locations or through licensing, dealerships, wholesalers, distributorships, or franchising. As one might expect, I am partial to franchising. The benefits seem to far outweigh the drawbacks.

Top 10 Benefits of Franchising Your Business

1. It is not as capital-intensive. Individual locations are capitalized by the franchisee.
2. The business is more duplicable.
3. Growth can be much faster.
4. Brand awareness is easier to attain and can be accomplished for less cost more quickly.
5. It is not as risky as other forms of expansion.
6. You have a better capability of getting higher-quality candidates to run the locations than you would if you had to recruit and pay employee managers to do it.
7. People work harder and smarter when they are vested in building their own business than they do when building yours.
8. It can turn your business into a much more salable commodity and do it much faster.
9. You can dominate the independents in the community.
10. Your profit potential is much greater and considerably less flexible. When franchisees pay royalties based on gross revenues, that royalty is consistent regardless of their expenses. They are committed to reducing their expenses rather than your having to control the expenses within a company-expanded business.

Regardless of how you may decide to expand, whether locally, regionally, or even nationally, and regardless whether you do this through franchising, company-owned locations, or other methods, don't be afraid to think big. Prepare for success and then go after it. I truly subscribe to the idea that anything the mind can believe it can achieve. You are responsible for your own success. If you are going to build something from a blueprint and spend a considerable amount of your time, money, and life doing it, you might as well set out to build a skyscraper instead of a shed. You may only be able to build that skyscraper one floor at a time, but that's okay so long as you don't give up and put your roof on to early.

> *"I like thinking big, if you are going to be thinking anything, you might as well think big."*
>
> DONALD J. TRUMP

Chapter 20

Defining Success

"All our dreams can come true, if we have the courage to pursue them."

Walt Disney

Is it even possible to define success? It depends on whom you are talking to. Success to one person may mean something totally different than it does to someone else. When will you know that you have succeeded in your business? Is it success the first month your income surpasses your expenses? Is it success when you have managed to eke out a decent living from your business? Is it success when you make it past the five-year mark and accomplish something that nearly 95 percent of other business owners aren't able to do? All of these things may be considered successful. It really all depends on how you define success for yourself.

I can't tell you how to define success; that is something you have to do yourself. But what I can tell you is that no matter how you define it, you should consider including some of these elements:

The Key Elements of Success

- Integrity and Character. Doing the right thing even when no one is looking. If you achieve success, but had to lie, cheat, and steal to get there, it probably won't feel much like success.

- Goals. One way to measure success is through achieving the business and personal goals that you have set for yourself. This is a tangible way of seeing the progress you have made.

- Family. Don't sacrifice the relationships you have with your family and friends to achieve your success. Success is empty if there's no one to share it with. Remember what is important in life and what isn't. Don't convince yourself you are doing what you're doing for your family, and then not spend any time with them while you're doing it. You absolutely must prioritize.

- Challenges. Success can truly only feel like success if it wasn't easy to attain. Nothing worthwhile in life comes easily. Cherish the challenges along the way. Look at the problems you are faced with as a signal that you are on the right track.

- Knowledge. Continue to learn something new every day, as knowledge truly is the root of success.

"True knowledge is when one knows the limitations of one's knowledge."

Confucius

- Like yourself. Don't be your own worst critic; instead, be your greatest fan. If you don't have confidence in yourself, no one else will either.

- Abide by the Golden Rule. We all have choices we get to make each and every day. Sometimes these decisions are not terribly important; other times they could mean the difference between life and death. There may even be times that doing the right thing will put you at risk. It's amazing how sometimes doing the right thing can ultimately end up even changing history.

I would like to expand on that last point with an Irish legend — and a true story — I heard many years ago.

There was a poor Scottish farmer by the name of Fleming. One day, while working hard on his farm, he heard a cry for help coming from a nearby bog. He dropped his tools and ran to the bog, where he found a terrified boy buried to his waist in thick, black muck. The boy was screaming and struggling in an attempt to free himself. Farmer Fleming rescued the boy from what would have been a slow and terrifying death. He did so at much peril. The next day, a fancy carriage pulled up to farmer Fleming's sparse surroundings. An elegantly dressed nobleman stepped out and introduced himself as the father of the boy the farmer had saved. "I want to repay you," said the nobleman. "You saved my son's life." "No, I can't accept payment for what I did," the Scottish farmer replied, waving off the offer. At that moment, the farmer's own son came to the door of the family hovel. "Is that your son?" the nobleman asked. "Yes," the farmer replied proudly. "I'll make you a deal. Let me provide him with the level of education my own son will enjoy. If the lad is anything like his father, he'll no doubt grow to be a man we both will be proud of." And that he did. Farmer Fleming's son attended the best schools, and in time, graduated from St. Mary's Hospital Medical School in London, and went on to become known throughout the world as the noted Sir Alexander Fleming, the discoverer of penicillin. Years afterward, the same nobleman's son who was saved from the bog was stricken with pneumonia. What saved his life this time? Penicillin. What was the name of the nobleman? Lord Randolph Churchill. And what was the name of his son who was saved a second time? Sir Winston Churchill. What goes around comes around. Consider the consequences. What if farmer Fleming had not saved the boy? What if the

Lord Randolph Churchill had not make the offer to put Fleming's son through school? Would penicillin have been discovered in time for Winston Churchill? How different would the world be today had Churchill died before World War II? Would Hitler still have been defeated? Always do the right thing and follow the Golden Rule. Not only is it the right thing to do, it can have an unexpected reciprocating effect.

The Universal Law of the Golden Rule

The number of different religions and beliefs that we have in this world amazes me. Some are so completely different than others. However, there is one universal law that exists in almost every organized religion and it is at least some version of the Golden Rule.

Bahá'í

"Blessed is he who preferreth his brother before himself."

Bahá'u'lláh, Tablets of Bahá'u'lláh, 71

Buddhism

"Hurt not others in ways that you yourself would find hurtful."

Udana-Varga, 5:18

Christianity

"Therefore, whatever you want men to do to you, do also to them, for this is the Law and the Prophets."

Yahshua (commonly known as Jesus of Nazareth), Matthew 7:12

". . . You shall love your neighbor as yourself."

Yahshua, Matthew 22:39

Confucianism

"Do not unto others what you would not have them do unto you."

Analects 15:23

Hinduism

"This is the sum of duty: Do naught unto others which would cause you pain if done to you."

Mahabharata 5:1517

Islam

"No one of you is a believer until he desires for his brother that which he desires for himself."

Sunnab

Jainism

"In happiness and suffering, in joy and grief, we should regard all creatures as we regard our own self."

Lord Mahavir 24th Tirthankara

Judaism

"What is hateful to you, do not to your fellow man. That is the entire law: all the rest is commentary."

Talmud, Shabbat 31a

Native American

"Respect for all life is the foundation."

The Great Law of Peace

Scientology

"Try to treat others as you would want them to treat you."

This is number 20 of the 21 moral precepts that form the moral code as explained in L. Ron Hubbard's booklet ***The Way to Happiness***.

Sikhism

"Do not create enmity with anyone as God is within everyone."

— Guru Arjan Devji 259. Guru Granth Sahib

Taoism

"Regard your neighbor's gain as your gain, and your neighbor's loss as your own loss."

— Tai Shang Kan Yin P'ien

Utilitarianism

"To do as one would be done by, and to love one's neighbor as one's self, constitute the ideal perfection of utilitarian morality."

— John Stuart Mill

Zoroastrianism

"That nature only is good when it shall not do unto another whatever is not good for its own self."

— Dadistan-i-Dinik, 94:5

Christians, Jews, Muslims, Hindus, Buddhists, atheists and all others in the world seem to be able to agree on the Golden Rule. It does not establish any religion, because it's common and universal in all religions and beliefs. Since all of us in the world seem to agree on the Golden Rule, all we have to do is start living it. Make it the core foundation of your business from the beginning and you will be sowing the seeds of a great harvest and reaping the rewards of much success.

"Every religion emphasizes human improvement, love, respect for others, sharing other people's suffering. On these lines every religion has more or less the same viewpoint and the same goal."

Dalai Lama

Defining Success

If you want to be successful, you have to truly know and understand success. I have been asked countless times how Kris and I were able to start and build such a successful business. My canned answer has always included the statement that it is a difficult question to answer because so many people define success differently. Invariably, the next question would always be, "How do you define success?" I would like to share my definition with you in the hopes that it will inspire you to come up with your own definition and motivate you to fulfill that definition within your own life.

> *"Success is reaching your goals by overcoming the challenges you face along the way and doing it without sacrificing your character or integrity or harming others in the process. It is being able to wake up each morning excited to be in your own shoes and having earned the confidence in yourself to realize that no matter what the day shall bring, you will meet it with much determination and fortitude. Treating each day as a new learning experience so you can continue to grow and succeed. Treating everyone you meet as you want to be treated. And then finally, sharing your success and the knowledge you gained from success with your family, friends, those who helped you to achieve it and those who truly need it."*
>
> Jerry L. Clum, Jr.

> *"Unless you choose to do great things with it, it makes no difference how much you are rewarded or how much you have."*
>
> Oprah Winfrey

The Greatest Gift

One of the greatest gifts Kris and I have ever received came from one of our first customers. We have been fortunate enough to work closely with the elderly. Society sometimes looks upon the elderly as frail and helpless individuals, as indeed some are. But it is more important to remember that they are often the true fountains of wisdom. People who have had seven to 10 decades of learning opportunities can share some of the most enlightening advice we'll ever hear, provided we listen. Because of our involvement with the elderly, we have seen firsthand many people dealing with end-of-life issues. One issue that almost always seems to come to the surface in the closing chapters of someone's life is referred to as an End of Life Review. It is a reflection of one's life, past and future. They consider their accomplishments, their family, and their spiritual connection and are sometimes faced with the question as to whether they made a difference in the world. Sadly, many people who perform an End of Life Review conclude their analysis with regrets — not having spent enough time with family, wishing they had done more for society or had been more spiritual, etc.

One of the most common regrets surprisingly does not fall into those categories. Instead it is the regret of not having taken enough chances in life or passing up an opportunity that may have presented itself. We all, at some time in our life, are faced with life-changing decisions. These decisions usually involve an element of risk that would take us out of our comfort zone, such as quitting a job and starting your own business. If your true life dream is doing just that, you will have to decide which worst-case scenario is the lesser of two evils. "I tried and failed, but at least I tried," or facing the possibility of having to sometime say to yourself, " I wonder what would have happened if . . ."

> ***"Of all the words of tongue or pen, the saddest are these: It might have been."***
>
> John Greenleaf Whittier

Tomorrow is the first day of the rest of your life. If you have always dreamed of starting your own business, then allow me to pass on this gift that was told to me by one of my first elderly customers. Quoting Henry David Thoreau, she said:

> ***"Go confidently in the direction of your dreams! Live the life you've imagined."***

Thank You

Though I would love to take credit for every idea and thought in this book, but fortunately, I cannot. I say fortunately because so many people have shaped my life over the years. It's difficult to analyze the individual impact that so many different people have had in one's life, but I do know I have been blessed by more than my fair share. I cannot express enough how much I have learned from people like Zig Ziglar, Brian Tracy, Anthony Robbins, Donald Trump, Jay Abraham, Stephen Covey, William Gates, Michael Gerber, Tom Hopkins, Harvey Mackay, Tom Peters, Stephen Wynn, Les Brown, Jim Rohn, and Denis Waitley by simply listening to their audio programs, reading their books, attending their seminars and studying how they built and managed their own businesses.

Thank you to my father for introducing me to the sales world and showing me the ropes, to my mother, mother- and father-in-law, siblings, grandparents, aunts, uncles, and closest friends for always supporting me in everything I do and building my self-confidence along the way.

My staff, board members and franchisees for always making me look good and giving everything they have and doing it every day to take our company to the next level and beyond.

My children Heather and Trey for letting me experience what life really is all about, and last, but certainly not least, my wife Kristina. I am most certain that I would not be where I am today without her. She deserves more gratitude than I can express in words for being my top supporter and for putting up with me and all my crazy ideas over the last 20 years.

"The sum of a man is directly proportionate to the people in his life."

Jerry L. Clum, Jr.

Answers to Brainteasers *from* Chapter 15

Look at the image below. Quickly count the number of squares. How many do you see?

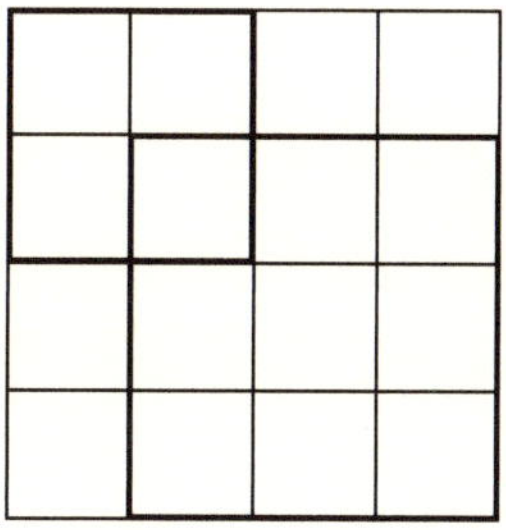

Answer: There are 30 squares in all. Most people have a tendency to first see 16, some will see the outside and count 17, but many do not see all of the inside squares. There are nine squares that are made up by four smaller squares. These are 2 × 2 squares, and there are three of these 2 × 2 squares in each of three rows (don't forget the center row). There are four squares that are made up of nine smaller squares. These are 3 × 3 squares, and there is one starting at each corner.

Here are nine dots arranged in a square matrix. Can you draw four straight lines that connect all nine dots without lifting your pencil from the paper?

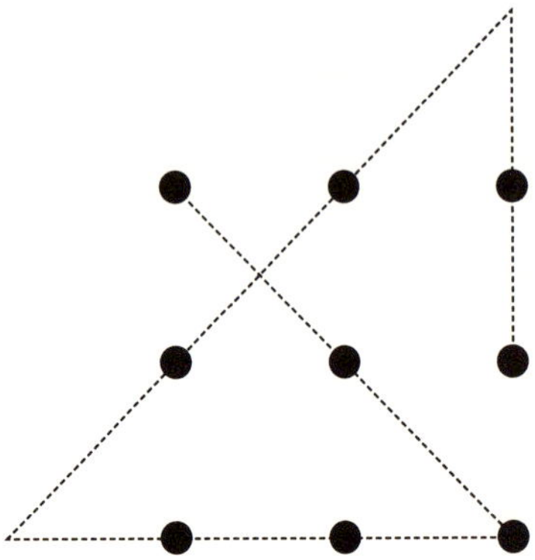

Answer (*above*): The instructions did not say that the lines had to be the same length or that you could not go outside the square matrix.

Answer (*right*): Each daughter would receive 187.5 acres, and to keep each plot as identical shapes, you would need to plot them as shown above.

A farmer owns 1,000 acres of land. He is getting on in age and has decided to give his farm to his five children. He has one son, and he would like his son to continue to farm. He realizes that to do so, his son will need a minimum of 250 acres. He also has four daughters. His daughters have always been critical about their father's fairness to them. He knows that to make them all happy he will need to give each of his daughters equal shares of the 750 acres that remain. They understand and accept the fact that their brother will get a larger parcel than they will to keep the farm running. The farmer also knows that to avoid other complaints among his daughters, each of their parcels will have to be exactly the same shape. Determine how many acres each of his daughters will get and draw out exactly how the parcels need to be divided up so that each of the four parcels of the remaining 750 acres are exactly the same size and shape.

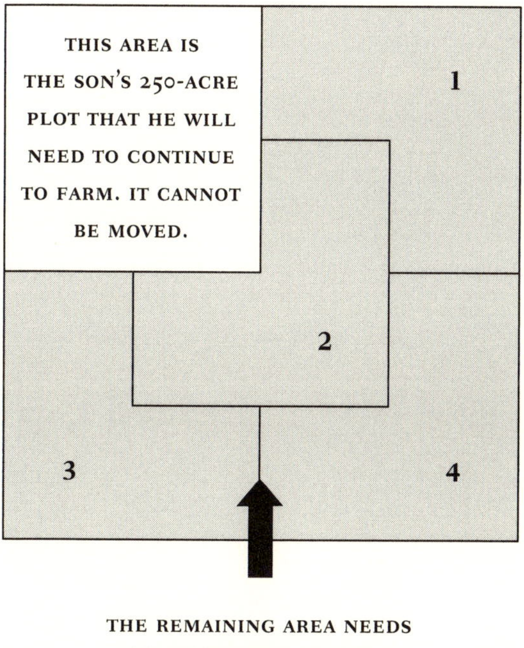

How many cubes do you see? How many cubes would you say are entirely hidden? How many cubes are there in all?

Answer: There are 14 different cubes that are at least partially visible. There are 27 cubes in all and 13 that are completely hidden. This puzzle was either easy or hard for you. Many people find it difficult to visualize things that are not visible to the eye. This puzzle requires both Right Brain and Left Brain thinking. You need to use both visual awareness and logic to solve this type of puzzle.

There are six lines shown below. Add five more lines and come up with nine.

Answer: The Dotted lines are the five added lines. As you can see, it is possible to come up with "Nine." Most people convince themselves that they somehow needed to come up with nine "lines." That wasn't what was asked for. Many times, especially when it comes to problem-solving, we have a tendency to overcomplicate things. Interestingly enough, this test was once given to a group of college graduates. It was also given to a group of third graders. The third graders, on average, were able to solve it in less than half the time of the college graduates.

Count the objects in the picture below. How many objects do you see? Describe the objects you see.

Answer: While many people would say there are five items shown, there are actually six separate objects. Your mind is telling you to see a white triangle on top of all the other items. It does not exist. Actually, there are three "Pac-Man" shaped partial circles and three partial triangles with one side missing on each.